Who Is Israel?
Past, Present, and Future

by

Batya Ruth Wootten

foreword by Angus Wootten

Who Is Israel? Past, Present, and Future
by Batya Ruth Wootten

© 2003, Batya Ruth Wootten, Saint Cloud, FL.
Edited by Michele Libin
Cover by Crystal Lenhart, Sheridan, Wyoming
Many of the graphics herein were designed by Michele Libin and
Batya Wootten and drawn by Rebecca Frazier and Sherry Scheitel.
Portions of this book have appeared in previous editions:
Who Is Israel? And Why You Need To Know. 1998.
ISBN 1-886987-01-7
Who Is Israel? Expanded Edition. 2000. ISBN 1-886987-03-3

Published and Distributed by:
Key of David Publishing, PO Box 700217, St Cloud, FL 34770
1.800.829.8777   http://www.mim.net/keyofdavid

Printed in the United States of America.
All quotations used by permission.
Unless otherwise noted, Scripture quotations are from the *New
American Standard Bible* (NASB), © 1995, The Lockman Foundation,
published by Holman Bible Publishers, Nashville; and the *New New
American Standard Bible*, Quick Verse for Windows, © 1992-1999,
Craig Rairdon and Parsons Technology.
Verses marked KJV are from the *King James Version* Bible.
Verses marked NRSV are from *The New Revised Standard Version
With Apocrypha*, © 1998 by Electronic Edition STEP Files, Parsons
Technology, Inc. Cedar Rapids, Iowa.
Verses marked NIV are from the *New International Version*, © 1995
by The International Bible Society, published by Zondervan
Publishing House, Grand Rapids.
Verses marked TAB are from *The Amplified Bible*, © 1994 by the
Zondervan Publishing House, Grand Rapids.
Verses marked TNKH are from the *Tanakh, A New Translation of The
Holy Scriptures*, © 1995 by The Jewish Publication Society. New York.
Verses from *26 Translations of the Holy Bible*, © 1985 by the
Zondervan Corporation, Mathis Publishers, Atlanta, are marked
according to the particular translation.
Note:
To emphasize some Scriptures, italics or an alternate word choice has
been used, especially for the names of the Father and Son. Also, with
all verses, except the Amplified Bible (TAB), brackets [] indicate text
added by the author.

ISBN 1-886987-17-3

Dedication

To my Father in Heaven, and to my earthly father,
who is now with my Father in Heaven.
And to all the sons of Israel
who follow after our Heavenly Father.

Special Thanks

Along life's way a number of people have
contributed bits and pieces to my books.
My deepest thanks to all
who helped in any way,
especially to my husband, Angus,
who has always encouraged me in my walk,
and to my editor and dear friend, Michele Libin,
who worked hard to make this book easy to read.
I also want to recognize my friend Judith Dennis for
checking the manuscript and for making suggestions.
Once more I am honored to be able to thank my friend
Crystal Lenhart for creating a truly beautiful book cover.
In addition, I want to extend special thanks to those
who contributed various helpful drawings and charts,
especially Sherry Scheitel who contributed so much.
For each one I pray that our Heavenly Father,
who sees all good things done in secret,
openly reward you for your kindness.
In Messiah Yeshua,
Batya

O house
of Ephraim Israel
and house of Judah...
the Father called your name,
a green olive tree, beautiful in fruit
and form. But because of your sins, He
pronounced evil against you. Yet take heart,
O house of Israel, take heart O house of Judah, for
the Father has promised: "It will come about that after I
have uprooted and scattered them, after some have become like
degenerate, foreign vines, then My compassions will again be
kindled and I will regather them. I will bring them back, each
one to his own inheritance, each one to his own land. Yes, this is
My promise to them. For these two olive branches are My
two chosen witnesses. And I will grant authority to them,
for they are the two sons of fresh oil who are
standing by the LORD of all the earth.
(Jeremiah
2:18–21;
11:10,16
–17; 12:15;
Hosea 1–2;
Zechariah 4:11–14;
Revelation 11:3–4.)

Long ago the Father
divided Israel into two houses,
Ephraim (Israel) and Judah.
As His "two witnesses" they were sent
in two different directions
to accomplish two different purposes.
And in this last day
He wants the two to come together,
that they might confirm His truth in the earth
(1 Kings 12:15,24; Hosea 1:11; John 8:17).

Simply stated,
that is the message of this book.
All else is commentary.
So as you read,
please remember
the simplicity behind it all:

Two houses—Two directions—
Two different purposes.
Now is the time to put them
back together again.

Contents

Part Three—The Future: Israel's Destiny

Part Four—Study Helps and More...

List of Major Illustrations:

Foreword

It is my observation that the GOD of Israel often uses men and women working together to keep His plan for Israel on course. Sometimes He especially chooses to use the female team member. For example, He used Sarah to insure that the promise went to Isaac rather than to Ishmael (the one Abraham would have chosen), and He used Rebekah to thwart Isaac's plan to pass the promise to Esau rather than to Jacob (whom YHVH had chosen) (Genesis 21:9-12; 27:4-10).

I am thankful that the Father has used my wife, Batya, and her faithfulness to help keep our team on course. Because of her tenacity, we can now understand "Israel," and can therefore be used by the Holy One to help accomplish His desire, which is to have a people for His own possession.

In the early Seventies we became deeply involved in the new Messianic Jewish Movement, where we faced two initial challenges. We needed to provide a way for Jewish Believers to come to know Yeshua as their Messiah without having to renounce their Jewish heritage. We also needed to present Israel's Messiah to the Church in a way that would encourage an appreciation for the Jewish people, for the eternal principles of Torah (the Law), and for the truths revealed in the feasts of Israel.

This new movement began to attract "Gentiles." In fact, more *non-Jews* were flocking to the standard being raised by Messianic Judaism than were Jewish people. These non-Jews wanted to support their Jewish brothers and to trade errant traditions for the Father's Torah and His feasts.

They too were being drawn to this reemerging Israel.

We strongly supported the fledgling efforts of our Jewish brothers and established a real first: The *House of David Messianic Materials Catalogue.*

The goal of this cutting-edge publication was to develop and distribute materials that would aid Believers in understanding their "roots."

However, the more we read and observed, the more we became concerned over the place of those regarded as "Gentiles" in the movement. At the time, Messianic Jewish heritage was based on one having "visible" Jewish parentage when they became involved in the movement, or they could be married to someone who met the requirement.

These "physical Jews" who accepted Messiah were then assumed to be "spiritual Jews" as well. On the other hand, "Gentiles" who joined the movement were considered to be only "spiritual" heirs, and there was no way for them to attain the Jewish "twice chosen" status.

This standard resulted in two classes of citizenship, which soon caused problems. Many non-Jews were made to feel like second-class citizens. Seeking resolution, I appealed to the leadership to establish a "conversion procedure" that would make everyone equal, both "physically" and "spiritually."

Not only was this proposal unacceptable to most of them, but after reflecting on the idea, it became completely unacceptable to my wife. She reasoned that whereas all must repent, if one also had to "be converted to be a first-class citizen," then one must have been born wrong in the first place. She would often say, *"A mortal man's declaration will not change the facts of who I am. What I need to know is, who am I to the Father?"*

The teachings being put forth about the roles of "Israel and the Church" did not seem to be adding up to what we saw in Holy Writ. This fact, plus the challenge of finding Scriptural books about Israel for our Catalogue led Batya to cry out to the Father with the question, *"Who is Israel?"*

This concise book offers His answer to that important question. Surely the Holy Spirit will use this book to help guide a believing Israel back onto the road of "Thy Kingdom come on earth, as it is in heaven." It will help get us back on course, thus preparing the way for Messiah's return and restoration of the Kingdom to Israel.

Batya asks and answers some life-changing questions: *Where is Israel now? What is Israel's destiny?*

On a profound level, this solution driven book will help you answer some personal questions: *Who are you to the Father? Why do you feel the way you do about Israel? What is your individual destiny?*

I believe my wife was called to write the first of our books because in our team she is the "nit-picker" (you need one of those for research purposes). She is never willing to settle for anything less than the absolute truth, regardless of consequences. Furthermore, between the two of us, she is more articulate. But her books speak for both of us. Every word.

However, I feel there is another reason that she especially has been called to write on this subject.

I think the Father wanted this latter-day truth to be presented first by the feminine side of His creation, because in order to reunite a divided Israel, we must all learn to *nurture* one another. We must learn to be patient, to love and encourage each other. In our restoration, we will first have to exhibit an encouraging, mother's type love to those who are somewhat different from us.

Batya's insights into what she calls "Mama's Torah" are absolutely invaluable. An excerpt from a forthcoming book by that title is included in this Third Edition of the now seminal classic, *Who is Israel?*

As reunited Israel emerges from their womb of dispersion, they will especially need to learn to heed some elementary "mother's instructions" (Proverbs 1:8; 6:20). They will first have to deal with their *heart attitudes*.

In the spirit of Deborah of old, Batya issues a call to those who are sitting and waiting like Barak. Hers is an encouraging call to "*Arise, O sons of Israel! Believe that the Father has given your enemies into your hands!*" (Judges 4-5). Her call is a declaration, for the day is upon us when the Holy One of Israel is making the two "sticks" of Ephraim and Judah one in His hand (Ezekiel 37:15-28). Today is the day when *YHVH Tsavaot*, the LORD of Hosts, is calling forth the overcoming armies of Israel!

It has been Sovereignly decreed that Ephraim and Judah ultimately will know victory over their enemies. They will help prepare the way for the return of our King and help establish His Kingdom here on earth (Isaiah 11:11-16). We want to partake of that victory. This book will help equip us for the battle that lies ahead.

Finally, I want to say that the God-given insights found in our books has brought radical change to my life. It has truly changed me. Further, I have seen this same understanding dramatically change the lives of tens of thousands. And I know it can change you! So I welcome you to the ranks of the radically changed—to the multitudes of forerunners being prepared for the day when the kingdoms of this world will become the restored Kingdom of Israel.

Shalom b' Yeshua,
Angus Wootten
Director
Messianic Israel Alliance

Introduction

Renaissance. Revival. Restoration.
The Holy One of Israel is doing a new thing in the earth. The ancient texts of Scripture are once again revealing previously hidden truths.

Renaissance speaks of enthusiastic and vigorous activity distinguished by a revival of interest in the past. A true renaissance is about rebirth, about an imaginative response to broader horizons. It is characterized by freshness, zest, productivity, and renewal of life.

Multiplied thousands of Believers in Messiah Yeshua,[a] Jewish and non-Jewish alike, are now experiencing a renaissance. Their faith is being renewed. They are being stirred. They are seeing "Israel" in a new light.

Believers around the world are finally seeing the truth about "both the houses of Israel" (Isaiah 8:14).

They are seeing Ephraim and Judah.

The Holy One once said of the heirs of Ephraim, the once lost children of the house of Israel:

---

a Believers: We call those purchased by Messiah Yeshua's blood *Believers* because the title *Christians* is often misused (Mat 7:23; 1 Cor 6:20; 1 Pet 1:17-19). *Yeshua* (ישוע): Our Messiah's given Hebrew name is Yeshus. It means "Salvation" (Mat 1:21). *Jesus* is derived from transliterating *Yeshua* into Greek, or *Iesous* (Ιησους), and then transliterating that name into English, or "Jesus." Also, the English "J" once had a "Y" sounded, but was hardened over the years. Thus we prefer the Hebrew Yeshua.

"Is Ephraim My dear son? Is he a delightful child? Indeed, as often as I have spoken against him, I certainly still remember him; therefore My heart yearns for him; I will surely have mercy on him" (Jeremiah 31:20).

In His mercy the Father is now allowing prodigal Ephraim to find the pathway that leads back home to his Father's house.

The people of Ephraim were destined to become a "*melo hagoyim*," or a "fullness of the nations." These were known as the Northern Kingdom of Israel before they were scattered among every nation, tribe, and tongue.

These wayward ones are now returning in repentance, and are experiencing a revival.

Judah too is being revived and renewed.

The Father has been re-gathering the people of Judah, bringing them back to the Land He promised to Abraham, Isaac, Jacob, and their heirs.

The Holy One has faithfully protected and guarded the apple of His eye. He has also begun to lift the veil from their formerly blinded eyes.

Scores among those of Judah now know Messiah Yeshua in all His glory. The eyes of their understanding have been enlightened.

Believers everywhere are now seeing how the Almighty has sovereignly used both the houses of Israel to accomplish His purposes in the earth. Formerly battling brothers are now reaching out to embrace one another.

Like the cherubim over the Ark in the Holy of Holies, glory is found in their embrace. In the midst of this holy embrace, regathered Israel is finding a true renaissance.

This book is about that renaissance.
We invite you to read it, to enter into the Holy of Holies. We invite you to the reunion for which your inner man longs —the restoration of the whole house of Israel.

Batya Ruth Wootten

Part One

Israel in the Past—
What Was Promised

1

Believing What Abraham Believed

The faith of the people of Israel begins with "the father of all who believe" (Romans 4:11). It begins with Abraham. We too must begin at the beginning. To do so, we travel across the sands of time to a desert mound under the night sky where an old man is experiencing a vision.

The Word came to Abram in a vision, saying, "Do not fear, Abram, I am a shield to you; your reward shall be very great."

Abram replied to the voice, "O *Adonai Yahhovee* [O Lord my GOD], what will You give me, since I have no child from my own loins? I am childless, my only heir is a servant born in my house, Eliezer of Damascus."

"Your servant," said the living Word, "shall not be your heir. Only one that shall come from your inward parts—only an heir from your own body shall inherit your blessing."

Then He said to the aged patriarch, "Come out here, Abram, and look up at the stars. If you can count them, then you will know the number of descendants that will come from your own body, in fulfillment of My sovereign promise to you."

Abram stepped out of his tent and gazed into the clear night sky. He could see no end to the countless stars and was comforted beyond measure by the pledge that had been made to him. His descendants would be as numerous as these countless heavenly bodies.

Abram smiled as he stood there in the desert contemplating this awesome promise. His body, though more than three quarters of a century-old, straightened as he looked toward the deep blue, light-sprinkled sky. Turning round and round, the man of faith saw myriads of stars arranged in twelve constellations, each telling a different part of the story of Redemption. Abram saw the Heavens declaring the glory of the God that he served. That night Abram believed YHVH (יהוה) [1] and it was reckoned to him as righteousness (see Genesis 15:1-6; Psalm 19:1-4).

Abraham's Descendants—A Noisy Multitude

The New Covenant says of Abraham: *"Without becoming weak in faith he contemplated his own body, now as good as dead since he was about a hundred years old, and the deadness of Sarah's womb; yet, with respect to the promise of God, he did not waver in unbelief, but grew strong in faith, giving glory to God, and being fully assured that what He had promised, He was able also to perform. Therefore, 'It was reckoned to him as righteousness'"* (Romans 4:19-22).

Abraham contemplated his aged body and Sarah's barrenness because he was looking for the *physical*

---

1 YHVH: We use these four letters to indicate the Name of the one true God, which is often mistranslated "the Lord." This is due to the Jewish tradition of not wanting to pronounce His Name. Christianity simply followed suit. The Father's Name is comprised of four Hebrew letters, יהוה, yod, hey, vav, hey, and there are various opinions as to how it is to be pronounced: Yahweh, Yahveh, Yahvah, Yehovah, etc. Some believe this Divine Name is made up of four vowels, and pronounce it, Ih-Ah-Oo-Ah. We use the four English letters that best duplicate the sound of the four Hebrew letters as pronounced in modern Hebrew (YHVH) and let the reader determine if, and how, to pronounce it. In the Greek Texts, "the Lord" is translated from the Greek κύριος *kurios*, meaning Supremecy. See Strong's # G2962.

fulfillment of YHVH's "star-filled" promise to him. Abraham was not satisfied with having only an adopted heir, and in response to Abraham's desire, YHVH said, "None but your very own issue shall be your heir" (Genesis 15:4, TNKH).

Based on this promise, Abraham looked for a biological heir that would result in a great number of descendants. The Holy One came to him again, this time when he was ninety-nine years old, and said, *"'I am the Almighty God, walk before Me and be blameless. And I will establish My covenant between Me and you, and I will multiply you exceedingly.' And Abram fell on his face, and God talked with him, saying, 'Behold, My covenant is with you, and you will be the father of a multitude of nations. No longer shall your name be called Abram, or "exalted father," but your name shall be called Abraham, "father of a multitude." For I will make you the father of a multitude of nations. I will make you exceedingly fruitful, I will make nations of you'"* (Genesis 17:1-6).

Abraham believed he would father a multitude of nations, a *hamon goyim* (המון גוים).

- *Goyim* (גוים) is the Hebrew word for Gentiles, or nations.[2]
- *Hamon* (המון) means "a noise, sound, tumult, wealth, multitude, crowd." [3]

With these words the Almighty decreed that from Abraham's loins would come forth a *"multitude of nations [Gentiles]"*—a people who would cause a tumultuous commotion, or a great noise (about Abraham's God), throughout the world. From Abraham would come a people destined to be "exceedingly fruitful."

---

2 *Strong's Exhaustive Concordance* (hereafter Strong's), # H 1471 says *goyim* means, "a foreign nation...heathen...people" (Thomas Nelson, 1984; also, Parson's Technology QuickVerse Bible Software Program, 1996-99, Cedar Rapids). *The New Brown-Driver-Briggs-Gesenius Hebrew-Aramaic Lexicon* (hereafter: BDBL) says the word means "nation, people," and is "usually [used to speak] of non-Hebrew people" (#H1471, Hendrickson, 1979; also Parsons Technology, 1999). The *Theological Wordbook of the Old Testament* 2 Vol., Moody, 1981 (hereafter TWOT), says, "goyim...usually refers to..the surrounding pagan nations" (# 326e).
3 Hamon: Strong's and BDBL # H 1995; also TWOT word # 505a.

Have We Missed the Miracle?

As New Covenant followers of The Way,[4] have we missed the full impact of Abraham's blessing? Have we painted a mental picture comprised of heirs who primarily are *not* related to Abraham—when Scripture explicitly states that he would have myriads of physical heirs? Have we misunderstood the promise that was given to Abraham, and thus overlooked a glorious wonder? If so, have we missed rejoicing in one of the marvels of the Holy One?

Yes we have.

YHVH said He would make the "fewest of all peoples.... as numerous as the stars of the sky" (Deuteronomy 7:7; Exodus 32:13). By not seeing this truth, we have missed the miracle of His sovereign multiplication of Abraham's seed.

Our Father promised He would bring forth from Abraham's loins myriads, literally *nations*, of biological heirs. That is the first and primary meaning of that blessing —the literal way in which it should be interpreted. We therefore begin our search by simply believing what Abraham believed: Out of his loins would come countless descendants.

It is this promise that we will follow throughout Scripture. We will not try to prove that Messiah Yeshua's sheepfold includes some who are *unrelated* to Abraham, for that topic has already been addressed by many. Neither will we deny legitimacy to any Believers who feel they are *not* related to Abraham. However, for the sake of those who believe they might actually be of Abraham's loins, we will pursue the Scriptural trail of the myriads that were promised to Abraham.

We acknowledge that our God can certainly choose to have "others" partake of Abraham's promise. Moreover, to believe that Abraham presently has myriads of physical heirs in the earth does not imply that *all* Believers must be

---

4 Acts 9:2; 19:9,23; 24:14.

related to Abraham in order to have a relationship with his God. Eliezer was dearly loved by Abraham, just as Abraham surely loves all who believe in the Holy One.

We do not examine this facet of Abraham's promise in an attempt to prove patriarchal descent for any person or group. Rather, we do so for the following reasons:

Most people define Israel based on some idea of physical descent—regardless of how abstract or vague their definition. Perceived physical descent from the patriarchs is generally the primary factor in one's "Israel decision." Therefore, if we are going to answer the question of "Who is Israel?" we are forced to address the issue according to this universal standard, since it is usually the underlying presumption of all who seek to know the truth about Israel.

Our intent is to question the validity of this misconceived standard.

To say Israel is most often measured this way is not to deny that sometimes people correctly use "spiritual" attributes to define Israel. Rather, it is to say that, "abstract biological division" is the standard most often applied, whether realized or not.

We question this standard because it determines the fundamentals of our faith. After coming to know Messiah Yeshua (Jesus[5] Christ), one naturally asks the questions: "Who are His chosen people? Who are Abraham's heirs? Who is Israel?"

Though we ask these questions, our study will be rooted in the basic understanding that most people cannot prove their genetic connection to the patriarchs, and we in no way

---

5 *Yeshua* (ישוע) is the Messiah's given Hebrew/Aramaic name. It means "Salvation" (Mat 1:21). *Jesus* is derived from the Greek rendering of *Yeshua*, which is *Iesous* (Ιησους). The name was changed because the Greek language does not have a "sh" sound. This Greek transliteration was then transliterated into English, and many years ago the English letter "J" had a sound like that of today's "Y." Thus the name was pronounced "Yesus." With the hardening of the sound of the "J," it became "Jesus." For these reasons we prefer to transliterate the Messiah's name from Hebrew into English as "Yeshua." (See the article Why Continue in Misunderstandings?, *Messianic Israel Herald*, Vol. 2, No. 2 at <www.messianicisrael.com>).

suggest they try to prove it. Nevertheless, there is a great deal of research being done in the science of genetics that is briefly outlined in Addendum A. [6]

It is pointless for anyone to argue, or to try to assert claims based on "unprovable genealogy." However, this in turn means that Jewish people cannot prove that they *are* physically related to Abraham. Conversely, no one can prove that non-Jewish Believers are *not* physically descended from Abraham.[7] Neither group can prove biological descent.

Because no one can demonstrate their genealogy, we shall pursue our course by faith alone, using Holy Writ as our guidebook. We press on in hopes that we might restore to a people of promise that which was once lost. [8]

With this understanding in place, we now return to our study of the patriarchs and the promises made to them.

---

6 "Addendum: Genetic Confirmation," Michele Libin, p 243.

The Jerusalem Report Magazine, in its cover story (May 10, 1999), states: "Under religious law, *kohen* status is obtained through patrilineal inheritance. Since the Y chromosome is passed from father to son..."
Various articles found in this issue reaffirm that tribal descent is determined "patrilineally."
Also, the following article appeared in the *Jerusalem Post International Edition* (Chicago), Jan 11, 1997:
Genetic link found among kohanim   by Judy Siegel
"Jews of the priestly tribe (kohanim)—both Ashkenazi and Sephardi—have been found to share a variation of the Y chromosome, linking them as descendants of Aaron the High Priest...
This was the result of a study conducted by Prof. Karl Skorecki, a senior nephrologist at Rambam Hospital in Haifa and head of molecular medicine at the Technion's medical school, along with colleagues in Haifa, London and Arizona. Their finding was published...in the British science journal *Nature*. [They]...took samples...from unrelated Jewish men...by swabbing the inside of their cheeks. The phenotypes of 188 secular and religious Jews who said they were kohanim were found to be very different from those who said they were not....The Y chromosome, carried only by men, is passed patrilineally; mitochondrial DNA is transmitted by the mother.
Skorecki...added that it was impressive how the characteristic Y chromosome was passed down to today's Kohanim despite periods of assimilation over the millennia.
Even secular Jews seem to know if they are of the priestly tribe..."
7 Jew and non-Jew must avoid trying to prove "endless genealogies" (1 Tim 1:4).
8 Deu 30:3; Isa 11:1-14; 49:6; Jer 31:21; 33:7; Hos 1-2; Acts 15:16.

Abraham, Isaac, and Jacob—Joint Heirs

By not seeing Abraham's promise of myriads of biological heirs, are his non-Jewish descendants robbed of a blessing? If Scripture indicates that they are his heirs, should they be denied that understanding?

We cannot dismiss this point as though it were unimportant, for all of the Father's truths must be received and revered. Additionally, non-Jewish heirs are robbed of their blessing when they are told, "You may be a spiritual heir of Abraham, but you are *not* an heir of Abraham, Isaac, and Jacob." We cannot rightly separate their inheritance because Scripture reveals that theirs is a common blessing.[9]

- YHVH said to Isaac, "To you and to your seed...I will establish the oath which I swore to your father Abraham" (Genesis 26:3).
- Isaac then passed the blessing to his son Jacob when he said, "May He [YHVH] also give you the blessing of Abraham" (Genesis 28:4).
- The Chronicler later reiterated the promise: "The covenant which He [God] made with Abraham, and His oath to Isaac, He also confirmed to Jacob for a statute, to Israel as an everlasting covenant" (1 Chronicles 16:16-17).
- The New Covenant (*Brit Chadashah*) reveals that Abraham "lived as an alien in the land of promise... with Isaac and Jacob, fellow heirs of the same promise" (Hebrews 11:9).

Scripture does not support the theory that one can be an "heir of Abraham" but not an heir of "Abraham, Isaac, and Jacob." You are either an heir of all three, or you are not an heir at all. It also reveals that "These were all commended for their faith, yet none of them received what had been promised...only together with us would they be made perfect" (Hebrews 11:39-40, NIV).

---

9 Gen 15:5; 17:4; 26:4; 24:60; 28:3,14; 48:4,16,19.

The Greek word translated here as "perfect," *teleioo* (τελειοω), can also mean: "complete, accomplish, consummate, finish, fulfill, perfect." [10] Without us, the New Covenant Believers, the blessing of the patriarchs is imperfect. It is incomplete.

Peter the apostle writes, "The prophets who prophesied of the grace that would come to you made careful search and inquiry, seeking to know what person or time the Spirit of Messiah within them was indicating....It was revealed to them that they were not serving themselves, but you, in these things which now have been announced to you through those who preached the gospel by the Holy Spirit sent from heaven" (1 Peter 1:10-12).

The Promised Kahal/Ekklesia

YHVH promised Abraham: "I will multiply your descendants as the stars of heaven" (Genesis 26:4).

Rabah (רבה), *or multiply*, means "to increase, exceedingly, become numerous, great." [11] The blessing given to Isaac's wife, Rebekah, was, "Be the mother of *thousands* of *millions*," or *myriads* (Genesis 24:60).[12]

Isaac and Rebekah then passed their multitudinous blessing to their son Jacob: "May God...make you fruitful and multiply you, that you may become a congregation of peoples" (Genesis 28:3).

From Jacob YHVH would call forth a *congregation*—a *kahal* (קהל).

This Hebrew word is primarily translated "congregation," and is especially used to describe "an assembly, company, congregation, or convocation," called together by the Almighty for religious purposes.[13]

According to the *Theological Wordbook of the Old Testament*," *qahal* is usually translated *ekklesia* in the LXX

---

10 Strong's # G 5048.
11 Strong's and BDBL # H 7235; TWOT # 2103, 2104.
12 Strong's and BDBL #'s H 505 and 7235.
13 TWOT # 1991a. Also see Strong's and BDBL # H 6951.

[*Septuagint*]." [14]   *Ekklesia* (εκκλησια) is the New Covenant word translated as church. It speaks of a calling out, or a meeting, especially a religious congregation or an assembly.[15]

In the *Brit Chadashah*, ancient Israel is called "the *ekklesia* that was in the wilderness" (Acts 7:38). Messiah Yeshua used *ekklesia* to describe the assembly that He would build (Matthew 16:18, 18:17). Just as our God is One, so in the end He will have but one called-out people.[16]

The Call

Abraham's heirs are to respond when *YHVH Elohim* calls to them, they are to then call on His Holy Name.

In addition to this great religious assembly that the Father vowed to call forth, He also promised Jacob:

"Thy seed shall be as the dust of the earth, and thou shalt spread abroad to the west, and to the east, and to the north, and to the south" (Genesis 28:14, KJV).

To spread abroad is translated from *parats* (פרץ), which means "to break through, burst out (from womb or enclosure), to increase." [17]

The common blessing given to Abraham, Isaac, and Jacob was that of a great congregation of physical descendants: Bountiful bunches of babies, lots and lots of little ones, exponentially growing groups of great-great-great-grandchildren. That is the promise that made old Abraham so happy that night in the desert!

This was the faith of our father Abraham.

---

14 TWOT word # 1991a; page 790. Septuagint: Greek translation of the Hebrew Old Covenant completed 200 years before Messiah's birth. Of the 122 KJV usages, more than 60 times *kahal*(*kehilat*) is translated *ekklesia* (*Hatch and Redpath Concordance to the Septuagint*, 1983, Baker, p 433); 36 times it is translated *synagogue*, as in Genesis 28:3 (TWOT word # 1991a). Like *ekklesia*, both *kahal* and synagogue also describe an *assembly* (Strong's word #'s H6951; G4864).

15 *Thayer's Greek-English Lexicon of the New Testament*, Baker, 1983, p 196a; Strong's # G 1577. In Acts 19:32 *ekklesia* is used to define the confused mob crying out against Paul. Thus *assembly* might be a more appropriate translation.

16 One God: Deu 6:4; Mark 12:29. One people: Num 15:15; Eze 37:19; John 17:11.

17 Strong's and BDBL # H 6555; TWOT # 1826.

Conclusions

- Abraham looked for multiple heirs from his own loins.
- He believed he would father a multitude of nations.
- Isaac was given the same oath.
- Jacob/Israel was given the blessing of Abraham.
- Abraham, Isaac, and Jacob are fellow heirs.
- The Father said that from Jacob would come forth a *kahal-congregation-ekklesia*.

Abraham's multitudinous blessing was passed to Isaac and then to Jacob. It was given to the one who was renamed *Israel*.

Now, as we search for answers to our "Israel" questions, and armed with an outline of the blessing of fruitfulness promised to Jacob, we move to the first time the name *Israel* was given.

Multitude

Abraham

2

Israel: A Blessing

The name Israel is mentioned more than 2,570 times in Scripture. It is first used in Genesis 32:28. There we find Jacob wrestling with an angelic being.

On that decisive night, the starlit sky served as a canopy for the match taking place in an otherwise quiet gorge. The whole world would ultimately be affected by the outcome of the battle, but on this moonlit night the only ones at ringside were the heavenly hosts. They looked on in awe as two beings rolled in the dust, limbs intertwined like a vine. They watched while Jacob clung to an angelic being with unyielding determination.

The heavenly beings saw that the angel mysteriously could not overcome Jacob, yet had the power to dislocate Jacob's hip with a touch.

After the two had wrestled all night, the angelic being spoke and said, "Let me go, for it is daybreak."

But Jacob contended. "I will not let you go unless you bless me." The angel then asked him, "What is your name?"

"*Ya'acov,*" answered the one whose name meant "heel holder."

The angelic being replied, "'No longer will it be said that

your name is *Ya'acov*, but *Yisrael*, for you have striven with the Divine and with human and have overcome'....and he blessed him there" (see Genesis 32:26,27,29-30).

Yisrael. It is a name that is given as a blessing. What does it mean to be Israel? How is it a blessing?

Suggested answers to these important questions provide both a picture of, and a standard for, the children of Israel.

Jacob is derived from the root word *a'kov* (עקב); which is said to mean "heel catcher." Some say, "to seize by the heel; to circumvent [tripping up the heels]; to restrain [holding by the heel]; to stay; to supplant." [18]

Jacob was apparently so named because he grabbed his brother's heel during their birth. Later, possibly fulfilling his name by seizing the moment, *Ya'acov* (יעקב) acquired the firstborn blessing of his father.[19]

Then change came. Our forefather met the angel in the wilderness. He met *YHVH Elohim Tsa'va'ot* (יהוה אלהים צבאות). He met the One known as *The LORD God of Hosts*.

It is written that Jacob "wrestled with the angel and prevailed," and that Jacob "wept and sought His favor." He also confessed his own name to be *Yaacov*, one who acquires by *supplanting.*

After Jacob made lamentation, and after he prevailed, YHVH called him *Yisrael* (Hosea 12:2-4). The Holy One appeared to Jacob and said to him, "You shall no longer be called Jacob, but Israel shall be your name" (Genesis 35:10).

In addition, Hosea wrote of Jacob: "He found Him at Bethel, and there He spoke with us, even the LORD, the God of hosts; YHVH is His name" (Hosea 12:4-5).

Our Father gave Jacob the name *Yisrael*, and through Jacob, "He spoke with us." In other words, through this blessing, the Father also spoke to Jacob's *seed*—the

---

18 Strong's and BDBL # 3290; *Interpreter's Dictionary of the Bible*, Vol. 2, Abingdon, 1962, pp 782-83.

19 Many overemphasize Jacob's season as a "supplanter" and summarily dismiss him (Gen 27:36; Jer 9:4; Hosea 12:3). We would do well to also see that with all his being Jacob wanted the privilege of being the patriarchal firstborn heir. Would not "the God of Jacob" (Exo 3:6) see that desire as a good thing?

multitudes who were in Jacob's loins when the Father called him Israel. He spoke to all who were to become part of Israel. Our Father spoke with *us* through Jacob. [20]

The Meaning of the Name...

The name *Yisrael* (ישראל) is derived from two words: *sarah*, (שרה) and *el* (אל). It is said to mean, "God prevails." [21] Many scholars have studied the etymology (origin and development) of this enigmatic name or title, yet only He Who gave it knows for certain its full meaning.

Strong's defines Israel as, "He will rule as God." *Gesenius Hebrew Lexicon* says, "contender, soldier of God," and that it means "to fight." [22]

- *Sarah* is listed as, "to have power, contend, persist, exert oneself, persevere," and "to prevail, have power (as a prince)." [23]
- *El* is rendered "strength...mighty; especially the Almighty," and as "El persisteth, persevereth." [24]

Scripture reveals that Jacob "wrestled with the angel" and that he "strove with God [Elohim]" (Genesis 32:24; Hosea 12:3-5). The *Angel* must therefore be *Elohim*. [25]

Further, *wrestled* and *striven* are both translated from *sarah*. In this encounter, Jacob demonstrated an ability to stand as a type of "limping prince." He depicts one who is flawed, yet has been granted a certain power in this earth.

The *Theological Wordbook of the Old Testament* says of Jacob's encounter:

---

20 Since "all Scripture is profitable for doctrine," this principle applies to those "brought nigh to Israel's covenants." They share "citizenship" in Israel (2 Tim 3:16; Eph 2:11-22). When this verse was written, it probably referred to the Old Covenant (Tanakh) texts, because the New Covenant texts had not yet been recognized as being Scripture.
21 *Brown-Driver-Briggs' Hebrew Definitions*, #H3478, Parsons, 1999, Findex.com.
22 Strong's # H 3478. *Gesenius*, Hendrickson, 1979, p 370, # 3478.
23 BDBL' # H 8280 (TWOT # 2287); Strong's # H 8280 (TWOT # 93) respectively.
24 Strong's # H 410; BDBL # 3478, Hendrickson, 1979, p 975 respectively.
25 Gen 16:7,13; 21:17; 22:11,15-16; 32:29-30; Exo 3:2; 13:21; 14:19; Dan 3:25,28.

"Jacob's struggle was spiritual, in prayer, as well as physical. And in it, the patriarch prevailed! Not that Jacob defeated God, but that he finally attained God's covenantal requirement of yielded submission....he persisted in refusing to let the Angel go until He had blessed him." [26]

Jacob held on. He prevailed. Thus his name was changed to *Yisrael,* which might be said to mean:

One Who Contends
A Powerful Prevailing Prince
A Soldier of YHVH
One Who Rules With the Almighty [27]

Jacob yielded, contended, and prevailed.

What can his heirs learn from his experience?

Through repentance and perseverance, in the power and strength of the Almighty, Jacob was given the name *Yisrael.* We too should seek our Father's favor, yield to His ways, and always hold on, even cling to Him. That is the secret to prevailing.

Jacob's call to be Israel was issued to him as a human being, which indicates that he was called to be Israel, to prevail here on this earth. Our call is the same. In the power and strength of the Almighty we must persevere and seek victory in this life.

Jacob walked with a limp after he wrestled with the Angel.[28] After we have had a personal encounter with our Messiah, we too should have a decidedly marked walk. Our walk should be so different that it is evident to everyone around us.

Lareshet et Ha'aretz! Possess the Land!

Abraham's heirs are to be victors. As YHVH said:

------

26 TWOT # 2287.
27 Not an actual definition but a suggested compilation of various interpretations.
28 Gen 32:25,31-32.

"I will greatly bless you, and I will greatly multiply your seed as the stars of the heavens and as the sand which is on the seashore; and your seed shall possess the gate of their enemies" (Genesis 22:17).

Israel is to *possess, yaresh,* ירש, (the verb is *lareshet*) both the gates of their enemies and the Land promised their fathers (Genesis 15:7; 28:4; Deuteronomy 1:8). Based on the meaning of *yaresh,* they are "to seize, dispossess, take possession of, inherit, disinherit, occupy."

As the heirs of Jacob, Israel is called to utterly succeed.[29] Yet Israel will only succeed if led by the *Ruach haKodesh* (the Holy Spirit). Those who think they are Spirit led—*but in truth are not,* will not succeed (Leviticus 18:28; 20:22). The sons of Israel who will inherit and possess the Land must in *truth* be led by YHVH's Spirit. This point is so vital that it cannot be overstated. *We must truly be led by the Father's Holy Spirit.*

Where is Israel to be a victorious possessor of gates?

She is to gain mastery in *this world.* In Heaven there is nothing to triumph over, since everything is already in order. Israel's possession of enemy gates must occur here—on the earth.

At the very least, we must desire that victory in our hearts. We must be a people who cry out to the Father and ask Him for victory over our oppressors as the Israelites did when they were slaves in Egypt.

YHVH said, "I have surely seen the affliction of My people who are in Egypt, and have given heed to their cry because of their taskmasters, for I am aware of their sufferings" (Exodus 3:7).

When He hears our cry, He will come and deliver us.

We "do not struggle against flesh and blood, but against the rulers, the powers and world forces of this darkness, against the spiritual forces of wickedness in the heavenly places." And we must master these evils in our own lives (Ephesians 6:12; Genesis 4:7).

---

29 Strong's and BDBL # H 3423. Also see Gen 27:29.

We war against the darkness that binds our people.

In this war, our first objective must be to take our own thoughts captive so that our motives are subject to Messiah. His Kingdom, which is not of this world, must first be established in our own hearts (2 Corinthians 10:5; John 18:36; Matthew 7:3-5). Only then will we be equipped to fight the battles here on earth.[30]

The Twofold Call of Yisrael

Our call to prevail must be tempered with the understanding that "flesh and blood cannot inherit the kingdom of God" (1 Corinthians 15:50). Our God is Spirit, and to be an inheritor of His Eternal Kingdom of Israel,[31] we must be spiritual. "God is spirit, and those who worship Him must worship in spirit and truth" (John 4:24).

The call to be Israel begins here, with people living in flesh and blood bodies. The Creator's established pattern is that first a seed is sown in a natural body, then it is raised in a spiritual body. [32]

The same is true for Israel. The call is twofold: It begins in the physical realm, but is culminated in the spirit realm.

Our call is like that of our forefather. Jacob was given his title because he refused to let go. He would not quit. He was therefore renamed Israel. Such is the call for all followers of Israel's Messiah. Yeshua said, "You will be hated by all because of My name, but it is the one who has *endured to the end* who will be saved" (Matthew 10:22).

May we be counted among those who endure.

Who Will Rule?

To be Israel is to be one who rules with the Almighty. The question of "Who is Israel" leads to the question: *Who*

---

30 2 Chr 20:15-22; Josh 10:25; Zech 10:5; 14:14;1 Tim 1:18; 2 Tim 4:7.

31 His Kingdom of Israel: See 1 Chr 14:2; 17:14; 28:5; 29:23; 2 Chr 9:8; 13:5,8; Isa 9:6-7; Luke 1:32-33; Eph 5:5; Heb 1:3; 3:6; 8:1; 10:12.

32 1 Cor 15:36-50; See the *House of David Herald*, Vol. 11, Book 7, The Seed Principle, by Ephraim and Rimona Frank.

will rule with the Almighty?

Whether realized or not, many fight over this unspoken issue of rulership. Some want exclusive rights to the title of Israel for the wrong reasons. They want to be preeminent. They want to be ones who reign (1 Corinthians 4:7-8; Galatians 4:17). However, Messiah declared, "If anyone wants to be first, he shall be last of all, and servant of all" (Mark 9:35).

To please the Messiah of Israel, one must first become a servant of servants.

Servant—Israel.

Inseparable concepts.

Israel is also a title that is bestowed. Jacob was given the name Israel. So it is for us. In this life men may temporarily take the title unto themselves, but in the end it will only be bestowed by the Almighty. The Father says, "Israel is My son, My firstborn" (Exodus 4:22; Psalm 89:27; Jeremiah 31:9).

Israel is a name given by the Father to His son(s). Only the Father can disinherit a son. Brothers may want to do so, but it is not their prerogative.

Israel, a son.

To find out what happened next to the blessing given to the one who wrestled and prevailed, we ask: To whom did Jacob give the precious blessing given to him by his fathers? Did he pass it on? What took place next? To whom does this title now belong?

Jacob's Firstborn Heir

Jacob's two wives, Leah and Rachel, and their handmaidens, Zilpah and Bilhah, gave Jacob twelve sons, who became known as the twelve tribes of Israel.

Leah was the mother of Jacob's firstborn son, Reuben, The title of "firstborn" should have been his, yet Chronicles reveals that Reuben was not Jacob's heir, but that "the birthright belonged to Joseph" (1 Chronicles 5:2).

"Reuben...was the firstborn, but because he defiled his father's bed, his birthright was given to the sons of Joseph the son of Israel; so that he is not enrolled in the genealogy according to the birthright" (1 Chronicles 5:1).[33]

Jacob gave the birthright to his beloved Rachel's firstborn son. He gave it to Joseph and to Joseph's sons.

In ancient Israel the birthright consisted of a double portion, as well as family preeminence (the right to act as the next family ruler). The Almighty commanded that the father must "acknowledge the firstborn...by giving him a

---

33 *Unger's Bible Dictionary*, Moody, 1974, says, "Jacob took away the right of primogeniture [see Deu 21:17] from Reuben because of his incestuous conduct... and transferred it to Joseph by adopting his two sons" (p 368). Also see *Wycliffe Bible Encyclopedia*, Moody, 1983, p 27.

double portion of all that he has, for he is the beginning of his strength; to him belongs the right of the firstborn" (Deuteronomy 21:17).

The firstborn was given a double portion, that he might be equipped to act as a kinsman-redeemer for his brethren.[34] This "right," or *mishpat* (משפט), of the firstborn (*bekor*, בכור),[35] speaks of preeminence, primogeniture, the right to act as family ruler, to dispense justice, to be the family redeemer.

Concerning this privilege of the firstborn, various textbooks note:

- "The promises...to the patriarchs were considered as attached to the...firstborn." [36]
- The "firstborn...belonged to Jehovah," and "was the priest of the whole family." [37]
- He "had respect as leader among the brothers...and a double portion." [38]
- "He received the right to inherit family leadership... (Genesis 43:33)." [39]
- "Preferential status...sanctity, authority, sovereignty, responsibility, and right of succession accrued to [him]....he became the next head of the family...and embodied the soul and character of the social group, becoming responsible for its continuance and welfare." [40]

Israel conferred the position of firstborn upon Joseph and his sons. Joseph was also given the double portion.

But Joseph had something else...

As a young man Joseph had two prophetic dreams in which his brothers bowed down to him (Genesis 37:5-28).

---

34 See, Ex. 6:6; Lev. 27:13; Ruth 3:9; 4:4; Isa. 59:20.
35 Strong's #'s H 4941 (also TWOT 2443); and 1062 respectively.
36 *Wycliffe Bible Encyclopedia*, Moody, 1983, p 609.
37 *Unger's Bible Dictionary*, Moody, 1974, p 367.
38 *Zondervan Pictorial Encyclopedia*, Vol. 2, Zondervan, 1976, p 540.
39 *The New Harper's Bible Dictionary*, Harper & Row, 1973, p 194; 2 Chr 21:3.
40 *Interpreter's Dictionary of the Bible*, Vol. 2, Abingdon, 1962, pp 270-271.

These "messianic" dreams spoke of Joseph's coming position of leadership. But telling of them greatly angered his brothers. They could not conceive of this eleventh son becoming the family leader. The very idea of him ruling over them made them so mad that when they got him alone they threw him into a pit and later sold him to a group of Ishmaelite traders on their way to Egypt.

After a difficult time in Egypt, Joseph nevertheless rose to power, becoming second only to Pharaoh. He married Asenath, daughter of Potiphera, priest of On, and together they had two sons, Manasseh and Ephraim.

The intriguing story of how the firstborn blessing was passed from Joseph to his sons is found in Genesis Forty-eight. To see the story unfold, let us once again look across the sands of time to a patriarchal tent located in Egypt.

"Your father is sick," the young messenger said as he bowed low before his master. Joseph, vice-regent of Egypt, gathered his sons, who followed him as he hurriedly headed for Jacob's tent. Tears welled up in his eyes as he approached his aged father's bed.

Upon seeing his beloved son, the old man gathered his strength, and sitting up, he said to Joseph:

"God Almighty...said to me, 'Behold, I will make you fruitful and numerous, and I will make you a company of peoples.'"

Jacob told this to Joseph because he knew it was time to convey the blessing that would result in the fulfillment of his promise from the Almighty: that he, Jacob/Israel, would father a great congregation of peoples.

"And now," said the aged Israel, "your two sons, Ephraim and Manasseh, bring them to me, that I may bless them."

Joseph moved his sons toward his father, deliberately choosing their places so Manasseh would be standing before Jacob's right hand.

But Israel deftly placed his *right* hand on Ephraim's head and his *left* hand on Manasseh's head. He then blessed them. (See illustration on page 25.)

"May they grow into teeming multitudes upon the earth."

Joseph heard his father speak precious Hebrew words over his sons, *Va'yig'de'lu la'rov...* (וְיִגְדְּלוּ לָרֹב):

"*May they multiply and proliferate abundantly, like multitudes of fish—may they become teeming multitudes.*"[41]

The patriarch continued to bless Joseph's boys:

"Manasseh shall become a people. However, his younger brother, Ephraim, shall be greater than he, and his descendants shall become "a fullness of Gentiles."

Again, Hebrew words hung in Egyptian air. Ephraim's descendants would become "*melo ha'goyim.*"

The words awed Joseph. The descendants of Ephraim would become a fullness of Gentiles—The abundance of the nations. They would be so numerous they would have to inhabit the lands of other nations! [42]

Joseph stood beside his father's bed. Though he was at first confused by his father's deliberate choice, and even tried to move his hand, Joseph nonetheless watched as his father defined how his promised blessing would be fulfilled. He watched as Israel gave the blessing of a single nation to Manasseh. He listened as Jacob declared that those of Ephraim would become the fullness of the nations.

Joseph's sons were part of YHVH's plan to give to Abraham myriads of descendants, and the way in which it would be accomplished was being declared:

First would come a single nation, and then would come a company, or congregation of nations.

---

41 The *ArtScroll Tanach Series* (commentary from *Talmudic, Midrashic* and *Rabbinic* sources; hereafter called *ArtScroll*) translates the verse, "May they proliferate abundantly like fish" (*Genesis*, Vol. 6, Mesorah, 1982, pp 2115-2117). This verse also can be translated, "May they multiply; may they grow into a multitude of fish" (as translated from *The New Concordance of the Tanach* by Rimona Frank, Hebrew editor). Perhaps this translation fits best, for "fishers of men" would one day be sent forth to gather scattered Israel (Mat 4:19).

42 *ArtScroll* says *m'loh* means a "fullness" and, "Connotes abundance...meaning: His seed will become the abundance of the nations....They will have to inhabit lands of other nations" (*Genesis*, Vol. 6, Mesorah, 1982, p 2121). *Melo* also is used in Psalm 24:1: "The earth is the LORD'S, and the [*melo*] fulness thereof, (KJV), or "all it contains" (NASB). Strong's defines melo (# 4393) as "fulness," and goy (#1471) as "Gentile, heathen, nation, people."

Joseph smiled. He felt honored to be part of it all.

"The God of my fathers will be with you, Joseph, He will bring you back to the land of your fathers," the patriarch said as he laid back on his couch.

Jacob had conferred his promised blessing to Joseph and his sons. Now he could rest. (See Genesis 48:1-22.)

The Allegory

The Father promised Jacob: "A nation and a company of nations shall come from you" (Genesis 35:11). Israel began as "a single nation," then the Shepherd God of Ezekiel 34 and John 14 came and began to gather a "congregation of nations."

In this way we can see how Manasseh allegorically depicts those of Old Covenant Israel—a single, ethnic *people*. Whereas, Ephraim depicts New Covenant Israel—a congregation of many ethnic *peoples*.[43]

Just as Paul used Sarah and Hagar to represent Heavenly and earthly Jerusalem (Galatians 4:24-27), so Manasseh represents Old Covenant Israel and Ephraim represents New Covenant Israel.

The Double Portion

The Almighty said to Jacob, "Behold, I will make you fruitful and numerous, and I will make you a company *[kahal]* of peoples, and will give this land to your seed after you for an everlasting possession" (Genesis 48:2-4).

Joseph was the son of Jacob's beloved Rachel, and Jacob "loved Joseph more than all his sons" (Genesis 37:3).

Jacob said to his firstborn heir, Joseph:[44]

"And now your two sons, who were born to you in the land of Egypt before I came to you in Egypt, are mine;

---

43 *In Search of Israel*, chapter 6, *The Allegory*, Batya Ruth Wootten, 1988.
  Ephraim Frank says Joseph's two sons were named Manasseh (meaning to *forget)* and Ephraim (*fruitful)*, and based on these meanings we see that Joseph's heirs were destined to *forget* their roots, yet would ultimately become a *fruitful* people.
44 Gen 48:21-22.

Ephraim and Manasseh shall be mine, as Reuben and Simeon are."

He also said, "May my name live on in them, and the names of my fathers Abraham and Isaac" (Genesis 48:5,16).

Through this action Israel "adopted" Joseph's two sons.

However, it was not an adoption in the normal sense, since these two boys were Jacob's *biological grandchildren.* They were actually adopted into the position of first and second born *sons.*

If viewed in context, we see that this adoption portrays natural (grand)sons being adopted into a position as "sons in the spirit."

Paul the apostle similarly speaks of his brethren "who are Israelites," saying, it is they "to whom belongs the adoption as sons" (Romans 9:4).

Jacob's statement, "May my name live on in them," could have been a recognized adoption formula in the times in which he lived. [45]

Through this adoption process, Joseph received the firstborn double portion (Deuteronomy 21:17). He would thereafter be known primarily as the two tribes of Manasseh and Ephraim, not as the tribe of Joseph.

Jacob next carried his blessing a step further.

When Joseph brought his sons before his father, "Joseph took them both, Ephraim with his right hand toward Israel's left, and Manasseh with his left hand toward Israel's right, and Joseph brought them close to him" (Genesis 48:9,13).

Scripture clarifies the position of each boy in relation to Israel's right hand because, as the *ArtScroll Tanach Series* states, "One traditionally blesses another by laying his hand on the person's head....The right hand is the preferred one for the performance of *mitzvos [mitzvot]*, and accordingly, has spiritual primacy."[46]

Further, Genesis reveals that "Israel stretched out his

---

45 *Wycliffe Bible Encyclopedia,* Moody, 1983, p 27.
46 *ArtScroll, Genesis,* Vol. 6, Mesorah, 1982, p 2098. *Mitzvot:* righteous acts of mercy.

right hand and laid it on the head of
Ephraim, who was the younger, and his
left hand on Manasseh's head, crossing
his hands, although Manasseh was the
firstborn" (Genesis 48:14).

Thus Jacob put Ephraim before
Manasseh and declared Ephraim to
be Joseph's heir.

Jacob/Israel further clarified what he meant when he
said, "Ephraim...shall be mine as Reuben." In other words,
"Ephraim shall be as my firstborn" (Genesis 48:20,5).

Writing Joseph's Will

Israel in essence wrote Joseph's will for him, which
Ezekiel confirms when he says, "The stick of Joseph...is in
the hand of Ephraim" (Ezekiel 37:19).

Possession of the "stick" indicates Ephraim's headship
over the tribe of Joseph. The Father instructed Moses:
"Speak to the sons of Israel, and get from them a rod for
each fathers household: twelve rods...You shall write each
name on his rod...one rod for the head of each of their
father's households" (Numbers 17:2-3). The *stick*, or *rod*,
serves as the symbol of family leadership,[47] and Ephraim
holds Joseph's rod.

Abraham's heir was Isaac. Isaac's heir was Jacob.
Jacob's heir was Joseph. And Joseph's heir was Ephraim.

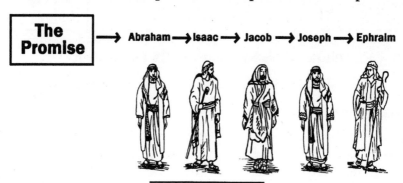

The Promise → Abraham → Isaac → Jacob → Joseph → Ephraim

---

47 *Matteh*, מטה (stick), "means 'staff' or 'rod.'" TWOT # 1352.

But why was Joseph's inheritance given to Ephraim, rather than Manasseh, who was Joseph's actual firstborn son? Why was the one who was naturally in line for the firstborn blessing be passed over in favor of another? Is there a message being conveyed in these actions? Is the Father teaching us a principle in the way the patriarchal firstborn were chosen?

Divine Election

Abraham's physical firstborn was Ishmael, but the Holy One elected Isaac, Abraham's second-born, as heir. Isaac's firstborn, Esau, was passed over in favor of Jacob. Then Jacob overlooked firstborn Reuben and chose Joseph, his eleventh son (the firstborn of Rachel). Finally, Manasseh was passed over in favor of Ephraim.

Each of these elected heirs had one thing in common: Though all were biological heirs, they became firstborn heirs through a type of adoption into that position.

YHVH's Elected Heirs

Abraham ⇨	Actual Firstborn: **Ishmael** YHVH's Elected Heir: **Isaac** ⇨	Actual Firstborn: **Esau** YHVH's Elected Heir: **Jacob** ⇨	Actual Firstborn: **Reuben** YHVH's Elected Heir: **Joseph** ⇨	Actual Firstborn: **Manessah** YHVH's Elected Heir: **Ephraim**

The Actual Firstborn and *YHVH's Elected Heirs*

Divine Intervention

With the exception of "mysterious Ephraim," each of the above listed firstborn heirs required divine intervention to bring them forth. We read of their mothers:

- "And Sarai was barren; she had no child." But the Father said, "I will bless her....and she shall be a mother of nations" (Genesis 11:30; 17:16).
- "Isaac prayed to YHVH on behalf of his wife, because she was barren; and YHVH answered him and Rebekah his wife conceived" (Genesis 25:21).
- "Rachel was barren....Then God remembered Rachel, and God gave heed to her and opened her womb" (Genesis 29:31; 30:22).

The wombs of the mothers of Isaac, Jacob, and Joseph each had to be opened by the Holy One, but this was not the case with Ephraim (a point we will return to later).

Isaac, Jacob, Joseph, and Ephraim, did not gain their position based on biological birth order. They became heirs by being adopted into a firstborn position.

What picture do these examples paint for us?

They portray the truth that even if one is a physical heir, it is still our Father Who brings forth the elected firstborn. They are determined according to His election.

Thus Paul wrote that inheritance is not based "on man's desire or effort, but on God's *mercy"* (Romans 9:16, NIV).

It all depends on the Father's *chesed*, on His *mercy*.

These examples teach us that the natural firstborn can be set aside for one who is a firstborn after the spirit. Similarly, in our first, or natural, birth we are found to be but sinners; whereas in our second, or spiritual, birth we become children of God.[48]

A Firstborn Profile

In Israel the firstborn belonged to YHVH (Exodus 13:2,15). As the family priest, he was the embodiment of the soul and character of the social group. As head of the family, he was given authority and respect as the leader among the brothers. As the firstborn, he received preeminent sovereignty and a double portion.

---

48 John 1:12; 3:1-7; Rom 9:8-13; 1 Cor 15:22,45-47

Despite this rule, "It was possible for the father to deprive the firstborn of the right....Primogeniture was always considered but was not always decisive....The cases of transfer of birthright appear as exceptions which exemplify divine election." [49]

Did Ephraim Become Preeminent?

In Israel the firstborn is preeminent, he is a priest, a sovereign, a redeemer, and he has a double portion.

Did Ephraim, as Jacob's firstborn heir, fulfill his call to become the next head of the family, the head who embodied the soul and character of Israel? Did Ephraim become a powerful prevailing prince?

---

49 *Wycliffe Bible Encyclopedia*, Moody, 1983, pp 609-610; 843.

4

Ephraim: A Profile

*E*phraim's name *as an individual* is mentioned only fourteen times in Scripture. [50] We are told he was born in Egypt, that he was the second son of Joseph and Asenath (the daughter of Potiphera the priest of On), and that he was named *Ephraim* because his father Joseph said, "God has made me *fruitful* in the land of my affliction" (Genesis 41:52).

Ephraim was brought before his grandfather, Jacob, who declared him to be Jacob's primary heir. Later we are told the names of his sons. He is last mentioned in Scripture in Genesis 50:23: "And Joseph saw the third generation of Ephraim's sons."

After that, elusive Ephraim disappears. He whose name meant "doubly fruitful," simply fades away[51]—with no record of him ever passing on his rich blessing to another.

The patriarchal firstborn blessing was passed to Ephraim, and its passing ended with Ephraim.

---

50 Gen 41:52; 46:20; 48:1,5,13,14,17,20; 50:23; Num 26:28; 1 Chr 7:20,22.
51 Strong's defines Ephraim (אפרים), as meaning "double fruit" (# H 669); *Gesenius Hebrew Lexicon*, Hendrickson, 1979, says, "double land" (# 69, p 73). Double land, double fruit is the meaning of the name of the one given the double portion.

A House Divided

After Jacob blessed Ephraim, Ephraim's descendants were thereafter regarded as a single tribe. Years later, ten of Israel's twelve tribes collectively became known as "Ephraim," or "Ephraimites," [52] but they were most often called after their firstborn birthright name, "Israel."

Some time after the children of Israel entered into the land of Canaan, they divided into two houses: Judah and Ephraim (or Israel).

Although all twelve tribes were Jacob/Israel's descendants, and thus could rightly be called "Israel," those of the Northern Kingdom of Ephraim were primarily called "Israel," and those of the Southern Kingdom were called "Judah" (2 Kings 17:34; 1 Kings 12:21).

Again, the Father says, "Israel is My son, My firstborn" (Exodus 4:22). Thus "Israel" is a birthright name. Just as the *birthright* was given to Joseph and then to Ephraim, so the birthright *name* of Israel was appropriated by the people of Ephraim.

The Lost Tribes

The Northern Kingdom of Israel consisted of ten tribes (1 Kings 11:35) and lasted a little more than two hundred years (975-721 B.C.).[53] However, because the Ephraimites often followed after the pagan customs of their Gentile neighbors, for a season some of them joined the more godly people of Judah.[54]

---

52 Isaiah says, "Ephraim" was shattered, and thus was no longer "a people." He also tells of the day "Ephraim separated from Judah (Is.7:5-9; 7:17). The Father calls the separated ten tribes "Ephraim" (1 K 11:31-37). We find "Ephraim-Judah" comparisons in 1 K 12:21; Hosea 5:12,14; 6:4; 10:11; Zech 9:13; Eze 37:16-19. We call the people of the Northern Kingdom "Ephraim" and sometimes use the term "Ephraimites" when referring to them (see Judges 12:4-6). We use "Judahites" to refer to those of "Judah," and "Israelites" to refer to those of "Israel."
53 *The Kings of Judah and Israel* by Christopher Knapp, Loizeaux Brothers, 1983, pp 27-28.
54 How many tribes joined Judah, even if only for a season? While we cannot find every tribe represented as being among them, we can find Levites (but not all (continued...)

These Israelites were considered to be subjects of Judea while they sojourned with them (1 Kings 12:17), but when Judah ultimately fell into the same sins,[55] the Ephraimites returned to their land, and both houses continued their distinct identities: Judah and Ephraim/Israel.

Although Scripture does speak of some intermingling and intermarriage between the two kingdoms,[56] and while men could move from their tribal land to that of another, they could not take their land inheritance with them.

Land could be sold on a "lease" basis, but not permanently (Leviticus 25:13,29-31; Judges 21:24). This restriction would have tended to limit intermingling, but more importantly, if someone did move to a different tribal territory, that move would not change their tribal lineage. For example, someone from the tribe of Asher could live among either the Ephraimites or the Judahites and be considered a citizen of either kingdom.

It is possible that each house—Israel and Judah—included representatives of each tribe, however small that representation might be. Yet each house remained a distinct entity until the very end. There was even continual warfare between them that ceased only when Ephraim's northern foe, Assyria, carried the people of Ephraim into captivity.[57]

So it is that those of Ephraim Israel became known as "The Ten Lost Tribes."

Ephraim and the Samaritans

Of the Israelites taken captive by Assyria, the *New International Version Study Bible* tells us:

---

54 (...continued)
Levites: see 2 Chr 11:14; 2 Ki 17:28; 1 Ki 12:21 and the *New International Version Study Bible*, Zondervan, 1985, footnote). We also see some from Ephraim, Manasseh, Simeon, Asher, Zebulun and Issachar (2 Chr 15:9; 30:11,18).
55 Ez 23:1-49; 2 Ki 16:2-4; 17:19; 2 Chr 31:1.
56 1 Ki 22:4; 2 Ki 8:18.
57 Their last war was in 735 B.C. See *Chronological Charts of the Old Testament* by John H. Walton, Zondervan, 1978, p 62; 1 Ki 14:30; 15:16; 2 Ki 15:37; 16:5-6.

"Israel experienced its first deportations under Tiglath-Pileser III (745-727 B.C.), a cruelty repeated by Sargon II (722-705 B.C.) at the time of the fall of Samaria. The latter king's inscriptions boast of carrying away 27,290 inhabitants of the city as booty.... they were sent to Assyria, to Halah (Calah?), to Gozan on the Habor River, and apparently to the eastern frontiers of the empire (to the towns of the Medes, most probably somewhere in the vicinity of Ecbatana, the modern Hamadan)." [58]

During this time the Assyrians practiced a unique method of controlling newly conquered lands. They scattered the leading citizens among different nations, then moved other conquered leaders into the newly subjugated land. All were thus destabilized and less likely to unite and revolt.

Assyrian records indicate that noble families were taken captive, whereas agricultural workers were left behind to care for the crops. [59] The farmers and fishermen who were forced to stay and feed their conquerors were ultimately assimilated into the Assyrian Empire.

Nevertheless, a few could have held out. Some Ephraimites could have lived for generations under the rule of their Assyrian conquerors without forgetting that they were Israelites.

After Israel ceased to be an identifiable people (Isaiah 7:8; Hosea 1:10; 2:23), and after some of the people of Judah returned from Babylon, all of the sons of Jacob who stood together began to be called "Jews." Thus there could

---

58 *New International Version Study Bible*, Zondervan, 1995, (hereafter: NIV Study Bible) Map, *Exile of the Northern Kingdom*, p 550.
Note: This number does not include all those ultimately taken captive. Scripture states that, "Tiglath-Pileser king of Assyria came and captured Ijon and Abel-beth-maacah and Janoah and Kedesh and Hazor and Gilead and Galilee, all the land of Naphtali; and he carried them captive to Assyria" (2 Ki 15:29). The total number of captives is unknown. However, Amos 5:3 does say, "The city that marches out a thousand strong for Israel will have only a hundred left; the town that marches out a hundred strong will have only ten left" (also see vs. 3:12).
59 NIV Study Bible, Zondervan, 1995, p 550.

have been Ephraimite fishermen, such as Peter the apostle, who were called Jews.

As to what happened to the Ephraimites, the Word reveals that Ephraim was scattered "in Halah, at the [River] Habor, at the River Gozan, and in the towns of Media," and that afterward, "The king of Assyria brought men from Hamath and Sephar-vaim, and settled them in the cities of Samaria in place of the sons of Israel. So they possessed Samaria [Israel's capital] and lived in its cities" (2 Kings 17:6,24, TNKH; 1 Chronicles 5:26).

Among this mix of assimilated and transplanted people were those who ultimately became known as "Samaritans." These people were generally despised by those of Judah. The Samaritans apparently returned this disdain. Each persisted with these attitudes even into New Covenant times.[60]

Miles Apart—Generations Later

To understand what happened to the people of Ephraim, we must see that at the time they were taken captive:

- They had their own king and functioned as a separate kingdom (2 Kings 17:1-3).
- They were taken to cities that varied in distance from 250 to 350 miles north of Babylon, which is where Judah was taken.
- It was 135 years, or several generations later, before Judah was taken captive.
- Judah was settled "by the river Chebar" (Ezekiel 1:1), whereas Ephraim was scattered "beyond the Euphrates River" (1 Kings 14:15).

There were many miles and several generations between the deportation of Ephraim to Assyria and the later deportation of Judah to Babylon. Note also that these two peoples were openly hostile toward one another when they occupied the Promised Land.

---

60 Luke 9:52-53; John 4:9; 8:48.

Despite these facts, many people do not see the differences between the two kingdoms. They do not realize that there were different deportations and times, as well as different prophecies and promises that apply to each group.

It is as though they were blinded to the truth...

Assimilated Into the Foreign Milieu

What happened to the Ephraimites as a people after their conquest by Assyria?

The *Encyclopaedia Judaica* says:

"It is evident that as a rule they did not possess the status of slaves or of an oppressed population. The exiles were first settled in Mesopotamia as land tenants of the king...the craftsmen among them were employed in state enterprises. Eventually, some of the exiles achieved economic and social status and even occupied high ranking positions in the Assyrian administration....The striking of roots in Mesopotamian society by a large part of the descendants of the Israelite exiles resulted in their eventual absorption into the foreign milieu."[61]

All Jews Were Israelites
But Not All Israelites Were Jews

To understand Israel, we must realize that these deported Ephraimites were *Israelites*, not *Jews*. When they lived in the Land *prior to their deportation,* these Israelites were not called Jews, they were called Israelites. [62]

Once dispersed from their native land, once scattered, they lived and worked in Assyria. As stated, they struck roots in Mesopotamian society, meaning they were absorbed. *For all outward appearances* these Ephraimites became "foreigners." As foretold, they became "Gentiles."

---

[61] *Encyclopaedia Judaica*, Keter Publishing, 1972, Jerusalem, Exile, Assyrian, p 1036.

[62] "Jew" is a derivative of "Judahite" (Hebrew: יהודי, *Yehudi*).

The Judahites were taken captive more than a century and a quarter later. In addition, wherever they have been scattered, the Jewish people have always sought to maintain a separate identity from the nations in which they lived. They have fought assimilation.

The Ephraimites, in contrast, wanted to be like the Gentiles. They liked the ways of the heathen. Because of this desire, the Father allowed them to become lost among the nations. He allowed them to outwardly become "Gentiles."

So went the fate of Ephraim.

From this brief history we see that the hallmark of the people of Ephraim is that they are lost to their own Israelite identity. With this lost identity they do not paint a picture of a great congregation of people mightily blessed by the God of Israel.

A Second Birth?

Where are the Ephraimites today?

The *Encyclopaedia Judaica* notes that Josephus, the first century historian, stated in his *Antiquities*: "The ten tribes are beyond the Euphrates till now, and are an immense multitude not to be estimated in numbers." [63]

Alfred Edersheim, the 19th century Jewish Believer and theologian, wrote in his respected work, *The Life and Times of Jesus the Messiah:*

"The great mass of the ten tribes was in the days of Messiah, as in our own, lost to the Hebrew nation." [64]

Edersheim also calls them:

"Those wanderers of the ten tribes whose trackless footsteps seem as mysterious as their after-fate." [65]

In his study of rabbinical thought regarding the lost tribes, Edersheim concludes:

---

63 *Encyclopaedia Judaica*, 1972, Keter, *Ten Lost Tribes*, p 1004.
64 *Life and Times of Jesus the Messiah*, 1973, Eerdman's, pp 15-16.
65 Edersheim, *The Life and Times of Jesus the Messiah*, p 14.

"As regards the ten tribes there is this truth underlying...that, as their persistent apostasy from the God of Israel and His worship had cut them off from His people, so the fulfillment of the Divine promises to them in the latter days would imply, as it were a second birth to make them once more Israel." [66]

As suggested by Edersheim, did the Ephraimites experience a second birth? Were the Divine promises made to them ever fulfilled? Having become lost among the Gentile nations, did they once again become Israel?

---

66 Edersheim, *The Life and Times of Jesus the Messiah*, p 15.

Yankees and Rebels

Before their division, the two houses of Israel were united under three successive kings.

- The first king was Saul, a Benjamite.
- Then from the tribe of Judah came King David, whom "all Israel and Judah loved" (1 Samuel 18:16).
- Afterward, David's son, Solomon, became king.

Solomon entered into sin by building places of idol worship for his foreign wives. This idolatry sounded a death knell for the unified kingdom of Israel.

The Holy One told Solomon, "Because you have done this...I will surely tear the kingdom from you, and will give it to your servant. Nevertheless, I will not do it in your days for the sake of your father David, but I will tear it out of the hand of your son" (1 Kings 11:11-12).

Judah, the Beloved

The united kingdom of Israel was torn from Solomon's son, Rehoboam, because of idolatry. However, the Father said, "I will not tear away all the kingdom, but I will give one tribe to your son for the sake of My servant David and for the sake of Jerusalem which I have chosen" (1 Kings 11:13).

Judah remained a kingdom because they were beloved for the sake of their father David, and because of YHVH's love for Jerusalem, His chosen city.

This will forever remain unchanged. Romans 11:28 says of the Jew: "From the standpoint of God's choice, they are beloved for the sake of the fathers."

The God of Israel loves the Jewish people and is always calling them to Himself.

Let us never forget this important truth. Let us always seek to make it known to those who do not realize it.

Divided Ten to One

Regardless of His eternal love for them, the Father took the greater portion of the kingdom away from Judah's sovereignty. As He swore He would, He gave ten parts to Solomon's servant, an Ephraimite named Jeroboam.

At that time the Father told Jeroboam, "I will tear the kingdom out of Solomon's hand and give you ten tribes" (see 1 Kings 11:11-12,26,31-35).

Ten tribes were given to Ephraim, and Israel was thus torn in two. It is most important that we see it was torn in two by the Almighty Himself. For the Holy One declared, *"This thing has come from Me"* (1 Kings 12:24). [67]

North and South—Brother against Brother

The Israelites separated into two houses after King Solomon's rule. Their division can be compared to that of the United States during the Civil War: Yankees and Rebels —Union and Confederacy—North and South.

During the American Civil War both sides continued to be Americans despite the bloody battle that raged between brothers. So it was in ancient Israel.

---

[67] See 1 Ki 11:31-32; 12:21 and NIV Study Bible footnotes for same; also see Joshua 21.

The Southern Kingdom of Judah and the Northern Kingdom of Ephraim repeatedly went to war against each other—cousin countering cousin, though both were part of the greater family of Israel. However, those of Judea were primarily called "Judah, Judeans, or Jews."

Considering our "Yankee and Rebel" comparison, it is ironic that one reason for ancient Israel's separation was a type of slave labor. Many in the house of Joseph had become conscripted laborers for the ruling house of Judah, thus King Solomon needed an overseer to control this considerable number of forced laborers.[68]

The Root Cause of Israel's Division

When Solomon saw that "Jeroboam was a valiant warrior" and that he "was industrious, Solomon appointed him over all the forced labor of the house of Joseph" (1 Kings 11:28).

After YHVH told Solomon that Jeroboam would receive ten tribes, Solomon was filled with jealousy and tried to kill Jeroboam. So Jeroboam fled to Egypt and remained there until after Solomon's death.

After Solomon died, his son, *"Rehoboam, went to Shechem, for all the Israelites had gone there to make him king. When Jeroboam son of Nebat heard this [he was still in Egypt, where he had fled from King Solomon], he returned from Egypt. So they sent for Jeroboam, and he and the whole assembly of Israel went to Rehoboam and said to him, 'Your father put a heavy yoke on us, but now lighten the harsh labor and the heavy yoke he put on us and we will serve you.'"*

Foolish Rehoboam ignored the wise counsel of his elders to relent. He instead "listened to his peers," who errantly advised him to make the service that was imposed on his brothers "even more harsh" (1 Kings 12:1-14).

Thus began Israel's division.

-----

68 See 1 Sam 8:11-19; 11:15; 1 Ki 9:15,21, and *NIV Study Bible* footnotes.

It Was From the LORD...

Scripture says of Rehoboam's refusal to listen to his elders: "It was a turn of events from the LORD, that He might establish His word...to Jeroboam the son of Nebat."

This division was "from YHVH," which means there is a reason why it happened. We will soon see this reason.

Nonetheless, Jeroboam's reappearance incited Rehoboam to make a move to retake all Israel. So, "King Rehoboam sent Adoram, who was over the forced labor, [apparently he had taken Jeroboam's place] and all Israel [Ephraim] stoned him to death. And King Rehoboam made haste to mount his chariot to flee to [his capital] Jerusalem."

"When all Israel [Ephraim] heard that Jeroboam had returned, they sent and called him to the assembly and made him king over all Israel [the Northern Kingdom]" (see 1 Kings 12:15-20).

David's Fallen House

The kingdom of Israel was thus divided: Rehoboam was the king of Judah, and Jeroboam was the king of Israel. David's once united house, his once glorious tent, was fallen. For it is written that, "a kingdom divided against itself cannot stand"—so David's house fell (Matthew 12:25).

It is essential that we realize that this kingdom was divided in two by the Almighty. It was a turn of events that came from His hand. [69]

It came from His hand because He had a plan. In spite of their innate differences, despite their many sins, the Father would yet use His two houses of Israel.

---

69 1 Ki 12:15,24; 2 Chr 11:4.

6

LoAmmi—Not A People

After they became a separate kingdom, the people of Ephraim began to mingle with the heathen. "Ephraim mixes himself with the nations," Hosea said. Ultimately it was written of them: "Ephraim has become a cake not turned" (Hosea 7:8).

Because they mixed themselves with the heathen, the Ephraimites became "a cake not turned." In other words, they were "*half-baked*," like a pancake cooked on one side. The metaphor suggests they had only a partial relationship with the finishing fire of God's Spirit—their other side was raw, or pagan.

The people of Ephraim entertained foreign gods and doctrines, which led to the sapping of their strength. This prevented them from being the powerful prevailing prince that Israel was called to be, for Israel was "not to be reckoned among the nations" (Numbers 23:9). They were called instead to be a holy people, set apart and belonging solely to YHVH.

Foreign ways. That was the trouble with Ephraim. It was also the reason the Father allowed the Assyrians to take their unrepentant tribes captive. But before He scattered them among the nations, the Father sent a prophet to His wayward children. He sent Hosea.

Hosea's family spoke prophetic volumes to the Ephraimites. It depicted their spiritual condition, their impending punishment, and the blessing the Father would ultimately pour out on the repentant descendants of these wayward Israelites. [70]

The Holy One judged them because of their lust for pagan ways. YHVH's wife was being unfaithful, so when He spoke through Hosea, He said, "Go, take to yourself an adulterous wife and [have] children of unfaithfulness, because the land is guilty of the vilest adultery in departing from the LORD" (Hosea 1:2, NIV). [71]

Hosea then married Gomer and they had three children.[72] YHVH said the names of these children depicted the punishment He would soon mete out to the Ephraimites. Once changed, their names would ultimately depict the blessings He would bestow on their scattered seed.

When Gomer had her first child, a son, the Father said to Hosea, "Name him *Jezreel;* for yet a little while, and I will punish...and I will put an end to the kingdom of the house of Israel" (Hosea 1:4).

Though it marked the end of the Ephraimite *kingdom,* it did not mark their end as *individuals.* The Father made some definite, yet unfulfilled, promises to these scattered ones.[73]

Gomer conceived again and gave birth to a daughter, and YHVH instructed Hosea to, "Call her name *LoRuhamah:* for I will no more have mercy upon the house of Israel; but I will utterly take them away" (Hosea 1:6, KJV).

Finally, when Gomer gave birth to their third child, a son, God said to Hosea, "Name him *LoAmmi,* for you are not My people and I am not your God" (Hosea 1:9).

---

70 Hosea 1:6,9-10; 2:1,23.
71 Eze 23; Isa 54:5; Hosea 2:19-20.
72 *Gomer* comes from a word that means *complete.* See BDBL # H 1586.
73 Hos 1:6,9-10; 2:1,23; Jer 31:20; Isa 11:13-14; Zec 10:7.

The Meaning of Their Names

The first child's name was *Jezreel*, which comes from two words: *zera* (זרע, seed), used in the agricultural sense of to sow, to scatter; and *El* (אל), one of the names of God.

This name speaks of the entire agricultural process. A seed is scattered, then hidden in the ground. It dies and is reborn, then comes forth in a new, more beautiful form; finally, it is harvested. [74]

- *Jezreel* (יזרעאל): *El will scatter—El will sow.* This name indicated the destiny of the Ephraimites. It foretold their beginning punishment and the blessing they would receive in the end.
- *LoRuhamah* (לא רחמה): *No Compassion; No Mercy.*[75] This second child was so named because the Father could no longer have pity on the Ephraimites. To do so would be to wink at sin. He had to correct them.
- *LoAmmi* (לא עמי): *Not My People.* The third child's name described their impending penalty.[76] The Father would punish them by scattering them. For a season they would be *"Not My People."*

Swallowed by the Nations

YHVH would *scatter (Jezreel)* the Ephraimites. He could no longer allow them to remain in His Land (Leviticus 20:22). Because they wanted to be like the Gentiles, He would allow them to have their fill of it. In other words, He would allow them to be scattered among the nations and appear to be Gentiles until they were tired of being like the Gentiles.

YHVH could not overlook Ephraim's heathen ways. As a Father He had to correct their errant behavior. Since they had sown their *zera* (seed) in harlotry in the land of His enemies, He would in turn scatter their *zera* (descendants)

---

74 *Jezreel.* Strong's # H3157; TWOT # 582; Hosea 1:4, 11 NIV Study Bible footnotes.
75 Strong's # H 3819.
76 Strong's # H 3818: *Lo,* means no, not; *Ammi,* means, a, (or my) people.

in the land of their enemies.[77]

Because they scattered seed of harlotry, their seed was scattered in humiliation. Thus it is written, "Israel is swallowed up; they are now among the nations like a vessel in which no one delights" (Hosea 8:8).

Swallowed is translated from the Hebrew *bala* (בלע), meaning, "to make away with by swallowing, to devour, to be at an end, to swallow down." [78]

When a piece of meat is swallowed, it virtually becomes part of the flesh. Similarly, all Ephraimite identity vanished. Once "swallowed up," the Ephraimites became part of the nations. They became *LoAmmi/Not a People*. Their hallmark was that they were not YHVH's people because they were not acting like set-apart people, but like the other *Gentile heathen nations.*

Our Father promised, "I will shake the house of Israel among all nations as grain is shaken in a sieve, but not a kernel will fall to the ground" (Amos 9:9).

Ephraim would be shaken among all nations. Those who were "not a people" were destined to be found everywhere.

There Remains a Promise

To the seed of these wayward ones the Holy One of Israel made a pledge. The names of Hosea's children would one day be turned to represent the blessings the Father would bestow on them. One day they would *"respond to Jezreel"* (Hosea 2:22). [79]

---

77 Hosea 8:8; 9:3,17; Amos 7:11; 9:9. *Zera/descendants.* See Genesis 12:7.
78 Strong's # H 1104.
79 Blessings: Hos 1:6,9-10; 2:1,23; *NIV Study Bible*, Zondervan, 1985, footnotes.

In its second meaning, *Jezreel* speaks of the blossoming forth of those once hidden like a seed, the emphasis being on the seedlings' *response—anah* (ענה). [80] In other words, one day Ephraim's scattered seed would begin to heed, to pay attention to, the Father and to His Word. They would begin to speak, to sing together, to shout, to testify, to announce. They would begin to bear witness to the world about the One called their Husband and Maker. [81]

Such was the destiny of those of the Northern Kingdom, which they were destined to fulfill in great numbers. YHVH had promised that "The number of the sons of Israel will be like the sand of the sea, which cannot be measured or numbered; and in the place where it is said to them, 'You are not My people,' it will be said to them, 'You are the sons of the living God'" (Hosea 1:10).

When the sons of Ephraim would begin to respond in their diaspora, and begin to hear and testify about the Almighty—in that day, they would also finally do as they were told: "Say to your brothers, '*Ammi*,' and to your sisters, '*Ruhamah*'" (Hosea 2:1).

From No Mercy to Vessels of Mercy

Those who once were "not my people" were destined to respond to YHVH. He would once again call them "My people." Those once called *LoRuhamah*, or *NoMercy*, would become *Ruhamah*—vessels on which He would show *mercy* (Romans 9:23):

"I will sow her unto me in the earth; and I will have mercy upon her that had not obtained mercy; and I will say to them which were not my people, Thou art my people; and they shall say, Thou art my God" (Hosea 2:23, KJV). They would tell their brothers of the Father's great mercy. They would come forth, even as the Psalmist prayed:

"*O God: hold not thy peace, and be not still...For, lo,*

---

80 Hidden Ones: See Psa 83:3-4; 27:5; 31:20; 91:1; Col 3:3.
81 See Strong's # H 6030 definition.

*thine enemies make a tumult: and they that hate thee
have....taken crafty counsel against thy people, and
consulted against thy hidden ones. They have said, Come,
and let us cut them off from being a nation; that the name
of Israel may be no more.... They have consulted together
with one consent: they are confederate against thee: The
tabernacles of Edom...the Ishmaelites...Moab...Ammon...
Amalek, the Philistines...." (Psalm 83:1-9, KJV).*

Ephraimite Hallmarks

We have enumerated certain hallmarks that will help us
identify the hidden ones who are often called the "Ten Lost
Tribes." Although their corporate footprints may be
trackless, their children are nevertheless decidedly marked.

- Ephraim would become a *melo ha'goyim*, a *fullness
  of the Gentiles* (Genesis 48:19).[82]
- They would be scattered among, and be regathered
  from, *all nations.*
- They would experience a second birth (*Jezreel: born
  anew)* and once more be known as "Israel."
- They would be like the sand of the sea in number.
- One of their names would be *Sons of the living God.*
- They would proclaim to their brothers the Good News
  of the great mercy of their God.

---

82 *ArtScroll, Genesis,* Vol. 6, Mesorah, 1982, says *m'loh* means a "fullness" and
"Connotes abundance...meaning: His seed will become the abundance of the
nations ....They will have to inhabit lands of other nations" (p 2121). Also see
Strong's # H 4393 and 1471.
It is important to note that Psalm 24:1 uses the word *melo,* and the King James
Bible translates it: "The earth is the LORD's and the *fullness thereof."* Also,
according to Gesenius' (Hendrickson, p 163a, word # 1471), *goyim* is "specially
used of the (other) nations besides Israel."

Many Israels—One Israel

For two thousand years, following the Father's call to Jacob, the twelve tribes of Israel—though ultimately divided into two houses by the Almighty (1 Kings 11:26; 12:24)—appeared to be Jacob's heirs.

Then in Israel a Son was born. He called Himself "the Son of Man." However, He also was a man with many names: Immanuel, the Lamb of God, the Son of David, the Good Shepherd, the Glory of Israel.

Paradoxically, incorrect interpretations of the life and death of the One called the Prince of Peace served to divide Israel once again. Because of Him another war began in Israel—a war over the title of Israel.

This conflict has continued for almost 2000 years, pitting brother against brother. It is a battle that brings much grief to the heart of our Heavenly Father.

Two groups of people today lay claim to the coveted title of Israel. Many adherents of Christianity and virtually all followers of Judaism proclaim themselves to be the true heirs of the patriarchs, and most deny the other the right to the title.

But what is the truth? Who really is Israel?

The question is crucial, because the true identity of the heirs of this important title must not be vague. As the chosen people of the Almighty, the Israelites are destined to reign with the Ruler of all the earth. So we ask: Who are they?

For centuries the Church claimed the title of *New Israel*. Many Christians claimed they had replaced the "rejected" Jewish people. They taught that *they* were God's chosen people. But when the modern State of Israel was established in 1948, it caused an identity crisis within the Church, because it was evident to the world that the God of Israel aided the return of the Jewish people to the Land.

Then in the 1970's there began a new move in the earth. Jewish Believers in the Messiah began to make their presence known, and their growing presence only added to the "Israel" question.

So again we ask: *Who is Israel?*

Traditionally, the most common responses to this crucial query have been:

- Jacob, Whose Name Was Changed to Israel
- The Sons of Jacob—The Twelve Tribes
- The Land Given to the Twelve Tribes
- The Old-Covenant People of the God of Israel
- The Ten Tribes of the Northern Kingdom
- The Church [83]
- The Jewish People
- The Present Jewish State

---

[83] "Church," like "Israel," is a multi-faceted name/title, and one must know what the author means with its use. There is a "church system" that persecutes true Believers (Rev 3:16; 2 Tim 3:1-12; Matt 5:20), and there is a true *church*, an eternal *ekklesia*—which includes all who truly seek to follow the God of Israel (Acts 7:38; 2 Thes 1:1; 2:13). There also is a "synagogue of Satan" that opposes Messiah (John 8:44; 10:33; Rev 2:9; 3:9). In this book, the word "Church" is sometimes used to include those who, in this life, "claim" to belong to "the Church." This same standard of including those who, in the end, the Father Himself may not include also is applied in references to "Jews/Judaism." We trust that in the end the Holy One Himself will decide who among both peoples is acceptable (Mat 7:23). Since the word "Church" is often misunderstood, we will prefer the Greek *ekklesia* (Strong's # G 1577) when referring to the *called out ones*.

The One True Israel

The above list includes the most common responses to the "*Who Is Israel*" question. However, it does not include an "Israel" that stands above the rest. It leaves out the most important Israel of all. It fails to recognize the only One Who is truly capable of being "A Prince Who Rules With The Almighty." It leaves out...

♈ *Yeshua*

The Israel Who Will Gather Israel

"Then you shall say to Pharaoh, 'Thus says YHVH, "Israel is My son, My firstborn" (Exodus 4:22).

There is an Israel Who is appointed the task of "raising up the tribes of Jacob/Israel." That Son named Israel is none other than Yeshua, the Man with many names, for He is also named *Yisrael.*

In Isaiah, both the Father and Yeshua speak:

"Listen to Me, O islands [the nations]....From the body of My mother He named Me [says Yeshua]. And He has made My mouth like a sharp sword....And He said to Me, 'You are My Servant, Israel, In Whom I will show My glory'....And now says YHVH who formed Me from the womb to be His Servant, to bring Jacob back to Him, in order that Israel might be gathered to Him...To raise up the tribes of Jacob and to restore the preserved ones of Israel; I will also make You [Yeshua] a light of the nations so that My salvation [Yeshua] may reach to the end of the earth" (Isaiah 49:1-6).

Yeshua fulfills these verses in numerous ways:

♦ Those of the "nations" were to listen to "the One *named* from the body of His mother."

✓ Our Heavenly Father named His Son Yeshua before He was born (Matthew 1:21).

♦ The One speaking has a mouth like sharp sword.

✓ A sword is in Yeshua's mouth (Revelation 2:16).

♦ The Father calls this One, "My Servant, Israel."

✓ The Father calls Yeshua, "My Servant Whom I have chosen" (Matthew 12:18).

♦ Isaiah's Servant named Israel cannot be Jacob, or his descendants, for this Servant will restore the tribes of Jacob and gather the people of Israel.

✓ Surely Yeshua is the Good Shepherd who is both restoring and re-gathering the scattered sheep of Israel (Psalm 23:3; Ezekiel 34:10-16; John 10:11-14; Matthew 15:24)

♦ This Israel is said to be the One in Whom the Father will show His glory.

✓ When presented in the Temple as a firstborn son, Simeon said Yeshua was: "A light of revelation to the Gentiles, and the glory of Thy people Israel" (Luke 2:32). As that Light, Yeshua, whose name means Salvation,[84] is causing the salvation of the God of Israel to reach to the ends of the earth.

We also see that Yeshua is *Israel* in that the Father said: "Out of Egypt I called My son" (Hosea 11:1). And Matthew, speaking of Yeshua's return from Egypt, says: "So was fulfilled what the Lord had said through the prophet: 'Out of Egypt I called My son'" (Matthew 2:15).

Whereas the Exodus verse applies to the Father bringing the sons of Jacob/Israel out of Egypt, it was also fulfilled when He brought His Son, Yeshua/Israel, out of Egypt.

Yeshua is the Israel through Whom the sons of Israel are being re-gathered to the God of Israel.

Yeshua is Israel.

In Isaiah the Father says of Yeshua, "It is too small a thing that You should be My Servant, to raise up the tribes of Jacob, and to restore the preserved ones of Israel. I will also make You a light of the nations so that My salvation may reach to the end of the earth" (Isaiah 49:6). He also

---

84 Yeshua/Salvation: See Gen 49:18, Strong's # H 3444.

says, "I will appoint you as a covenant to the people, as a light to the nations, to open blind eyes, to bring out prisoners..." (Isaiah 42:6-7).[85] And, "The people who walk in darkness will see a great light..." (Isaiah 9:2). [86]

The Glorious Light of Israel

Yeshua came "to fulfill what was spoken through Isaiah: The land of Zebulun and the land of Naphtali, by the way of the sea, beyond the Jordan, Galilee of the Gentiles [former Ephraimite territories]—The people who were sitting in darkness saw a great light, to those who were sitting in the land and shadow of death, upon them a light dawned" (Matthew 4:14-16).

Yeshua said of Himself, "I am the light of the world, He who follows Me shall not walk in the darkness, but shall have the light of life....While I am in the world, I am the light of the world."

In and through the Messiah and His people, "The true Light is already shining" (John 8:12; 9:5; 1 John 2:8).

YHVH has given Yeshua the throne of His father David. From this throne He rules over the house of Jacob both now and forever. His is a Kingdom without end. He has made purification for our sins and He now sits at the right hand of the Majesty on high (Luke 1:32-33; Hebrews 1:3).

Yeshua's eternal Kingdom of Israel is now, yet it is also to come.[87] Yeshua made a New Covenant with Israel that is both now, and is yet to come in all its fullness. When we all know Him, and are thus no longer teaching neighbor and brother about YHVH, then we will have entered into the fullness of Yeshua's New Covenant Kingdom (Jeremiah 31:31-33; Hebrews 8:8-12).

---

85 Covenant: See Jer 31:31-33; Luke 22:20; 1 Cor 11:25.
86 Hosea 8:8; Amos 9:9; Isa 8:14; Rom 11:11,25.
87 Exo 19:6; 2 Sam 7:12-16; Luke 1:32-33; Dan 7:22; Luke 12:32; Rev 5:9-10; 20:6:1 Peter 1:1; 2:5-10; Heb 1:3; 8:1; 3:6; 10:19.

The Primary Player

To understand Israel, we must see that the Primary Player in the game is Yeshua. For the Father is "summing up all things in Him" (Ephesians 1:10). In Him, He is gathering "together in one all things" (KJV). He is bringing "all things in heaven and on earth together under one head, even Messiah" (NIV). For He is the appointed "heir of all things" (Hebrews 1:2).

Yeshua. If all teaching and leadership does not point to Yeshua, it points in the wrong direction. If it does not lift up Yeshua, it should not be lifted up. If we want to see Israel, we must lift up and look to Messiah Yeshua (John 12:32).

Israel: From Genesis to Revelation

In Scripture our God is called the God of Israel. [88] The Bible is a book about the people of Israel. In the Book of Genesis, or Beginnings, our God names a man *Israel*, and He begins to call forth a people named *Israel*. In the final Book, Revelation, His Son, Yeshua, the epitome of all that is Israel, invites His people to come into the New Jerusalem. His followers must enter through gates named after the Twelve Tribes of Israel, for there is no other entrance.[89] Moreover, Scripture tells us that ultimately, we will "name Israel's name with honor" (Isaiah 44:5).

The *Theological Wordbook of the Old Testament* says of this verse: "In the Restoration, Israel's title will be a truth, not a misnomer." [90]

Those who would follow the God of Israel should walk in His truth regarding Israel. They should *not* use the name of Israel as a misnomer.

This means that if non-Jewish Believers in Messiah are not part of Israel, then they should not use Scriptures pertaining to Israel when referring to themselves.

---

88 Exo 5:1.
89 Rev 21:12; Ezek. 48:31.
90 *Theological Wordbook of the Old Testament*, Moody, 1980, Vol. 1, # 997, p 444.

On the other hand, if they are part of Israel, then a clear definition of the exact basis on which they may lay claim to the title must be developed.

Likewise, if the Jewish people are Israel, then their right to the title must neither be demeaned nor denied, but instead should be encouraged.

Thus we continue our search for the full Scriptural truth about Israel.

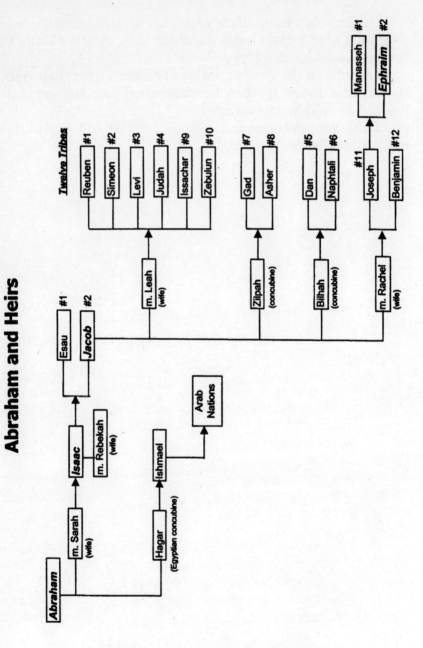

Chart Contributed by Ashton Lemonus

8

Chosen To Choose

When Moses came down from the mountain after conversing with the Almighty, he presented an offer from the Holy One to all of the sons of Israel. It was an offer they could not refuse.

"You yourselves have seen what I did to the Egyptians, and...now if you will indeed obey My voice and keep My covenant, then you shall be My own possession among all the peoples, for all the earth is Mine; and you shall be to Me a kingdom of priests and a holy nation" (Exodus 19:4-6).

That was it. Israel was forever "chosen."

Because the Father loved their fathers, He *chose* their descendants after them (Deuteronomy 4:37). He *chose*, *bachar* (בחר), *appointed*, the children of Israel. [91]

Moses said:

"You are a holy people to YHVH your God; YHVH your God has chosen you to be a people for His own possession out of all the peoples on the face of the earth. YHVH did not set His love on you nor choose you because you were more in number than any of the peoples, for you were the fewest

---

91 Strong's # H 977.

of all peoples, but because YHVH loved you and kept the oath which He swore to your forefathers ....On your fathers did YHVH set His affection to love them, He chose their descendants after them, even you above all peoples as it is this day" (Deuteronomy 7:6-8; 10:15).

Because Israel is *chosen*, Israelites must make a *choice:* "I call heaven and earth to witness against you today, that I have set before you life and death, the blessing and the curse...so *choose* life in order that you may live, you and your descendants" (Deuteronomy 30:19).

Believe and Be Blessed

"Now it shall be...if you will diligently obey YHVH your God, being careful to do all His commandments which I command you today, YHVH your God will set you high above all the nations of the earth. And all these blessings shall come upon you and overtake you, if you will obey YHVH your God: Blessed shall you be in the city, and blessed shall you be in the country. Blessed shall be the offspring of your body and the produce of your ground... Blessed shall be your basket and your kneading bowl. Blessed shall you be when you come in, and blessed shall you be when you go out" (Deuteronomy 28:1-6).

If Israel will obey, they will be blessed. Their enemies will flee before them. The Father will bless all that they put their hands to do. And thus all the people of the earth will know that the God of Israel does indeed bless His people (Deuteronomy 28:7-14).

Doubt and Be Debased

However, if the sons of Israel refuse to obey, then curses will come upon and overtake them.

"It shall come about, if you will not obey YHVH your God, to observe to do all His commandments and His statutes with which I charge you today, that all these curses shall come upon you and overtake you: Cursed shall you be

in the city, and cursed shall you be in the country. Cursed shall be your basket and your kneading bowl. Cursed shall be the offspring of your body and the produce of your ground...Cursed shall you be when you come in, and cursed shall you be when you go out" (Deuteronomy 28:15-19).

If the chosen ones do not obey, then curses, confusion, defeat, and rebuke will reign in all they undertake to do, because they have forsaken Him who chose them. If they do not obey, they will be a scattered, miserable, wretched, and accursed lot (Deuteronomy 28:20-68).

Chosen Forever

"You are My witnesses," the Father says of the children of Israel (Isaiah 43:10). Regardless of the path they choose, Israelite sheep are always being a witness, though that witness may be positive, negative, or a mix. Because, "The gifts and calling of God are without repentance" (KJV).

All Israelites have an "irrevocable call" on their lives (Romans 11:29). For our "God is not a man that He should lie, ...has He said, and will He not do it? Or has He spoken, and will He not make it good?" (Numbers 23:19).

YHVH makes good on His promises. And He has chosen Israel—forever. Israel is forever chosen to choose: Choose this day whom you will serve O Israel (Joshua 24:15).

Chosen to Be Witnesses

The Father called Israel to be His witnesses, which means they were chosen for a specific purpose: to be a witness to the world that He and He alone is God. They are to proclaim to the world that He is the "I AM" and that none can deliver out of His hand. They must tell the world that before Him there was no God formed and there will be none after Him. They must declare that there is no Savior besides Him. "Is there any God besides Me, or is there any other Rock? I know of none," declares the Holy One of Israel (Isaiah 43:8-13; 44:8).

Israel must be a witness for the Holy One.

However, that presents a potential problem. The Holy One inspired the divine words of the Torah. [92] He is the ultimate Author of Israel's Book of Covenants: Old and New. In those Books He established a law in Israel that He Himself must keep.

YHVH Must Have Two Witnesses

Our Father established the rule in Israel that, "two or more" must bear witness before a matter can be established, confirmed, and/or believed as being the truth (Numbers 35:30; Deuteronomy 17:6; 19:15). This principle of dual testimony is also upheld by both Messiah Yeshua and Paul the apostle:

"It is written that the testimony of two persons is reliable and valid" (John 8:17).

"Every matter must be established by the testimony of two or three witnesses" (2 Corinthians 13:1).

We must understand this salient point of Biblical law: In Old Covenant and New, the Father and Yeshua established the principle that: for a matter to be confirmed and/or believed in the Earth, it first must be upheld by "two or more witnesses." [93]

---

92 The Five Books of Moses: Genesis to Deuteronomy.

93 This law also reveals the plurality of the Almighty. He declared that "No person shall be put to death on the testimony of one witness" (Num 35:30; Deu 19:15). In Israel, there first must be a plurality of witnesses to the crime before someone can be executed. In these verses, *one* is translated from *echad*, which can mean a numeral, united, first, alike, alone, a man, only, other, together, same, single, each (Strong's # H259; TWOT # 61). *Echad* also is used to define our God in the Shema, the Deuteronomy 6:4 affirmation of faith: "Hear, O Israel...the LORD is one [*echad*]."

Echad can mean both alone—as in only, or it can mean together—as in one/united/same. In the verses that deal with human witnesses, "*echad*" must be taken in its "diversity within unity" meaning. While it is true that our God is to be the *One* and *Only* God of the Israelites—it is also true that His *echad* claim must be understood in its plural form. For "Scripture cannot be broken" (John 10:35). In Scripture, YHVH is depicted as a "witness" against the people of Israel (Mal 3:5; Lev 20:5; Deu 32:35; Psa 96:13). And if He is "singular," and has been a "witness" against a man that leads to the death of that man, then He has broken Scripture. To be a Scripturally correct witness against that man, He must be understood in the "diversity within unity" sense of *echad.* Scripture declares that He is plural with

(continued...)

It is logical to conclude that they too must have confirming witnesses before their collective truth (Genesis to Revelation) can be established in the Earth.

Yeshua Himself said that "Scripture cannot be broken" (John 10:35). Could this be the reason why the Father and Yeshua have historically had two witnesses in the Earth, Judah and Ephraim, both of whom can now potentially serve to confirm the whole truth of their Word to the Earth?

Two Chosen Families

Remember, when Israel was divided and Rehoboam wanted to make Ephraim come under his "Jewish" rule, YHVH warned, "You shall not go up or fight against your relatives...for this thing is from Me" (2 Chronicles 11:4).

When enemies came against this segmented Israel, He said, "Have you not observed what this people have spoken, saying, 'The two families that YHVH chose, He has rejected them'? Thus they despise My people. No longer are they as a nation in their sight.

"But thus says YHVH, 'If My covenant for day and night stand not, and the fixed patterns of heaven and earth I have not established, then I would reject the descendants of Jacob....But I will restore their fortunes and will have mercy on them'" (Jeremiah 33:23-26).

Family of Ephraim　　　　　　　　**Family of Judah**

---

93 (...continued)
Messiah Yeshua—Who ultimately will be both Judge and Jury (John 5:22-24,30-34: 12:48). For Yeshua is the Living Word, and His Word that will one day be used to judge all mankind (John 1:1; Heb 4:12). (See the *House of David Herald*, Vol. Eight Book Nine, One Witness? by Batya Wootten and Judith Dennis.)

Israel is comprised of the "two families" whom the Father chose. They are His two *mishpachah* (משפחה), or families.[94] They are His "two nations," His two "kingdoms" (Ezekiel 35:10; 37:22). He calls them, "Both the houses of Israel" (Isaiah 8:14). Both are called to confirm His truth in the world. Historically, they have been His two witnesses in the Earth.

Chosen to Be Tested

Chosen Israel also is called to a test, because the word *chosen* also can be translated tested:

"Behold, I have refined you, but not as silver; I have *tested* you in the furnace of affliction" (Isaiah 48:10).

The *Theological Wordbook of the Old Testament*, by Moody Press, says of the Hebrew word, *bachar*, or chosen:

"The root idea is evidently to 'take a keen look at'...thus... the connotation of 'testing or examining' found in Isa 48:10 ....The word is [primarily] used to express the choosing which has ultimate and eternal significance." [95]

To be chosen Israel is to be tested.
Blessing or curse?
Which will Israel choose during its earthly sojourn?
This eternal call to choose continues on all Israel—both houses—Judah and Ephraim.

Shema Yisrael... Hear, understand, and obey, O Israel.
Choose this day whom you will serve (Joshua 24:15).
Set your face this day to pass the test.

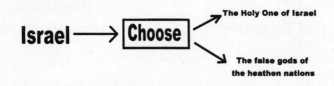

Israel ⟶ Choose

The Holy One of Israel

The false gods of the heathen nations

---

94 Strong's # H 4940, a family, circle of relatives; a tribe or people, kindred.
95 TWOT, Moody, 1985, # 231, Vol. I, p 100.

Part Two

Israel in the Present—
Truths and Errors

A Priceless Gift

Who is Israel? Why do we even need to know? Is it not enough to be in Messiah?

We need to know, because the way we define Israel determines how we interpret Scripture. How we define Israel determines who we believe are God's chosen people. It sets the course for what we envision to be the life-call of those people, as well as what we believe about Messiah Yeshua's purpose in the earth.

Whether we realize it or not, our answer plays a profound role in our lives, because in the game plan of the God of Israel, the people of Israel are the players. If we do not know who the players are, how can we possibly play the game, or even understand the game plan?

The people of Israel are the family of the God of Israel. They are the chosen people. But who makes up this family? Are they the Jewish people or the New Covenant Believers?

For ages the answer given by many excluded those of Judaism; but in this day and time many give an answer that excludes New Covenant Believers from being *part of* the chosen people of Israel. [96]

---

96 To say they are "part of" Israel is *not* to say they are "all" of Israel, nor does it
(continued...)

Messiah Yeshua said He is One with the Father, and this means:

- He is One with Him Who calls Himself "the God of Israel" [97]
- He is One with Him Who calls Israel, "a holy people ...chosen...for His own possession out of all the peoples on the face of the earth."
- He is One with Him Who swears that only "if the heavens above can be measured" will He "cast off all the offspring of Israel."
- He is One with He Who avows, "If I have not established my covenant with day and night and the fixed laws of heaven and earth, then I will reject the descendants of Jacob" (NIV) (Deuteronomy 7:6; Jeremiah 31:37; 33:25-26). [98]

The unmeasured Heavens remain. The offspring of Israel continue to be the chosen people of the One God. And the God of Israel continues to love the people of Judah. However...

The New Covenant Chosen Ones

In the New Covenant, Peter the apostle says he is writing to "the aliens," and of them he says, "You are a chosen race, a royal priesthood, a holy nation, a people for God's own possession" (1 Peter 1:1; 2:9). [99]

So what is the truth? Who are the chosen people? The "aliens" to whom Peter writes, or the Jewish people?

Another way we might ask our Israel question is:

If the God of Israel were to once again call His people

----

96 (...continued)
imply that they have "replaced" Judah, nor is it "Replacement Theology." This issue is addressed in Chapter 13.

97 His claim to "Oneness" was the reason the "Jews took up stones to stone Him" (see John 10:30-31; 17:22; 1 Cor 8:6; 1 Tim 2:5; Deu 6:4; 7:6; 14:2; Mk 12:29; Exo 5:1-2; 2 Sam 7:24).

98 Jer 30:1; 33:22,24; 46:28; Rom 11:2-5,26-29.

99 Chosen: see 2 Thes 2:13.

into the desert, where would His non-Jewish followers pitch *their* tents?

Again, understanding Israel will help us better grasp the Father's end-time plan. It will also answer a question many non-Jewish Believers ask about themselves:

"*Who am I to the God of Israel?*"

To answer this question, and to see the importance the Father places on the title of Israel, we need to remember that He declares, "Israel is My son, My firstborn" (Exodus 4:22) Therefore, it must be conversely true that:

- The Father's "firstborn is Israel."
- Israel is a "firstborn" title.
- To be God's "firstborn" is to be "Israel."

As followers of the Messiah we are called "to the general assembly and church/*ekklesia* of the firstborn...to Yeshua, the mediator of a new covenant" (Hebrews 12:23-24). We belong to His *ekklesia* of the firstborn.

Non-Jewish Believers are specifically said to belong to the "commonwealth of Israel" (Ephesians 2:11-22).

Yet when it comes to this vital call, many are content to apply the title to themselves in an abstract spiritual sense. They dismiss the importance of the title as being anything but hypothetical. Still others feel it makes no difference whether or not they are part of the people of Israel. "We're the Church" they proudly assert, "So why should we care about being part of Israel?"

No Place for Repentance

Why be concerned about our attitude toward being the Father's firstborn?

One reason is because we do not want to follow in Esau's foolish footsteps. The New Covenant warns about this when it says: "See that no one is...godless like Esau, who for a single meal sold his inheritance rights as the oldest son." Because, "afterward, as you know, when he wanted to inherit this blessing, he was rejected. He could bring about no change of mind [no place for repentance], though he sought for it with tears" (Hebrews 12:15-17, NIV).

Esau missed an extraordinary blessing. He lost out on something exceptionally important. Though he wept over his mistake, he could never regain what he had lost. We are dealing with an issue that the Father Himself may liken to "the sin of Esau."

Esau's Folly

Esau's sad story began after Rebekah conceived. When her children struggled within her, a prophet proclaimed, "Two nations are in your womb; and two peoples shall be separated from your body; and one shall be stronger than the other; and the older shall serve the younger."

"When she gave birth to the twins, the first came forth red, like a hairy garment; and they named him Esau. Then his brother came forth, his hand holding on to Esau's heel, so his name was called Jacob" (Genesis 25:22-26).

For Beans!

In regard to primogeniture,[100] Esau was the firstborn son of Isaac. But Esau ultimately sold his birthright to his younger brother, Jacob, for a bowl of beans.

Beans!

Esau missed out for a bowl of beans!

Returning from a hunt, a hungry Esau said to Jacob, "Feed me now with some of that red stew, for I am famished." Therefore his name was called *Edom* (meaning "Red").

Jacob saw something priceless in the opportunity that lay before him. To be the firstborn heir was precious to him. So Jacob seized the moment. With the smell of his fresh stew wafting through his tent, he said to his brother, "First sell me your birthright."

Ravenous, Esau retorted, "I am about to die; so of what use then is the birthright to me?"

---

100 The right to the birthright (Deu 21:17).

Before parting with the coveted stew, Jacob said, "First swear to me." So Esau swore, and with his foolish decision, he sold his birthright.

Jacob then gave Esau bread and lentil stew, and he ate, drank, arose and went on his way.

Thus Esau despised his birthright (Genesis 25:28-34).

"I am about to die," the famished hunter said to his brother, "Of what use then is the birthright to me?"

In other words, "I'm not long for this old world, Jacob, and it's difficult for my flesh to try to hold onto this title. Besides, in this life what difference does it make whether or not I'm the heir of Abraham and Isaac?"

So Jacob gave Esau a few lentils and Esau went his way. But the Father decreed that with the uncaring attitude shown by this mournful man, he despised his birthright.

Esau Will Be Eliminated

Esau was supposed to inherit the *right of the firstborn* —to be the next head of his family.[101] But he did not esteem the privilege. Therefore the Holy One said of him:

"Was not Esau Jacob's brother? Yet I have loved Jacob; but have hated Esau...[and]...have appointed his inheritance for the jackals" and I will be "indignant forever" toward Esau. He "will be ransacked...I will...destroy wise men from ....Esau....everyone will be cut off...by slaughter....covered with shame...forever...Jacob will possess their possessions ....but...Esau will be stubble....there will be no survivor" (Malachi 1:2-4; Obadiah 1:6-9,17-18; Jeremiah 49:10).

In the end it will be said that Esau and "his offspring have been destroyed...and he is no more."

Esau. Erased. Eternally.

New Covenant Believers and Esau

What does YHVH's eternal indignation with Old Covenant Esau have to do with New Covenant Believers?

---

101 Deu 21:17, Strong's #'s H 4941 and 1062.

Paul writes that what happened to our forefathers is recorded for us as examples: "Now these things happened to them as an example, and they were written for our *instruction...*" (1 Corinthians 10:1,11).

In a comparative teaching from Hebrews we read, *"For you have not come to a mountain that can be touched and to a blazing fire....but...to Mount Zion and...to the general assembly and ekklesia of the firstborn...and to Yeshua, the mediator of a new covenant....See to it that you do not refuse Him who is speaking. For if those did not escape when they refused Him who warned them on earth, much less will we escape...."*

Even as the Father's *"voice shook the earth then...[so] He has promised...'Yet once more I will shake not only the earth, but also the heaven.'...removing those things which can be shaken ...that those things which cannot be shaken may remain. Therefore, since we receive a kingdom that cannot be shaken, let us show gratitude, by which we offer to God an acceptable service with reverence and awe"* (Hebrews 12:18-28).

Giving Up Our Birthright

Because he did not appreciate being a firstborn heir, Esau was called a "profane" man (KJV). He was not in awe of, did not revere, his privilege. Thus he was easily shaken and "sold his birthright" (Hebrews 12:16)—the Greek word being *apodidomi* (αποδιδωμι), to give away, give up, to yield.[102]

For New Covenant Believers to sell off, give away, despise, or yield up their call to be the "*ekklesia* of the firstborn" is to risk a sin like that of Esau.

We do not want to be like him, nor do we even want to be be one of his neighbors, for they too were destroyed (Jeremiah 49:10).

To have Father call us His firstborn is to have Him give us a priceless gift. It means He sees us as one with His

---

102 Strong's # G 591. See Gen 31:15; 37:28,36; Psa 73:18; 74:3.

Israel—Yeshua. We must therefore not be shaken from our position as part of His chosen people. We must not be talked out of our God-given birthright. With unflinching determination we must cling to the truth of who we are in and to the Holy One of Israel.

Let Esau's indifference serve as a warning to all who lightly esteem the call. Beware to all who feel being of the firstborn is not really important, or in the New Covenant the Father still warns: "Esau I hated" (Romans 9:13).

On the other hand, let us not accuse Believers who do not yet understand the truth about "Firstborn Israel" of sin. There are times and seasons for everything. Furthermore, there are mysteries in Scripture that sometimes are not revealed "until..." [103] For this reason, many New Covenant Believers have not yet realized the full truth about all Israel.

In contradistinction to those who simply do not see, there are still those who *will* themselves not to see. Yeshua said of people like these, "If you were blind, you would have no sin; but since you say, 'We see,' your sin remains" (John 9:41). When we think we know all we need to know and are unwilling to learn, then it becomes sin. "If we go on sinning willfully after receiving the knowledge of the truth, there no longer remains a sacrifice for sins" (Hebrews 10:26).

Let us be a people who do not harden our hearts in the day that we hear His voice. Let us not cast away nor think lightly of our glorious call in Messiah Yeshua—in *Yisrael.* Instead, let us be like Jacob and cling for all we are worth to Him in all His fullness. Let us receive that priceless gift from our Father's hand.

Right now ask YHVH to bless you as he did Jacob. Ask Him to empower you, that in that final day you might be counted worthy to be called *"His Yisrael."*

---

103 See Ecc 3:1; Dan 12:4; Rom 11:25-26; Lev 4:22-23; Heb 4:12; and Chapter 12.

10

The Blood, The Redeemer, and Physical Israel

Who are the biological heirs of Jacob/Israel? The science of genetics teaches us that: "The Y chromosome is the keeper of family history on the male side." Because, "Written in the letters of DNA...[is] a record of a man's paternal ancestors." [104]

Judaism teaches that those of the Jewish priesthood, the *Cohanim*, descend from a single male ancestor—Aaron. Studies in molecular genetics have shown that the Y chromosomes of the *Cohanim* males bear resemblance to one another because of an unbroken link. Researchers have discovered that *Cohanim* from all over the world have genetic markers that confirm this oral tradition.

As stated on the PBS Web Site:

"Researchers may have found...a marker indicating paternal connection... [which is] potentially a powerful tool that enables us to look into...history...."

---

[104] "NOVA Online: Lost Tribes of Israel | Why the Y Chromosome." http://www.pbs.org/wgbh/nova/israel/familyy.html
See Addendum: Genetic Confirmation, by Michele Libin, p 243.

Is this true?

Is Israelite descent determined patrilineally?

According to *The Jerusalem Report Magazine* in its cover story in the "Jewish World" section (May 10, 1999):

"Under religious law, *kohen* status is obtained through patrilineal inheritance." (For more info see footnote 6, page 6, and the Addendum: Genetic Confirmation.)

Kohen status is determined by the father. The genetic makeup of the sons of Levi is the determining factor, the standard, that makes them physical Levites. Therefore, the same standard should apply to all the descendants of Levi, as well as all the other tribes, regardless of their faith. [105]

In other words, some of the first century Levites followed Messiah Yeshua; whereas, others continued in traditional Judaism, yet all of their descendants would still be physical Levites, or *Israelites*.

The standard is still the genetic makeup. You cannot apply it in one place and not in the other.

Tribal affiliation was determined according to one's father. Scripture repeatedly confirms that bloodline, meaning one's sequence of direct ancestors, or one's direct line of descent, their pedigree, is accounted according to their fathers. [106]

For example:

• The covenant of circumcision is with the male, that he might bring forth offspring dedicated to YHVH (Genesis 17:10-11; Jeremiah 4:4; Romans 4:11).
• "They shall receive their inheritance according to the names of the tribes of their fathers."
• All female heirs of their father's estate had to marry within their father's tribe so the inheritance would

---

105 Scripture reveals that "many among the leaders" (priests?) believed in Yeshua (Luke 8:41; 18:18; John 3:1; 12:42). Surely this could not cause these First Century "leaders" to lose their "genetic markers." Therefore we ask, "Where are *their* heirs today?"

106 Bloodline: *Webster's Third New International Dictionary*, 3 Vol. Encyclopedia Britannica, 1981; *American Heritage Dictionary*, Third Edition, Houghton Mifflin, 1992, respectively.

remain with his tribe. It could not pass from tribe to tribe. Further, when a woman married into another tribe, her children were considered to be of their father's tribe (Numbers 26:55; 36:5-12; Ezekiel 47:13-14).

- To eliminate the children of Israel, the king of Egypt said to kill their male children, but they were to let their daughters live (Exodus 1:12-22).
- The Father cut off the houses of both Jeroboam and Ahab by killing every male child (1 Kings 14:10; 21:21-22; 2 Kings 9:7-9).
- The Father told Abraham that nations and kings would come from his loins (Genesis 35:11, KJV).
- Jacob's house was defined as those who "came out of his loins" (Exodus 1:5, KJV).
- Jacob's house was further defined as, "All those belonging to Jacob, who came to Egypt, his direct descendants, not including the wives of Jacob's sons, were sixty-six persons in all" (Genesis 46:26).
- Hebrews speaks of Levi being "in the loins of his father [Abraham]" (Hebrews 7:9-10).

In addition to the Biblical evidence, the *Apocrypha* (which offers an early view) states:

"I too am a mortal man like all the rest, descended from the first man, who was made of dust, and in my mother's womb I was wrought into flesh during a ten-months space, compacted in blood from the seed of her husband." (Wisdom of Solomon 7:1-3, *The New English Bible With the Apocrypha*). [107]

To further confirm this concept and find answers to almost unanswerable questions, we next examine the redeeming qualities of Messiah's bloodline.

---

107 *Apocrypha* (Greek: things hidden): Fourteen books written after the closing of the Hebrew canon. Included in the *Septuagint* and Latin Vulgate, considered uncanonical by Protestants, 11 books are included in the Catholic Douay Bible. In spite of its lack of "Inspiration," the *Apocrypha* is nonetheless an ancient writing that potentially offers a view of early understanding in this matter.

The Blood of Our Redeemer

Messiah's blood must be unique. For Him to be our Redeemer, His blood cannot be like the blood of any other man. Seeing this truth reveals another aspect of our Israel question, because the Word declares that:

"No man can redeem the life of another or give to God a ransom for him....But *Elohim* will redeem my life from the grave" (Psalm 49:7,15, NIV).

Yeshua is our Redeemer, and only Elohim (God) can redeem us from the grave. A mere mortal man, an *eesh* (איש), an individual male person,[108] cannot eternally redeem the life of another. Such redemption can only come from God. Although we can, and should, be redeemers in earthly situations, we cannot redeem another from death.

As for man trying to redeem another man from the grave, we are told that, "The redemption of his life is costly, and he should cease trying forever" (Psalm 49:8).

Only *Elohim* can pay the high price of eternal redemption, and the price of that redemption is sinless blood.

"The life of the flesh is in the blood, and I have given it to you on the altar to make atonement for your souls; for it is the blood by reason of the life that makes atonement." "According to the Law, one may almost *say*, all things are cleansed with blood, and without shedding of blood there is no forgiveness" (Leviticus 17:11,14; Hebrews 9:22).

In his book, *The Chemistry of the Blood*, the late M. R. DeHaan, M.D., states that mortal man cannot pay the price of redemption because mankind suffers from a universal "blood poisoning." [109] He explains that man's blood cleanses his body from impurities, and this process relates to the way Messiah's blood cleanses us—His body—from sin. DeHann further clarifies by noting that when the Father made Adam's body from the ground he was not a living being until our Creator breathed the breath of life into him.

---

108 Strong's # H 376.
109 *The Chemistry of The Blood*, Zondervan, 1971, p 16.

"The LORD God formed man of dust from the ground, and breathed into his nostrils the breath of *life*; and man became a *living being*" (Genesis 2:7).[110]

Life is in the Blood

DeHaan says that the life YHVH breathed into Adam had to do with blood because it was life, and "the *life/ nephesh* of the flesh is in the blood" (Leviticus 17:14).

The Father warned Adam not to eat of the tree: "For in the day that you eat from it you shall surely die" (Genesis 2:17). Adam bit anyway, and the poison in that bite condemned mankind to death. Since we are all descended from Adam, we all suffer from his "blood disorder," because YHVH "Made from one [blood], every nation of mankind to live on all the...earth" (Acts 17:26).

Without exception, every one of us is destined to die. Everyone. Jew, Gentile, bond, or free—all are corrupted by the blood of Adam.

Everyone except Yeshua.

He is the one exception to the corruption of Adam because He does not have Adam's blood flowing in His veins. He has the undefiled blood of His Heavenly Father.

The Origins of the Blood

During pregnancy the woman contributes no blood at all to her fetus. God created woman this way so that one day He could use her to bring forth a new Adam (1 Corinthians 15:45).

DeHann writes:

"The blood which flows in an unborn babe's arteries and veins is not derived from the mother but is produced within the body of the foetus. Yet it is only after the sperm has entered the ovum and a foetus begins to develop that blood

---

110 *Breath, neshamah*, wind, divine inspiration, intellect, soul, spirit. *Life, chai,* alive; living, beast; lively, quick, running (Strong's #'s H5397; 2416 respectively). Adam became a "*living soul*," a "*chai nephesh*." Nephesh: Strong's # H 5315.

appears. As a...simple illustration...think of the egg of a hen. An unfertilized egg is simply an ovum on a much larger scale than the human ovum. You may incubate this unfertilized hen's egg, but it will never develop. It will dry up completely but no chick will result. But let that egg be fertilized by the...the male sperm and incubation will bring to light the presence of life in an embryo. After a few hours it visibly develops. In a little while red streaks occur, denoting the presence of blood. And life is in the blood."[111]

The mystery of life began in Eden's garden when the Holy One breathed life into a lump of clay. We see this truth in a corn seed. If we take a single corn seed and plant and nurture it, we reap a harvest. In a few years we can have acres and acres of corn. All from the life in one little corn kernel.[112]

There is a similar, enigmatic "life factor" found in the seed of man that began with Adam. Scripture indicates that this life factor in the seed is transferred from father to son.[113]

According to the *New International Version Study Bible*, "The blood actually possesses a living principle, and that the life of the whole body is derived from it, is a doctrine of revelation, a doctrine which the experiments of the most accurate anatomists have served strongly to confirm..." [114]

The Precious Blood of Yeshua

The blood of mankind is tainted, so mortal man cannot redeem us. But Messiah Yeshua's Blood is different...

---

111 *The Chemistry of The Blood*, Zondervan, 1971, pp 30-31.
In her *Parade Magazine* column, Marilyn Vos Savant was asked, "Is there any interchange of blood between a mother and her fetus?" Her answer: "Actual blood cells and bacteria are too big to pass through the placenta...." (*Parade*, 2/16/92).
112 YHVH says of Ephraim's seed: "I will shake the house of Israel among all nations as grain is shaken in a sieve, but not a *kernel* will fall to the ground" (Amos 9:9).
113 This does not demean the mother's role. One might even say she determines which tribes will be "carried forth."
114 *NIV Bible*, Quick Verse for Windows, 1992-1999, Craig Rairdon and Parsons Technology, Lev 17:11 footnote.

- The blood of Messiah was offered to the Lord on our behalf (Hebrews 9:14).
- Yeshua sanctified us "through His own blood" (Acts 26:18; 1 Corinthians 1:2; Hebrews 13:12).
- He is our Redeemer (Luke 24:21; Galatians 3:13; 4:5). He gave "Himself for us to *redeem* us...to purify for Himself a people for His own possession" (Titus 2:14).
- We are "not redeemed with perishable things...but with precious blood, as of a lamb unblemished and spotless, the blood of Messiah" (1 Peter 1:18-19).

Yeshua is our Redeemer. He redeems us with His blood.

If it were possible for mothers to contribute their own blood to their offspring, then Yeshua would have acquired Adam's blood from His mother Miriam (Mary). If this had been the case, He would then have offered Adam's blood to the Father as a ransom for us. This action would have meant that Yeshua broke "unbreakable" Scripture (John 10:35; Psalm 49:7,15).[115]

The Mysterious Secret

We know that Yeshua never broke Scripture. Nevertheless, we know that as a "God-man" He did *share* in humanity (Hebrews 2:14, NIV). [116] Yeshua took *part* of humanity, yet did not partake of Adam's sin-filled blood. He partook of flesh,[117] but not of blood.

Yeshua's blood came from His Heavenly Father. Thus, Acts 20:28 speaks of "the church of God which He purchas-

---

115 "There is no other God besides Me...and you were not to know any God except Me, for there is no Savior besides Me" (Isa 45:21; Hos 13:4). Only YHVH Elohim can be our *Savior*. And Luke 2:11 says, "Today in the city of David there has been born for you a Savior, Christ the LORD." In John 4:42 it is said of Yeshua, "We have heard for ourselves and know that this One is indeed the *Savior* of the world." Yeshua is our Savior and there can be but *One*. YHVH says, "I...am your... Redeemer" (Isa 49:26). Yeshua can redeem us by His blood, because He is "One," *Echad*, with our God. He is *Elohim* in the flesh (John 10:25-30,33; 8:58-59).

116 NIV translation of Heb 2:14: "Since the children have flesh and blood, he too *shared* in their humanity..." Also, *metecho*, μετεχω, *shared* (Strong's G 3348), in 1 Cor 9:10, is translated as "sharing" the crops—meaning, to "take only part."

117 *Flesh: sarx* (σαρξ), external flesh, Strong's # G 4561.

ed with His own blood." "He" speaks of God, because it was "God['s]...blood."[118]

As the *Amplified Bible* says, "Great and important and weighty, we confess, is the hidden truth—the mystic secret —of Godliness. He (God) was made visible in human flesh" (1 Timothy 3:16, TAB).

It is this mystery that we must believe: Yeshua was a God-man sent to redeem us. It is faith in His undefiled blood shed on our behalf that gains us entry into the eternal "general assembly and *ekklesia* of the firstborn who are enrolled in heaven" (Revelation 5:9; Hebrews 12:23-24).[119]

The sinless blood of Yeshua does not merely cover or atone for our sin—it totally annihilates it!

The Spirit of Antichrist

John the apostle warns, *"Who is the liar but the one who denies that Yeshua is the Christ?" The antichrist... denies the Father and the Son....every spirit that confesses that Messiah Yeshua has come in the flesh is from God; every spirit that does not confess Yeshua is not from God; and this is the spirit of the antichrist....those who do not acknowledge Messiah Yeshua as coming in the flesh. This is the deceiver and the antichrist" (1 John 2:18,22; 4:2-3; 2 John 1:7-11).*

John says, They do not "acknowledge Messiah Yeshua as coming in the flesh."[120] He then explains what it is that they must accept: "There is One who came by water and

---

118 Also see see Romans 3:25.

119 *YHVH Elohim*, the self-Existent, Eternal, Mighty, *plurality* said we could "have no other Gods" (Strong's #'s 430; 259; Gen 1:26; Isa 51:2; Exo 20:3; Deu 5:7). Yeshua's Divinity cannot be such that He is separate from the Father. He could not have come into being after the preexistent God: "Before Me there was no God formed, and there will be none after Me" (Isa 43:10). He could not have been created later as a "mini-Deity." One cannot be "a little bit pregnant," and Yeshua cannot be "a little bit Deity." He is fully Divine or not at all. He shares the Father's pre-existent nature or He is not true Deity. To simultaneously live in the hearts of many Yeshua must be Omnipresent. And it is written of Him: "In the beginning was the Word, and the Word was with God, and the Word was God. He was in the beginning with God. All things came into being through Him, and apart from Him nothing came into being that has come into being. In Him was life, and the life was the Light of men. The Light shines in the darkness, and the darkness did not comprehend it" (John 1:1-5).

120 *Flesh*: Strong's # G 4561. *sarx*, external flesh.

blood, Messiah Yeshua" (1 John 5:6).

We must believe that Yeshua came to this Earth "by water and blood." We must also believe that, "When His mother Mary had been betrothed to Joseph, before they came together she was found to be with child by the Holy Spirit" (Matthew 1:18). As to this truth, "It is the Spirit who bears witness, because the Spirit is truth" (1 John 5:7).

We must believe that Yeshua is our Redeemer, that He is more than a mere man, and that He came by water and blood.[121] To believe anything less is to be deceived by the spirit of the antichrist.

Israelites Remain Bloodline Israelites

Just as Yeshua's blood came from *His* Father, so the bloodline of the sons of Israel comes from *their* fathers.

Regardless of where they are and how they look to man, blessed or cursed, Israelites forever remain bloodline Israelites. For God "does not withdraw His gift and His call" (Romans 11:29, *Lamsa).*

Biological Israelites are forever biological Israelites. Our actual grandfathers will always be our grandfathers, regardless of what we believe or do not believe.

A Judean Ethiopia? An Ephraimite West?

Let us look to 1 Kings 10:1-13 to illustrate our point about the ethnicity of Israelites. We are told in these verses that the queen of Sheba "Heard about the fame of Solomon," and came to Jerusalem to visit him. And "according to Ethiopian tradition, Sheba (called Makeda) married Solomon, and their son, Menelik I, founded the royal dynasty of Ethiopia." [122]

Assume for a moment that Sheba numbered among the hundreds of women who were Solomon's wives (1 Kings

---

121 Our Heavenly Father calls Himself "the fountain of living waters" (Jer 2:13). *Fountain* (*maqowr*, מקור) can speak of progeny, living (*chai*, חי), flesh; and waters (*mayim*, מים), seed (Strong's # 4726, 2416, 4325). Yeshua gives living waters and life is found in His blood (John 4:11-14; 7:38; Jer 17:13; John 6:53-55).
122 *The New Encyclopaedia Britannica*, 29 Vol., 1985, Vol. 10, Sheba, p 714.

11:3), and that a son was born of their union. Assume that when he was born he looked just like his dark-skinned Ethiopian mother.

Because of his father, this son would have been from the tribe of Judah, regardless of his looks. Taking this idea a step further, let us assume that he grew up and married an Ethiopian woman and that they had sons, all of whom grew up to marry Ethiopian women and have sons. On and on the process goes. While we are asleep at night, He Who has in the past both opened and closed wombs[123] could have been turning all of Ethiopia into the tribe of Judah.

Likewise, descendants of the twelve tribes could be anywhere. They could be everywhere. And we would never know.

We also note that "an east wind" was sent against Ephraim, and that east winds carry toward the west. Thus the Father says that in the last days, Ephraim "will come trembling from the *west*" (Hosea 13:15; 11:9-10).

Joseph's Coat of Many Colors

We see many ethnic colors in Joseph's coat of many colors (Genesis 37:3, KJV). Colors, or *pac* (*pas*, פס), comes from a word that can mean palm of the hand or sole of the foot.[124] His coat depicts the idea that he would father many *shades* of people.[125] His descendants are likely found in every nation and are of every skin shade and hue known to man.

Israelites can be anywhere and can have any and every ethnic look known to man. So who is Ephraim and who is Judah? Where are they?

Only the Father in Heaven knows for sure.

Perhaps one of the myriads of biological children promised to Abraham, Isaac, and Jacob is reading this book right now....

---

123 Gen 20:18; 30:22.
124 Strong's # H 6446.
125 Joseph's coat was dipped in the blood of an animal. Animals only atoned for, or covered sin. In His Second Coming, as "Messiah ben Joseph," Yeshua wears a coat dipped in His sinless, eternally redeeming blood (Gen 37:31; Rev 19:13).

11

Literal or Spiritual Interpretation?

New Covenant Believers often wonder whether to interpret Israel's promises *literally* or *spiritually*. Once the Church began to emphasize the concept of "spiritual Israel," many began to divide the Word in this way (2 Timothy 2:15). But is it right to do so?

As followers of Messiah Yeshua, we worship in the Spirit and put no confidence in the flesh. We are a dwelling in which our God lives by his Spirit. He also desires that "our spirit and soul and body be preserved complete" (Philippians 3:3; Ephesians 2:22; 1 Thessalonians 5:23).

While we are called to worship the Holy One in spirit and in truth, He nonetheless uses physical men to accomplish His spiritual purposes on the Earth.

For instance, when He wanted to redeem His children from a wicked Pharaoh, He used Moses. When He wanted to punish Amalek, He used King Saul (Exodus 3:9-10; 1 Samuel 15:2-3). He calls men by His Spirit and they physically act out the call. If we will make ourselves available to Him, He will use us to accomplish His earthly purposes.

Worms and Butterflies

1 Corinthians 15:42-44 likens man to a seed: "So it will be with the resurrection of the dead. The body that is sown perishable, it is raised imperishable; it is sown in dishonor, it is raised in glory; it is sown in weakness, it is raised in power; it is sown a natural body, it is raised a spiritual body."

Separating the physical and spiritual man is like forcefully removing the embryo from its outer seed covering —or like forcefully removing the butterfly from the worm.

In this life, man is in the process of being "transformed" (2 Corinthians 3:18). Like the butterfly, he too is going through a *metamorphois.*[126]

In a *House of David Herald* Newsletter titled "The Seed Principle," Ephraim and Rimona Frank asked a question:

"If we were to call the worm, 'Adam,' what would we call the butterfly? Are they two different insects, or are they one and the same? They are one and the same. This spirit of oneness is spoken of in Yeshua's prayer, in the Garden: 'I pray for those who will believe in me through their [the Apostles'] message that all of them may be one, Father, just as you are in me and I am in you. May they also be in us, that the world may believe that you have sent me...' (John 17:20-23). The behavior of the worm and the behavior of the butterfly are completely different. The worm is a consumer of life, the butterfly a giver of life. How can the butterfly be in the worm and the worm in the butterfly? Though very different, even opposites, nevertheless, they both come from the same source or seed.

"Many separate these two, and in so doing take away any hope that the poor worm...may have in knowing that God has so designed this perishable, dishonored weakling to become just the opposite. [We liken the worm to the first Adam, to natural man, of whom it is said: 'Just as we have

---

126 Strong's # G 3339.

borne the image of the earthly, we shall also bear the image of the heavenly.' (1 Corinthians 15:49)] Scripture types the natural man as grass (perishable), sheep (weak), flowers (glory that fades), and as dust (earthy). That may be the condition of the seed, or the worm, but there is a life hidden within.

It is a life (embryo) made in the image of the parent, or Father, of that seed. That seed is imperishable, glorious, honorable, powerful, and spiritual.

"As Believers, when we look into a mirror and see our natural man, we should look deeper into the recesses of our hope, for our God has declared: 'We shall all be changed, in a moment, in the twinkling of an eye, at the last trumpet.' (1 Corinthians 15:51-52) As [our Father's seed]...our lives must be used to bring forth His truth. Our lives must show forth His oneness, His unity of purpose, and His harmony in bringing forth the plan of the ages.

"As Believers, it is imperative that we cease from any distorted teachings about separation of the physical and the spiritual. For both species of the seed are part of the Father's great plan!" [127]

Allegories: Word Pictures That Convey Much

YHVH often uses allegory to speak to us in Scripture. His word pictures can be understood by a child, yet can confound the wise. He reveals much with few words.

As we try to understand His parables and mysteries, we must not read more into the Word than He intended. On the other hand, we must also be free to enter into the many glorious Scriptural truths that He is now revealing.

Methods of Interpretation

Many Believers are becoming aware of Hebraic roots and Jewish tradition, and some are seeing that in Hebrew thought there are four main methods of interpretation:

---

127 "The Seed Principle" by Ephraim and Rimona Frank, Vol 11, Book 7.

- *P'shat:* Simple, literal, historical meaning.
- *Remez:* Allegory, hints.
- *Drash:* Complex, moral, homiletical, personal.
- *Sod:* Secret. Claims the meaning and numerical value of Hebrew letters hide an inner, mystical meaning. Condemned by most rabbis, this kabbalistic, mystical method often leads to heresy. [128]

We warn against all errant interpretations, especially when rooted in mysticism. On the other hand, we do believe that many of our Father's promises have multiple meanings.

For example, the simple meaning of Exodus 4:22 that was understood for ages was that *ancient Israel* was the son that was delivered from slavery out of Egypt. However, Matthew uses the verse to speak of YHVH's Son, Yeshua, who was also named Israel, and who was also in Egypt, "Until the death of Herod, that what was spoken by the LORD through the prophet might be fulfilled, saying, 'Out of Egypt did I call My Son'" (Matthew 2:15). [129]

This same Exodus verse likewise symbolizes each of us as sons who are being called out of the world system (Egypt) and into the eternal Kingdom of Israel.

Land and Fruitfulness

We also see multiple meanings in YHVH's fruitfulness, multiplication, and land promises, which are first to be taken in a *p'shat*, or literal sense.

- The Father said to the living creatures, "Be fruitful and multiply...on the earth."
- To Adam, "Be fruitful and multiply, and fill the earth."
- To Noah, "Be fruitful and multiply; populate the earth" (Genesis 1:22,28; 9:7).

---

128 This form of exegesis—peshat (simple), remez (hinting), derash (complex), sod (secret)—came to be known by the acronym, "PaRDeS," or "Garden" in the Middle Ages. *Sod* interpretation is dangerous. It is strongly rooted in Kabbalah, or Jewish mysticism. See *The Encyclopedia of Jewish Life And Thought*, 1996, Carta, *Pardes*, pg 343; and *The Encyclopedia of Jewish Symbols*, 1992, Frankel & Teutsch, Jason Aronson Inc., Northvale, NJ, *Pardes* and *Kabbalah*, pp 126 & 86-87.

129 Exo 4:22; Hosea 11:1; Isa 49:3,6; Psa 2:7; Pro 30:4; Isa 9:6-7; Mat 1:18-25.

- To Abraham, "I will make you exceedingly fruitful, and I will make nations of you [and] all the land which you see, I will give it to you and to your *seed* forever."
- To Isaac, "I will multiply your *seed* as the stars of heaven, and will give your *seed* all these lands."
- And finally, to Jacob, "Be fruitful and multiply....and I will give the land to your *seed* after you" (Genesis 17:6; 13:15; 26:4; 35:11-12).

Parah, or fruitful, means to bear fruit, to literally cause to grow, to increase, or make fruitful.

Rabah, or multiply, means to cause to multiply, increase, make great, to excel, exceedingly, and to be in authority. [130]

The Eretz and the Melo

YHVH promised the *eretz* (ארץ) to our forefathers. This can mean a particular land, such as Canaan, or Israel, or it can mean the whole earth. [131] It can mean the Land that was given to the twelve tribes, or the Earth that will yet be given to Israel's sons (Ezekiel 45:1). For "the *eretz* is YHVH's, and the fullness/*melo* thereof" (Psalm 24:1, KJV).

Abraham and his offspring were promised that "he would be heir of the world," or *cosmos* (κοσμος) (Romans 4:13, NIV). This fits with the idea of the fullness/*melo* [132] of the earth belonging to the Father and His reigning children.

Melo is translated "fullness thereof," or "all that is therein" in Psalm 24:1. Thus Ephraim's promised *"melo ha'goyim"* blessing could mean that the *eretz-world* is full of them.

The Bridegroom and the Bride

Our Messiah will one day return to a particular Land, to chosen Jerusalem. From there, the King of Israel will rule the Earth. Although the *eretz* is YHVH's, Jerusalem is still its center. She is depicted as the promised Bride.

---

130 *Parah:* Strong's # H 6509; TWOT # 1809; BDBL p 826. *Rabah:* Strong's # H 7235; TWOT # 2103.
131 Strong's # H 776; TWOT #167.
132 *Melo.* ArtScroll, Mesorah, *1982, Gen,* Vol. 6, p 2121; *Strong's* #'s H 4393; 1471.

We learn much by seeing ourselves as Messiah's Bride, and by seeing that He is the *Bridegroom* and we as His *Body*. In this way, we see ourselves as Jerusalem's Bridegroom/ protectors. One day we will go into her and become one with her. Thus we pray without ceasing for her well being. [133]

The Greatly Multiplied Seed

YHVH promised: "In your seed all the nations of the earth shall be blessed...and...I will multiply your seed as the stars of heaven, and will give your seed all these lands; and by your seed all the nations of the earth shall be blessed" (Genesis 22:18; 26:4).

The God of Israel made promises to the enigmatic *seed* of the patriarchs, and they looked for its physical fulfillment. Moses said to Israel, "YHVH your God has multiplied you, and behold, you are this day like the stars of heaven in number" (Deuteronomy 1:3,8,10). Joshua further stated, "Of all the good words which YHVH your God spoke concerning you...all have been fulfilled for you" (vs. 23:14).

The promise to Abraham saw a measure of fulfillment in the days of Moses and Joshua, yet the promise continues to see fulfillment today. Although Moses said at that time that Israel numbered like the stars, he also prayed, "May YHVH, the God of your fathers, increase you a thousand-fold more than you are and bless you, just as He has promised you" (Deuteronomy 1:11).

Moses knew there were far more heirs to come, and that Abraham was given a promise for all time.

The Son of David

YHVH promised David: "I will establish your seed forever, and build up your throne to all generations." He also promised that, "His throne...will be established forever like the moon" (Psalms 89:3-4,36-37). Additionally, YHVH

---

133 Jerusalem: Luke 19:41; 1 Ki 11:13. King: Matt 27:42; Mark 15:32; John 19:12-13. Rule: Zech 8:3; 14:4; Micah 4:2,7. Bridegroom and Bride: Mark 2:19; Eph 5:24-31; Isa 62:4-5; Rev 21:2; Psa 122:6.

said He would raise up this Seed after David died, and David said He spoke of his "house in the far distant future" (2 Samuel 7:19, TAB).

"When your days are complete and you lie down with your fathers, I will raise up your seed after you...I will establish his kingdom. He shall build a house for My name, and I will establish the throne of his kingdom forever. I will be a father to him and he will be a son to Me....your house and your Kingdom shall endure before Me forever; your throne shall be established forever" (2 Samuel 7:12-16).

The Father called this "Son of David" His Firstborn, saying: "He will cry to Me, 'Thou art my Father, My God, and the rock of my salvation.' I also shall make him My first-born, the highest of the Kings of the earth...and My covenant shall be confirmed to him. I will establish his seed forever, and his throne as the days of heaven" (Psalms 89:26-29).

David wanted to build a house, or a temple, for YHVH. In return, the Father is building a house, or a dynasty, for David through David's Greater Son (1 Chronicles 17).

Although David's natural son, Solomon, built up David's throne, Yeshua is the Seed who truly fulfills this promise. He cried to His Father from the cross and was resurrected as the Firstborn from the dead—the Highest of the Kings of the earth (Colossians 1:18; Revelation 1:5). In and through Him, Israel's New Covenant and David's eternal throne and house is forever being established.[134]

The Multiple Seed and the Individual Seed

In Hebrew, the word *seed* is *zera*. The *Theological Wordbook of the Old Testament* says of this word:

"The primary meaning comes from the realm of agriculture....Thus, the whole agricultural cycle is practically summed up in the word zera'; from the act of sowing, to the seed planted, to the harvest taken....Zera [also] refers to semen....The word 'seed' is regularly used as a collective

---

134 See Col 1:16; Jer 23:5; 30:9; Amos 9:11; Acts 3:20-23; 15:14-18; Hosea 3:5; Zec 12:10.

noun in the singular (never plural)." And, *"This...is an important aspect of the promise doctrine, for Hebrew never uses the plural of this root to refer to 'posterity' or 'offspring'....Thus the word...is deliberately flexible enough to denote either one person who epitomizes the whole group (i.e....Christ), or the many persons in that whole line...."*[135]

There are many possible meanings to be found in the blessing of the seed of Israel: *Zera* can be used in the agricultural sense of sowing and reaping; it can mean the whole line of people; or it can mean Messiah.

Scripture uses seed in these three ways:

- **Sowing and reaping:** Hosea named his first child *Jezreel*, because YHVH would scatter the seed of the Ephraimites among all nations. One day they would respond and thus be harvested. [136]
- **The whole line of people:** "If you belong to Messiah, then you are Abraham's seed, and heirs according to the promise" (Galatians 3:29, NIV).[137]
- **Messiah:** Galatians speaks of Yeshua as "the Seed to whom the promise referred" (Galatians 3:19, NIV).

One Seed—One People

In Galatians 3:16, Paul speaks of the Seed: "Now the promises were spoken to Abraham and to his seed. He does not say, 'And to seeds,' as referring to many, but rather to one, 'And to your seed,' that is, Messiah."

Paul reads many meanings into this text, bringing forth a glorious teaching, for like *posterity* and *zera*, the Greek *sperma* (σπερμα) can be used in the singular as a collective noun.[138] Thus Paul reveals that:

---

135 *Theological Wordbook of the Old Testament*, Vol. I, Moody, 1980, p 581, #582.
136 *Jezreel* comes from *zera* (seed) and *El* (Strong's # H 3157; TWOT # 582; Hos 1:4,11 NIV Study Bible, Zondervan, 1985, footnotes). Respond: Hosea 2:21-22.
137 Multiply Abraham's seed: Gen 12:1-3; 15:1-6; 17:4,6-8; 24:60; 26:3-4; 28:3-4,14; 48:4,19; Deut 7:7; Exo 32:13; 1 Chr 16:16-17.
138 *Sperma*: something sown, seed, including the male "sperm," by implication, (continued...)

- The people of Israel are God's son.
- Messiah Yeshua is God's Son.
- The biological children of Israel descend from Abraham and are his seed/descendants.
- The Messiah is "The Seed" promised to and descended from Abraham.
- All who have the seed of faith and trust in the promised Seed are one with *the Seed*.
- Abraham's faith-filled children trust in the Son.
- They are Yeshua's Body and are one with Abraham.
- All of YHVH's promises are fulfilled in the Messiah.
- All promises are being summed up in Abraham's Seed.

All these truths are found in this verse that so gloriously speaks of Messiah. [139] Remember, all of YHVH's promises are "yea and amen" in Yeshua (2 Corinthians 1:20).

A Nation and a Company of Nations

YHVH promised Jacob: "A nation and a company of nations shall come from you" (Genesis 35:11).

Restated, a *goy* (nation) and a *kahal [of] goyim* (nations) would come from Israel.

These words also have multiple meanings:
- *Goy* is used to describe the nation of Israel. YHVH promised Abraham, "I will make you a great *goy*..." (Genesis 12:2).
- Moses pleaded with YHVH, "Consider too, that this *goy* is Thy people," (Exodus 33:13).
- When Israel crossed the Jordan, the entire *goy* was circumcised (Joshua 3:17; 4:1; 5:8).

Goy/goyim (גוי/גוים) is used in Scripture to define political, ethnic, and territorial groups (without ascribing moral connotation); and to speak of a "governed body of people."

---

138 (...continued)
offspring; a remnant, issue, seed. Strong's # G 4690.
139 See Exo 4:22; Hosea 11:1; Mat 2:15; John 17:20-26; Rom 9:6-9; 2 Cor 1:20; Gal 3:2; 4:7,21-31; Eph 1:10; Heb 1:2; and *Jewish New Testament Commentary* by Stern, Jewish New Testament Publications, 1995, p 549.

It was not until after Israel received their covenant and entered into Canaan that the words *goy/goyim* were used among the Israelites to primarily mean the non-covenant, non-believing, pagan, foreign nations surrounding them. The word came to mean the *Gentiles*, [140] which is the way it is principally used today. The most important question is, "What did, or what does, the word mean to our Heavenly Father? That is the meaning we seek.

A Congregation Called Out

Kahal (קהל) means a congregation, a multitude of people called together, an assembly.[141] This word can be translated into the Greek *ekklesia* (εκκλεσια), which also speaks of an assembly, or congregation.[142]

Since it is the Almighty Himself who is declaring who will come forth from Jacob, then his promised *kahal [of] goyim* is a people from many nations who are being called together by the Holy One.

Jacob first produced a *single cultural nation* (*kahal*) that was Old Covenant Israel. But now, in and through Messiah Yeshua, Israel is producing *a congregation of nations*—an *ekklesia*—those being "called out" from every ethnic tribe and tongue by the Almighty. [143]

Let us determine in our hearts to literally respond in the Spirit to that Holy call!

---

140 Strong's and BDBL # H 1471; TWOT # 326; *Young's Bible Dictionary*, Tyndale, 1984, *Gentiles*, p 230. BDBL says it is usually used of non-Hebrew people.
141 Strong's # H 6951; TWOT # 1991.
142 *Kahal*: TWOT # 1991; *Hatch and Redpath Concordance to the Septuagint*, 2 Vol., 1983, Baker, p 433; Strong's # G1577; Acts 7:38. TWOT #1991a; p 790. Used 122 times (KJV), more than 60 times it is translated *ekklesia* (*Hatch and Redpath Concordance to the Septuagint*, 1983, Baker, p 433), 36 times as *synagogue* (TWOT word #1991a). *Ekklesia*, *kahal* and synagogue are used to describe an *assembly* (Strong's #'s H6951; G4864).
143 Manasseh was a type of the single ethnic nation that was Old Covenant Israel, Ephraim a type of New Covenant Israel. The actual tribe of Manasseh eventually became part of the confederation of tribes known as Ephraim. Old Covenant Believers belong to the "congregation of Nations" that is New Covenant Israel. Yeshua sits on the "throne of His father David" and reigns over all of the house of Jacob who will submit to Him (Luke 1:32-33; Heb 1:3; 10:12; 12:2; Rev 3:21).

12

Israel: A Mystery Until...

E cclesiastes 3:1: "There is an appointed time for everything, and a season for every activity under heaven."

Daniel 12:4: "At the end of time, many will go back and forth, and knowledge will increase."

Romans 11:25-26: "For I do not want you, brethren, to be uninformed of this mystery—so that you will not be wise in your own estimation—a partial hardening has happened to Israel until the fullness of the Gentiles has come in; and thus all Israel will be saved...."

There are appointed times.

There is a set time for knowledge to increase.

There are seasons when mysteries are revealed.

The *musterion* (μυστήριον) of Scripture tell of information shrouded in an imposed silence that may last for a season, or simply be imposed on the unhearing. [144]

Yeshua spoke to His apostles of Biblical mysteries: "To you it has been granted to know the *musteria* of the kingdom of heaven," but to certain others, "It has not been granted."

---

[144] *Musterion*, a derivative of "*muo* (to shut the mouth)," means "a secret" or 'mystery'"—specifically "through the idea of silence." Strong's # G 3466.

Messiah Yeshua often spoke in parables, lest those of "calloused heart" should hear and misuse the hidden truths of the kingdom (Matthew 13:11,13-15).

Similarly, Paul often spoke of truths that had been "kept secret for long ages past," but in his day were being "manifested to the saints."

Among these mysteries: "Messiah in *you*, the hope of glory" (Colossians 1:26-27).[145]

The Mystery of Israel

Concerning the mysterious partial hardening that happened to Israel, Paul says it will last "*until...*" But until when? When will the veil be lifted? When will Israel's shrouded eyes be opened to the secret that has so long been hidden?

Not "until the fullness of the Gentiles has come in."

A partial hardening, a hiding of certain of the Father's truths, was imposed on Israel. This hardening would last until a *fullness* of Gentiles had come into Israel's fold (Romans 11:25).

What is this fullness of Gentiles? Is it a specific number of Gentiles who will join Israel?

Surely that cannot be the full meaning, because to have Gentiles join Israel does not qualify as a *musterion.* Gentiles have *always* been allowed to join Israel.

Three Requirements—One People

"If a stranger who dwells with you would offer the passover to the YHVH, all his males must be circumcised; then he shall be admitted to offer it; he shall then be as a citizen of the country" (Exodus 12:48, TNKH).

"If a stranger sojourns with you, and celebrates the Passover to the YHVH, let all his males be circumcised, and then let him come near to celebrate it; and he shall be like

---

145 Mysteries: See Rom 16:25; 1 Cor 2:7; Rev 10:7; 2 Cor 12:4. As the Father reveals mysteries to us, we must remember, "Stewards of the mysteries of God" are called to present revealed truth in "love" (1 Cor 4:1; 13:2).

a native of the land " (Exodus 12:48, NASB).

One joined the people of Israel by observing circumcision, Passover, and sojourning. Once a person met these three requirements, he was thereafter considered a citizen, a native Israelite. It was so important to the Father to not make a distinction between native and sojourner that He re-affirmed the principle on more than twenty-five occasions.[146]

Moreover, He declared this rule to be a *perpetual statute* in Israel: "The community is to have the same rules for you and for the alien living among you; this is a lasting ordinance for the generations to come. You and the alien shall be the same before the LORD. The same laws and regulations will apply both to you and to the alien living among you" (Numbers 15:15-16, NIV).

YHVH also instructed those who joined the people of Israel on how they were to regard themselves:

"Let not the foreigner who has joined himself to YHVH say, 'YHVH will surely separate me from His people....The foreigners who bind themselves to YHVH...these I will bring to my holy mountain and give them joy in my house of prayer....for My house will be called a house of prayer for all the nations.' The LORD God [*YHVH Elohim*], who gathers the dispersed of Israel, declares, 'Yet others I will gather to them, to those already gathered'" (Isaiah 56:3,6-8).[147]

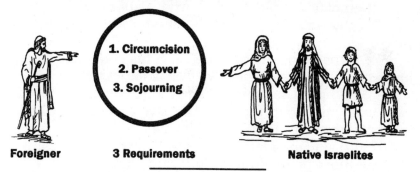

Foreigner   **3 Requirements**   **Native Israelites**

1. Circumcision
2. Passover
3. Sojourning

---

146 The primary verses are: Exo 12:48-49; Lev 19:34; 24:22; Num 9:14; 15:15-16,29; Eze 47:22. Also see Exo 12:19; 20:10; 22:21; 23:9,12; Lev 17:8,10,12; 18:26; 19:33; 20:2; 22:18; 24:16; 25:6; Num 15:30; 35:15; Josh 20:9; Psa 146:9; Mal 3:5.
147 The Father even promises these "others" whom He will gather, "a name *better than that of sons and daughters*" (Isa 56:3).

There is no mystery in having Gentiles join Israel!
Gentiles have always been able to become full members
of the house of Israel.

However, Israel's prophets long ago declared that the
Father would gather some *mysterious others* to the fold.

What is the Mystery?

Paul speaks of a secret concerning the salvation of all
Israel: "And so all Israel will be saved," he writes in Romans
11:26.   Could he possibly mean that all the biological
Israelites alive at that time will be saved?

That cannot be the answer, because elsewhere Paul
writes, "They are not all Israel who are descended from
Israel," meaning that in Israel unfaithful, fruitless branches
are broken off (Romans 9:6; 11:22; Exodus 12:15).[148]

Paul instead speaks of the *manner* in which the Father
has determined that salvation will come to those in Israel
who want to receive His salvation. Thus, in *The New
Testament* by Williams, this verse is translated, "And so in
that way..."

This meaning is clarified when we note that the Greek
houto (ουτο) means, "In this way (referring to what precedes
or follows); on this fashion; thus." [149]

An amplified explanation of what Paul is saying might
be: "In this manner will all Israel who will be saved, be
saved."

We translate it this way because his comment follows
his explanation about the olive tree of Israel.

Preceding his statement, "Thus will all Israel be saved,"
Paul explains the divine mandate given to those called a
"wild olive branch" (Romans 11:17,24).

That divine mandate is: The wild olive branches are to
provoke those of Judah to jealousy (Romans 11:14).

---

148 Gen 17:14; Lev 7:20-27; Mat 12:34-41; 1 Cor 6:9; Rev 22:15.
149 *The New Testament* by Charles Williams, from *26 Translations of the Holy
Bible*, Zondervan, 1985. Also see Strong's # G 3778.

Holy provocation is what will make those of Judah want what the wild ones already have. Thus salvation will come to whosoever will.

The Plan of Salvation

The name "Yeshua" means *Salvation*.[150] Those who once were wild olive branches are to bring Him to those of Judah.

Giving a somewhat similar clue about the time of the end, Messiah Yeshua says, "Jerusalem will be trampled under foot by the Gentiles until the times of the Gentiles are fulfilled" (Luke 21:24).

In our day, Jerusalem is no longer completely under Gentile control. In 1917 she was delivered from Moslem control by Allied Armies under the command of General Edmund Allenby. (An Ephraimite?)

In 1967, the Father returned the city to Jewish hands (minus the Temple Mount). As promised, once again He has begun to choose Judah and Jerusalem (Zechariah 2:12).

To fully understand the Divine Plan, we must see that the Father Himself imposed a type of blindness on Israel. This blindness is "partial," or *meros*, meaning: in part, section, division, share, partly, somewhat.[151]

Most people believe this partial blindness speaks of the Jewish people being hardened to the truth about Messiah Yeshua. There is some truth in this explanation, because in the past those of Judah have been blind to the truth about Yeshua. But in our day the veil is being lifted from their eyes, as Jewish people all over the world are seeing that Yeshua is their long awaited *Mashiach* (Messiah).

Are the Other Sheep Also Blinded?

Is there something more to Paul's mystery than just Judah's inability to see Yeshua?

Paul speaks of a fullness of Gentiles that will come into the sheepfold of Israel. And Yeshua said, "I have *other*

---

150 Yeshua/Salvation (ישוע): See Gen 49:18 and Strong's # H 3444.
151 Strong's # G 3313.

sheep, which are not of this fold; I must bring them also, and they will hear My voice; and they will become *one flock* with one shepherd."

Yeshua also said, "I was sent *only* to the lost sheep of the house of Israel" (John 10:16; Matthew 15:24).

Did the Messiah change His mind, or are we missing something? Could that unseen something have to do with the Romans 11 mystery?

Almost 2000 years ago Paul said he was revealing a *mystery*. He says those who would be blinded to that mystery would not be able to see the truth until...

In essence, Paul was saying that we would not fully understand the mystery until this point in time.

All Israel was afflicted with an inability to see clearly. They could only see in part. Both houses were afflicted with this inability to see the whole truth about Israel.

This means that if we are part of the people of Israel, then we too were partially blinded for a season.[152]

To clearly see the *who* and *how* of this hardening, we will now examine the primary theories put forth about the Church and Israel. [153]

Our study will compare each theory to Scripture, then if we find a hole in its fabric, we will discard it. Furthermore, we will continue to look until we find the perfect Israel tapestry being woven by our Heavenly Father.

The Good Shepherd　　　　**One Flock**

---

152 The punishments and promises made to Ephraim differed from those of Judah. And just as the promises made to Judah are literal, so the promises made to Ephraim are likewise literal. See Eze 4:3,6, and *Restoring Israel's Kingdom*, Angus Wootten, 2000, Key of David, Saint Cloud, FL. The Book of Hosea tells of Ephraim's punishment and is often referenced in the New Testament.

153 Church and Israel: Rev 3:16; 2 Tim 3:1-12; Acts 7:38; 2 Thes 1:1; 2:13; John 8:44; 10:33; Rev 2:9; 3:9; Mat 7:23.

13

Defective Doctrines

There are numerous teachings about the Church and the Jewish people. Many of these teachings either deny, disparage, or disregard the other party. Although most teach that the two olive branches of Romans Eleven symbolize these two groups of people, they are otherwise seriously flawed.

Let us examine the following popular theories:

- Replacement Theology
- Separate Entities—Separate Covenants
- Physical and Spiritual Israel
- The Adopted, Grafted-in Gentile
- The Jewish People Represent All Israel

Replacement Theology is a theory that claims the Church has replaced the Jew. Adherents of this theory proudly assert that "God is through with the Jew."

Although Peter the apostle states that the aliens being called forth are a "chosen race/nation" (1 Peter 1:1; 2:9), they are not chosen to *replace* Jewish Israel. Those who assume this stance violate Paul's Romans 11:18 warning that they are not to be arrogant toward the Jewish branches. Yet arrogance is clearly evident in the tone of those who promote this doctrine.

Moreover, it was this insidious ideology that added fuel to the flame of Hitler's Holocaust. This theory leads people to expect persecution of the so-called "rejected" Jew. It also encourages a condescending placidity in the presence of gross evil. In contrast, Scripture warns us:

"Do not look down on your brother in the day of his misfortune, nor rejoice over the people of Judah in the day of their destruction, nor boast so much in the day of their trouble."

"Do not be arrogant toward the branches [Judah]," *because you only "stand by your faith. Do not be conceited, but fear; for if God did not spare the natural [cultivated] branches, neither will He spare you [formerly wild, uncultivated, branches]" (Obadiah 1:12, NIV; Romans 11:18-21).*

Once before, some Israelites felt they were more spiritual than their neighbors: "No harm will come to us," they said.

But to this haughty claim, YHVH said: "Because the people have spoken these words, I will make my words...a fire, and these people the wood" (Jeremiah 5:12-14).

Yeshua spoke of a similar judgment:

"Do you think these Galileans [those killed by Pilate] were worse than all the other Galileans because they suffered this way? I tell you, no! But unless you repent, you too will all perish" (Luke 13:1-5).

When Christians look down on the Jewish people they run the risk of being considered haughty by the God of Israel and thus incurring His wrath.

Our God is Not Finished With the Jew

Our God is by no means finished with Judah. There is coming a time when, "On Mount Zion and in Jerusalem, there will be deliverance....In those days and at that time, I will restore the fortunes of Judah and Jerusalem," says YHVH Elohim (Joel 2:32-3:1).

In Isaiah 11:11-13, YHVH says, He "will again recover *the second time* with His hand the remnant of His people ...and will...gather the dispersed of Judah." He then caps this promise with a fearsome pledge: "Those who harass Judah will be cut off."

Judah is once again in the Land of our forefathers, yet this tiny nation is continually being pressured on every front. It is imperative that Believers not be counted among those who come against her with unrighteous motives. For in Joel 3:2 the Father warns that after He restores Judah's fortunes, He then "will gather all the nations, and bring them down to the valley of Jehoshaphat." There He "will enter into judgment with them."

The Term "Gentile Christian" is a Contradiction

Many teach that non-Jewish Believers are "Gentiles," or "Gentile Christians." But Ephesians 2:11-22 calls them *former* Gentiles. Specifically, verse 2:19 states, "You are *no longer* strangers and aliens, but you are fellow citizens with the saints, and are of God's household [of Israel]."

- In *Webster's* Dictionary, a Gentile is defined as a heathen.
- In Greek, Gentile is *ethnos* (εθνος), and can mean: foreign (non-Jewish), pagan, heathen.
- In Hebrew, *Goy/goyim* is now primarily understood to mean: foreign, heathen, Gentile. [154]

Nationhood is determined by its government. The difference between a heathen *goy* and the Father's *goy* has to do with its government. When you are governed by Him, you are of His *nation*. True Believers in the Messiah are governed by the Father and are part of His *holy goy*.

However, be warned: Let all who feel called to this goy not take the call lightly, for His goy is called to be holy,

---

154 *Webster's Third International Dictionary*, Encyclopedia Britannica, 1981, *Gentiles*, Vol. 1, p 947. Greek: Strong's # G 1484; *Young's Bible Dictionary*, *Gentiles*, Tyndale, 1984, p 230. Hebrew: Strong's # H 1471; TWOT #326.

meaning set apart to Him. They are not to be ruled by heathen practices.

Since those who truly believe in the God of Israel and in His Messiah are not foreign to Him, we conclude that the title, "Gentile Christian," is really a contradiction in terms. It is an unbiblical paradox.

Remember, the doors to the commonwealth of Israel were always open to whomsoever would *sojourn*, or live in harmony with them. But Israel was forbidden to join the Gentiles. They were to be set apart. Their customs were to be different.

YHVH made a distinction between Israel and the heathen. He said they were to be set apart to Him. This is His plan for evangelism—to provoke others to want to be like His chosen people, and eventually to join them. [155]

Yeshua said there was to be a difference between "Gentiles" and "Israel." He likened Gentile religion to that of Babylon and warned His followers to "Come out of her." He intended to have His purchased people "belong to God" alone. [156] Furthermore, He said that if a brother refuses to listen to us, then we must "Tell it to the *ekklesia;* and if he refuses to listen even to the *ekklesia*, let him be to you as a *Gentile* and a tax collector" (Matthew 18:17).

Yeshua's New Covenant people are not to be like the Gentiles. Instead, they are to come out from them and be separate (Matthew 5:47; 6:7; 2 Corinthians 6:17; 1 Thessalonians 4:5; 1 Peter 2:12).

Separate from What?

Historically, when followers of the Christ (Messiah) sought to separate themselves from the heathen, they often referred to their collective body as "New Israel." They believed that as His followers, they were the "New Israel," whereas the people of Judah were the "Old Israel."

---

155 Exo 11:7; Deu 4:20; 7:6; 14:2; Psa 33:12; 135:4; Isa 43:1; Est 3:8; Titus 2:14; 1 Pet 2:9.
156 Acts 20:28; Eph 1:14; Tit 2:14; Rev 18:4; 1 Pet 2:9.

In these latter days, the Father is now allowing the issue over the title of "Israel" to surface in a new way.

The Identity Crisis of the Church

When the Almighty brought the people of Judah back to the Land and began to bless them, it caused a certain identity crisis within the Church. Suddenly a vital question loomed large on the horizon: If our God is the God of Israel, and the Jewish people are Israel, then *who* is the Church?

As people began to study the subject of who is the Church and who is Israel, many of them began to question, and often reject, incorrect and antiquated teachings about Israel and the Church. Suddenly things were different. The Jewish people were in the Promised Land. That Land became the nation of Israel, and the God of Israel showed them great favor.

It is interesting to note that the returning Judahites were initially planning to name their new state, *Judea.* [157] However, at the last minute their Prime Minister, David Ben Gurion, decided to name the new homeland *Israel.*

Surely it would not have bothered the anti-Jewish people in the Church if Israel had been named Judea. They would have said that although the'"rejected Jews" were back in Judea, the Church was still the "New Israel." They could have continued to teach Replacement Theology.

But the God of Israel was in control. David Ben Gurion *did* name the Land Israel, and the return of the Jews to their new state ignited an identity crisis in the Church.

At this point many Christians began to call themselves "Spiritual Israel," as opposed to "New Israel." They also began to put great emphasis on interpreting Scripture in types and shadows, and to paint their concepts of Israel in spiritual, ethereal, intangible other-world colors.

---

157 Many names were proposed: Zion, Judea, Ivriya, etc. "Postage stamps printed in advance...were marked '*Doar Ivri* (Hebrew mail) since no one knew what the name would be." *Israel: A History* by Martin Gilbert, 1998, William Morrow & Company, *The War of Independence May 1948 to the first truce*, p 187.

For many the call to be Israel was for the next life. To others the issue was immaterial. Adherents of this theology taught that to be the Church was sufficient, and that the title of "firstborn heir" was unimportant. Those who could not embrace this belief were simply left with an abundance of questions.

Separate Entities

Many people believe that the Church and Israel are separate entities. They think of Israel as being the Jewish people, and the Church as being the non-Jewish people.

Some even claim that the Father's people are the Jews, whereas Yeshua's people are the Christians.

However, this teaching opposes the truth, because:

- We have "one hope of our calling" (Ephesians 4:4).
- Yeshua claimed, "I have other sheep, which are not of this [present Jewish] fold, I must bring them also, and they shall hear My voice; and they shall become one flock with one shepherd" (John 10:16).
- Yeshua prayed that His people might be "one, even as He and the Father are one" (John 17:11).

Separate Covenants

The idea of separate identities leads people to conclude that the Jewish people have a separate covenant. Is this so?

Whether realized or not, this concept is based on the idea that our Father made a promise to Abraham that could only be fulfilled through Abraham's biological heirs, and that only the Jewish people are those promised physical heirs.

As previously shown, Abraham was promised *myriads* of descendants.[158] His servant, Eliezer of Damascus, was not a physical heir, but equivalent to an "adopted Gentile." And YHVH had told Abraham, "This man will *not* be your heir; but one who will come forth from your own body shall be your heir" (Genesis 15:2-4).

---

158 Gen 12:3; 15:5; 17:4; 26:4; 24:24,60; 28:3,14; 32:12; 48:4,16,19.

For this reason, the Jewish people tend to believe that at least the majority of Jews came from Abraham's own body and are actual physical descendants.

The Children of the Children—Are They Jews?

At this time in history it would be impossible to separate Christians and Jews based on genetic heritage, because the Early Church was comprised almost exclusively of "Jewish Christians." These people had children, who had children, and so on. It is most likely that these descendants of the Early Church would have remained in the Church. If they had returned to Judaism they would have had to hide or deny their faith in Yeshua.

Assuming these Believers loved Yeshua too much to return to Judaism and deny Him, we ask: Are their descendants also biological heirs? Are not the descendants of Peter, James, and John still just as much Abraham's heirs as the Jewish people?

Cut Off for Following the Messiah?

If we say they are no longer physical heirs, we are in essence saying that the reward for following the Jewish Messiah is to be cut off from being part of Israel.

This idea contradicts Romans 11:17,20, which tells us the Father "broke branches off the olive tree for unbelief." This passage means those who did *not* follow the Messiah of Israel were broken off Israel's olive tree, not vice-versa.

To say the Early Believers and their descendants are no longer part of Israel on a physical basis—because they believed in and followed the Messiah—opposes Scripture.[159]

Furthermore, if we say that the children of First Century Rabbinical Jews[160] are Abraham's heirs because they are Jews, but that the children of the First Century Jewish

---

159 Paul writes to, "All the saints in Messiah Yeshua," and says to them, "We are the true circumcision, who worship in the Spirit of God..." (Phil 1:1; 3:3).
160 Rabbinic Judaism: A religion developed by rabbis after the destruction of the Temple (70 A.D.); their basic doctrine being that "Messiah has not yet come."

Believers are no longer heirs, then we are basically saying that these Believers were disinherited because they did not follow Rabbinic Judaism.

Scripture declares that those who *do* follow Messiah were, and are, rooted in the olive tree of Israel. [161]

What then will be our standard for inclusion in Israel?

- Genetics?
- Observance of Rabbinic Jewish customs?
- The standard of Scripture—Genesis to Revelation?

Gentile Jews?

While the Father Himself surely knows who is descended from whom, it is foolish for *mankind* [162] to try to divide His people based physical descent. There are too many variables that influence genetic heritage.

For instance, the sin of adultery was included in the Ten Commandments (Exodus 20:14), thus indicating that mankind has a problem in this area. If a Jewish person had even one unfaithful grandmother, her secret sin would send the family tree in an entirely unknown direction. Her descendants may believe they are related to King David, yet they could be the offspring of a nameless heathen.

Additionally, since Judaism has always accepted converts, [163] and the biological children of these converts live among the Jewish people, are not they and their children considered Jewish?

To say they are Jews, but that the descendants of the Early Jewish Christians are *not* biological heirs, means we are using different measures, and the Father calls this practice "abominable" (Proverbs 20:10).

---

161 This is not to say that those in the "Church" have truly followed the Messiah, but neither have those of Judaism. They resemble the two sons of whom Yeshua spoke in Matthew 21:28-31; neither has a perfect record of obedience.

162 While *mankind* cannot know who is or is not a biological Israelite, the Father in Heaven does know: "I know Ephraim, and Israel is not hidden from Me" (Hos 5:3). For "there is no creature hidden from His sight..." (Heb 4:13).

163 Exo 12:38; Est 8:17; Ezra 2:59; Acts 2:10.

Factors such as intermarriage, conversions, rape, and adoption must be considered if we are to determine actual physical descent. Anything less would not be scientifically valid.

Rape has been so commonly perpetrated on Jewish women throughout the centuries that many believe this is the reason Judaism began to determine Jewishness based on the mother. Out of compassion for the plight of these women and their offspring, Judaism decided to love and accept children of unknown fathers.

Another important factor is adoption. For instance, during the Holocaust when some men who claimed to be Christians were killing the parents of little Jewish children, many of those children were adopted by truly caring and loving Christians.

Bloodline Inspectors?

Let us assume for a moment that Abraham's biological heirs do have a covenant that is separate from that of the "Gentile Christian."

Then how do we establish a biological "Who's Who" among Christians and Jews? Do we envision YHVH one day sending out a squad of DNA Inspectors to separate the true Jews from the rank and file Gentiles?

Of course not.

Isaiah says, *"Let not the foreigner who has joined himself to YHVH say, "YHVH will surely separate me from His people....For thus says YHVH, "To the eunuchs who keep My sabbaths, And choose what pleases Me, And hold fast My covenant, To them I will give in My house and within My walls a memorial, And a name better than that of sons and daughters; I will give them an everlasting name which will not be cut off. Also the foreigners who join themselves to YHVH, To minister to Him, and to love the name of YHVH, To be His servants, every one who keeps from profaning the sabbath And holds fast My covenant; even those I will bring to My holy mountain And make them joyful in My house of prayer. Their burnt offerings and their sacrifices will be acceptable on My altar; For My house will be called a house of prayer for all the peoples (56:3-7).*

Furthermore, in the New Covenant, the Father continues to call His people Israel: "Out of Judah will come forth One Who will shepherd His people, *Israel*" (Matthew 2:6).

Conclusions

We conclude the following:

- Our God is not through with the Jew.
- He prohibits those who join themselves to Him from saying that they are separate from His people, Israel.
- Yeshua does not separate Himself from the Father.
- The Good Shepherd does not have separate sheep folds.
- Concerning dividing Jacob's heirs based on biological descent, only the Father knows "Who is Israel."
- Believing or not believing a particular doctrine cannot change the facts of one's genetic makeup.
- Biological descendants of both houses of Israel can be found anywhere and everywhere.

Armed with these conclusions, we look at the Separate Covenant theory from yet another perspective.

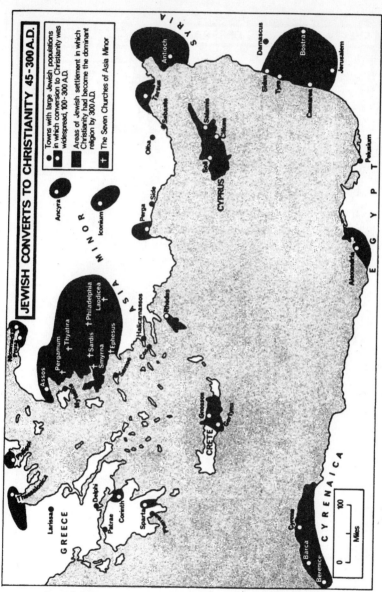

Jewish historians agree that millions of Jews became Believers
and were assimilated into the church/ekklesia.
Map from the *Atlas of Jewish History* by Martin Gilbert, p 19.
New York: William and Morrow, 1992. Used by permission.
The map lists the "Seven Churches of Asia Minor" (Rev 1:4-20).
So where and who are the children of these Jewish Believers in Messiah?

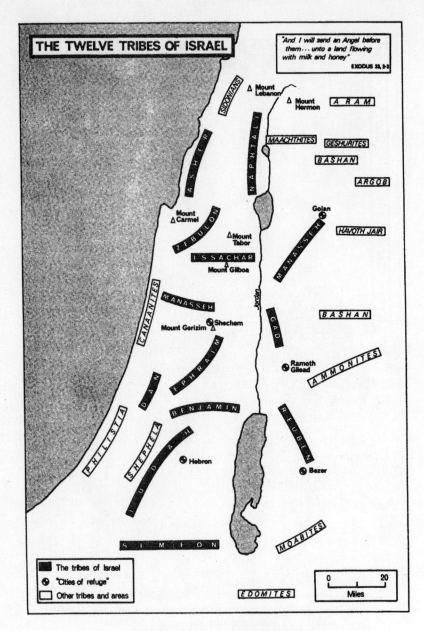

Territories of the Twelve Tribes of Israel.
From the *Atlas of Jewish History* by Martin Gilbert, p 19.
New York: William and Morrow, 1992. Used by permission.

14

More Tattered Theories

Some people claim that the Gentile Church has a *separate Covenant* from that of Israel. However, there is no record of the Almighty ever making a New Covenant with Gentiles. Yeshua made His New Covenant with the children of *Israel.*

"Behold days are coming when I will make a new covenant with the house of Israel and with the house of Judah, not like the covenant which I made with their fathers in the day I took them by the hand to bring them out of the land of Egypt, My covenant which they broke, although I was a husband to them,' declares YHVH. But this is the covenant which I will make with the house of Israel after those days, I will put My law within them and on their heart I will write it; and I will be their God, and they shall be My people'" (Jeremiah 31:31-33).

The Father promised a New Covenant to the house of Israel, and Yeshua said to His disciples, "This is the New Covenant in My blood." He spoke this to the sons of Israel who were seated at His New Covenant Passover table. With this statement the promised New Covenant was instituted (Luke 22:20; Hebrews 8:6-12; 1 Corinthians 5:7).

These disciples were following the Messiah promised to Israel. They continued to meet in synagogues and in the Temple. Scripture refers to them as a sect of the Jews known as "The Way" (Acts 24:5,14; 26:5; 28:22).

The Ekklesia in the Wilderness

When making his defense before his persecutors, the martyr Stephen spoke of the "*church/ekklesia* that was in the wilderness" (Acts 7:38).

The Greek word *ekklesia* is used to describe both those of ancient Israel and those who followed Israel's Messiah.

Moreover, Believers are called to "the *ekklesia* of the firstborn" (Hebrews 12:22-23).

Scripture does not separate Israel and the Believer. Those of the Early Church did not separate the *ekklesia* from Israel, because there is only one called out people of God.

Physical Israel—Spiritual Israel Conclusions

As noted earlier, many people try to divide Israel into physical and spiritual camps. However, Scripture makes no such distinction. Yeshua declared: "An hour is coming, and now is, when the true worshipers shall worship the Father in spirit and truth; for such people the Father seeks to be His worshipers" (John 4:23).

All Israel, Jew and non-Jew alike, are called to worship the Father in spirit. Moreover, every Believer in Messiah is a physical being. Everyone descends from *someone*. The question is: who do they descend from?

What this theory is really proposing is that non-Jewish Believers in Yeshua are *not* descended from Abraham.

But Abraham was promised myriads of biological heirs and they have to be *somewhere*. Why not among the followers of Messiah?

We conclude that it is not reasonable to try to divide Israel along these lines. Such theoretical conclusions are based on assumption and are rooted in the unscriptural idea of separating the Church from Israel.

Clarifying the Issue of Adoption

Many teach that "Gentile Believers" have to be adopted into Abraham's family, but that physical Jews do not. This misconception about Abraham's faith usually goes hand-in-hand with a misunderstanding about Israel's olive tree.

We will examine the olive tree in detail in subsequent chapters, but for now we will briefly address this issue.

Most Believers gain their first impression of Israel's olive tree from Romans Eleven, where Paul tells of wild olive branches being grafted in among the others (vs 17).

In this letter, Paul is referring to the Believing Jews of his day. Although he calls them "natural" branches, he is principally addressing *their natural disposition*, not their biological descent.

In this tree, branches can both be broken off and grafted in.[164] Relationship to the *root,* Yeshua, (Revelation 22:16) determines the state of the *branch*.

One must be in right relationship with the Cultivator in order to remain in the tree. The Cultivator is the Father—The One Yeshua calls the Vinedresser. [165]

The Effects of Errant Adoption Teachings

Many people interpret Paul's references to the olive tree to mean that former "Gentile" (non-Jewish) Believers are not natural children, but are "spiritually adopted, grafted-in" children.

On the other hand, Jewish people are thought to be *natural* children who are neither adopted nor grafted-in, they are thought to naturally be His children.

This interpretation usually produces one of two reactions in the non-Jewish Believers:

---

164 The principle is that Judah is "*natural*" only when he abides *according to* the rules of the Vinedresser (John 15:1). Otherwise, he is "cut off for unbelief." When Judah embraces Messiah, he is "grafted in again" (Rom 11:17,23, 24).

165 Strong's #'s G 5449, 2798; Isa 5:1-7; Ecc 5:9; Eze 36:9; John 15:1; Rom 11:17,24.

1) They see themselves as being adopted and therefore somehow inferior to the "natural," Jewish children.

2) They see themselves as more *spiritual,* and the Jewish people as more *carnal.*

The first group, those who feel inferior because they believe they are the adopted children, can be likened to a child who is adopted into a family. Adopted children have obstacles to overcome regardless of how much they are loved by the adoptive parent. They frequently do not feel the same sense of being loved and accepted as a natural child does. The above described age-old teaching often produces a similar feeling of inferiority in some Believers.

Still others believe they are more *spiritual* because they think they are "spiritually adopted." Some adherents of this theory actually believe they are superior to the "spiritually void," or supposedly carnal Jewish person.

Sadly, those who behave as though they are superior usually do so to cover up feelings of inferiority. This misconceived feeling of false superiority will likely remain as long as these people live under the false conclusion that they alone are adopted.

False Racial Pride

This errant teaching tends to produce a different reaction in some Jewish Believers. Some feel they have a superior position in the family of the God of Israel. They frequently believe they are the natural sons, and because they are descended from the "chosen race of the Jews" they are somehow "twice chosen." This thought spawns a false racial pride that only brings contention.

Since genealogy cannot be proven, their conclusion is based on presumption, and "through presumption comes nothing but strife" (Proverbs 13:10; 16:18; 1 Timothy 1:4).[166]

These feelings of inferiority or superiority are not befitting of the children of the Holy One of Israel.

---

166 Pride: See Isa 27:1; Job 41:34.

The Spirit of Adoption

What is the truth? Are the non-Jewish Believers adopted into Abraham's family?

No, they are not. Scripture uses the word *adoption* only five times, and those five verses tell us the following:

- "For you did not receive a spirit of slavery leading to fear again, but you received a Spirit of adoption as sons by which we cry out, 'Abba! Father!' The Spirit Himself bears witness with our spirit that we are 'children of God'" (Romans 8:15,16).
- "We to whom the first fruits of the Spirit have been given as a foretaste of our coming inheritance—we groan within ourselves while we eagerly await our full adoption as sons, which is the redemption of our bodies" (Romans 8:23).
- My brethren, "Who are Israelites, to whom belongs the adoption as sons and the Glory and the Covenants and the giving of the Law and the Temple services and the promises" (Romans 9:4).
- "God sent His Son, who was born under Law, that He might redeem those who were under Law, that they might receive the adoption as sons" (Galatians 4:5).
- "To the saints at Ephesus," Paul declares, "He predestined us to be adopted as his sons through Messiah Yeshua, in accordance with his pleasure and will" (Ephesians 1:5, NIV).

The Father gives the spirit of adoption to free us from the fear of death and thus enable us to call Him *Abba*, or *Father*.

As His sons, we await the fullness of our adoption, which is the redemption of our bodies.

This spirit of adoption belongs to the sons of Israel. The Father sent His Son to redeem those under the Law (Judah) as well as the saints (Ephraim).

He predestined both to adoption as His sons through Messiah Yeshua.

We must all first receive the spirit of adoption through Messiah Yeshua before we can join Abba's family and become sons of God, for "all have sinned and fallen short of the Glory of God" (Romans 3:23).

Abraham not Mentioned in Adoption Verses

The adoption verses listed above do not mention Abraham. Neither do they support the teaching that Believers are adopted into his family. Furthermore, if a Jewish person comes to faith in Messiah, he is "again" grafted into Israel's olive tree: "And they also, if they do not continue in their unbelief, will be grafted in, for God is able to graft them in again" (Romans 11:23).

Little Errors—Big Problems

With such high stakes riding on what we believe, we must ask ourselves: Is what we believe true? Is the foundation on which we have built our understanding of Israel one of Scriptural truth, or do we need to reexamine our basic beliefs regarding Israel?

In his book, *Ten Philosophical Mistakes*, Mortimer J. Adler, America's foremost philosopher, explores the ten major errors in the development of modern thought. He examines the serious consequences these errors have on our everyday lives. Adler points out the common, disastrous mistake of the world's greatest thinkers: They invented new kinds of wisdom in order to continue building on a faulty foundation. They failed to go back to ground zero and begin to build on original truths. They did not dig down to a solid foundation of original truth.

Adler quotes a 4th Century B.C. assertion made by Aristotle: "The least initial deviation from the truth is multiplied later a thousandfold."

He also paraphrases the words of Thomas Aquinas: "Little errors in the beginning lead to serious consequences in the end."

Adler himself writes: "Instead of retracing the steps that lead back to their sources in little errors at the beginning, modern thinkers have tried in other ways to circumvent the result of the initial errors, often compounding the difficulties instead of overcoming them."[167]

New Wisdom on a Faulty Foundation

Do Christians and Jews suffer from this same disastrous mistake? Have we invented new kinds of wisdom not built on original truths? If so, do these errors compound our problems?

Yes, they do.

In particular, the New Covenant *ekklesia* has never recovered from its early doctrinal divisions and theological mistakes. Especially crippling to them are their mistakes concerning Israel. These mistakes blind Believers. They prevent us from seeing the Father's plan for His people.

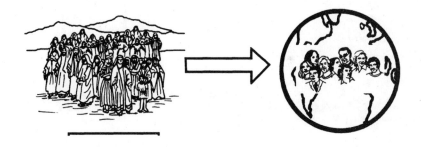

The Ekklesia
← **First in the Wilderness**
Scattered Throughout the World
Regathered by the Shepherd: Yeshua →

---

167 *Ten Philosophical Mistakes*, pp xiii,xv. New York: MacMillian, 1997.

Our Israelite Roots

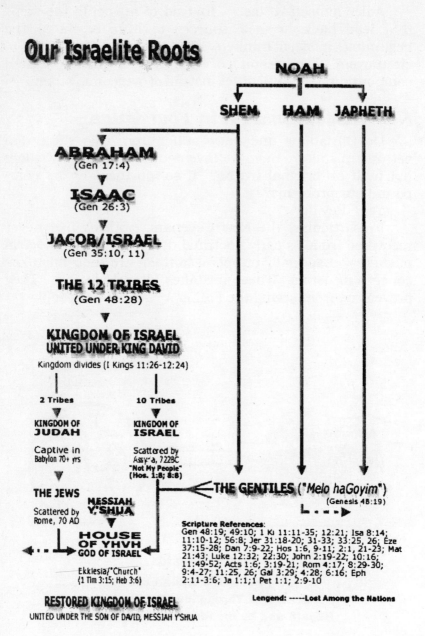

NOAH

SHEM   **HAM**   **JAPHETH**

ABRAHAM
(Gen 17:4)

ISAAC
(Gen 26:3)

JACOB/ISRAEL
(Gen 35:10, 11)

THE 12 TRIBES
(Gen 48:28)

KINGDOM OF ISRAEL
UNITED UNDER KING DAVID

Kingdom divides (I Kings 11:26-12:24)

2 Tribes   **10 Tribes**

KINGDOM OF   **KINGDOM OF**
JUDAH   **ISRAEL**

Captive in   Scattered by
Babylon 70+ yrs   Assyria, 722BC
             "Not My People"
             (Hos. 1:9; 8:8)

THE GENTILES ("*Melo haGoyim*")
(Genesis 48:19)

THE JEWS

MESSIAH
Y'SHUA

Scattered by
Rome, 70 AD

HOUSE
OF YHVH
GOD OF ISRAEL

Ekklesia/"Church"
(1 Tim 3:15; Heb 3:6)

Scripture References:
Gen 48:19; 49:10; 1 Ki 11:11-35; 12:21; Isa 8:14;
11:10-12; 56:8; Jer 31:18-20; 31-33; 33:25, 26; Eze
37:15-28; Dan 7:9-22; Hos 1:6, 9-11; 2:1, 21-23; Mat
21:43; Luke 12:32; 22:30; John 2:19-22; 10:16;
11:49-52; Acts 1:6; 3:19-21; Rom 4:17; 8:29-30;
9:4-27; 11:25, 26; Gal 3:29; 4:28; 6:16; Eph
2:11-3:6; Ja 1:1; 1 Pet 1:1; 2:9-10

RESTORED KINGDOM OF ISRAEL
UNITED UNDER THE SON OF DAVID, MESSIAH Y'SHUA

Lengend: -----Lost Among the Nations

15

Is Judah All Israel?

The last on our list of flawed theories is the belief that the Jewish people represent *all* Israel.

Those who teach this theory claim that the two houses were reunited when some from the house of Judah returned from Babylon. They conclude this because, after their return, and during their dedication of the rebuilt temple, they offered "a sin offering for all Israel" (Ezra 6:17; 8:35).

Was "all Israel" present at that time?

Scripture and historical records provide answers:

More than a hundred years after the end of the Northern Kingdom, [168] the Father said, "'Is Ephraim My dear son? Is he a delightful child? Indeed, as often as I have spoken against him, I certainly still remember him; therefore My heart yearns for him; I will surely have mercy on him" (Jeremiah 31:20).

We read in 2 Kings, written around 562-538 B.C.,[169] "The people of Israel were taken from their homeland into exile in Assyria, and *they are still there*" (2 Kings 17:23, NIV).

---

168 100 years: Jeremiah, NIV Study Bible, Zondervan, 1985, Author and Date.
169 NIV Study Bible, Introduction 1 Kings, pp 464-465.

Moving forward to around 520 B.C., we see Zechariah breaking his "staff called Union, [thus] breaking the brotherhood between Judah and Israel" (Zechariah 11:14, NIV).

The *New International Version Study Bible* says this action signifies "the dissolution of...the unity between the south and the north."[170]

The Twelve Prophets calls the broken staff "Binders," saying, "The...staff Binders, is now shattered, denoting the dissolution of all unity and harmony between Israel and Judah." [171]

Zechariah broke his staff *after* Judah's return from Babylon, not before. The brotherhood between Judah and Israel was broken after Ezra offered a sin offering for all Israel. They offered a sin offering for their lost brothers. Zechariah's prophetic act confirmed that they were lost, and thus they needed intercessory prayer.

Prior to this, and while still in Babylon, Daniel wrote, "Righteousness belongs to Thee, O Lord, but to us open shame, as it is this day—to the men of Judah, the inhabitants of Jerusalem, and all Israel, those who are nearby and those who are far away in all the countries to which Thou hast driven them" (Daniel 9:7, KJV).

Judah was *nearby*, in Babylon, but according to the *ArtScroll Tanach Series*, "'All Israel' would mean the ten tribes of Israel who were exiled and lost." [172]

Around 440 B.C., Ezra wrote that Ephraim was scattered in "Halah, Habor, Hara, and to the river Gozan, to this day" (1 Chronicles 5:26). The prophet penned these words more than 250 years after Ephraim was scattered, and more than 50 years after Judah's return from Babylon to rebuild the Temple.[173]

Obviously Ezra did not consider Israel reunited.

---

170 520 B.C.: NIV Study Bible, Introduction Zechariah, p 1405; NIV quote (same Bible), Zechariah 11:14 footnote, p 1412. Also see, *Binders, The Twelve Prophets*, Soncino, 1980, p 267.

171 *The Twelve Prophets*, Soncino, 1980, pp 316-317.

172 *ArtScroll*, Mesorah, 1982, *Daniel*, p 248.

173 NIV Study Bible Zondervan, 1995, Introduction Ezra, p 662-663.

After Judah's partial return to the Land, we move to the time of Yeshua and the apostles. At that time, Paul wrote that Messiah Yeshua came and preached peace to you who were "far away," and to those who were "near" (Ephesians 2:17). (See Daniel 9:7 above for "near" and "far away.")

Judah Says of the Ephraimite Exiles

The *Encyclopaedia Judaica* says of the Ephraimites once exiled to Assyria:

"It is evident that as a rule they did not possess the status of slaves or of an oppressed population. The exiles were first settled in Mesopotamia as land tenants of the king...the craftsmen among them were employed in state enterprise. Eventually, some of the exiles achieved economic and social status and even occupied high ranking positions in the Assyrian administration...The striking of roots in Mesopotamian society by a large part of the descendants of the Israelite exiles resulted in their eventual absorption into the foreign milieu." [174]

Assimilated But Not Lost

Ephraim was "swallowed up...among the nations." However, YHVH said of them: "I will shake the house of Israel among all nations as grain is shaken in a sieve, but not a kernel will fall to the ground" (Hosea 8:8; Amos 9:9).

In Deuteronomy we read, "YHVH will scatter you among all peoples, from one end of the earth to the other end of the earth; and there you shall serve other gods, wood and stone, which you or your fathers have not known" (verse 28:64).

Although they were scattered among all peoples and would become idolaters serving and bowing down to gods unknown to their fathers, still, the God of Israel would have mercy on the house of Israel. Not even a *kernel* of their scattered seed would be lost to Him:

"I know Ephraim, and Israel is not hidden from Me,"

---

174 *Encyclopaedia Judaica*, Keter, 1972, Exile, Assyrian, p 1036.

says the Almighty One (Hosea 5:3).

Ephraim is certainly not lost to the Father, but has he been reunited with Judah?

All Israel?

"Ezra rose and made the leading priests, the Levites, and all Israel, take an oath...so they took the oath"? (Ezra 10:5).

Did the Holy One reunite the two houses during Ezra's sacrificial ceremony

No, He did not. "All Israel" means those who were present at the ceremony. It specifically defines "they" as those "who took the oath. It speaks of "the offering...all Israel present there had offered" (Ezra 8:25).

Those who try to prove that Ephraim is now part of Judah say that use of the words "all Israel" proves that Judah represented all Israel after this sacrifice. However, these verses do not prove that Ephraim returned at this time, nor that Judah now represents all Israel, because the term "all Israel" is also used to describe those of the Northern Kingdom:

"And it came about when all Israel heard that Jeroboam had returned, that they sent and called him to the assembly and made him king over all Israel. None but the tribe of Judah followed the house of David" (1 Kings 12:20).

In this case, "all Israel" absolutely excludes Judah. Both cases refer only to "all Israel present" at those times.

Biology Does Not Change

Just because Judah was interceding for all Israel at the sacrifice, and because some from the other tribes were present, does not mean that Judah thereafter represented all Israel. Prayers do not change biology.

All scholars agree that not every biological Israelite was present at this ceremony. And the biological Ephraimites who did not take the oath were still Israelites. They were not cut off because they were not present for the ceremony.

If not being present meant they were cut off, then this rule would also mean that any Jew who did not take the oath was also cut off. This would indicate that most of today's Jews are not Jews, because the majority of them descend from those who stayed behind in Babylon.

The reasoning behind this teaching is illogical.

Judah continued to be Judah. and Ephraim continued to be Ephraim. Our Father does not withdraw His call (Romans 11:29).

Judah Was Still Called Judah

That Jews were sometimes called Israel does not prove the Northern Kingdom of Israel was reunited with Judah.

The name *Israel* was principally used to designate the house of Israel, or Ephraim. It was a birthright title given to Jacob's firstborn heir (1 Chronicles 5:1-2). However, Israel was also used to describe *all* the sons of Jacob:

"YHVH commanded the sons of Jacob, whom He named Israel." In some cases, both the houses were called Israel (2 Kings 17:34; Isaiah 8:14). But after their return from Babylon, Scripture continued to call the Jews "Judah." We read that: The agitators "discouraged the people of Judah" from building (Ezra 4:4). And that returning Jews were called "The Jewish remnant that survived the exile" (Nehemiah 1:2, NIV).

| Lost Ephraimites | All Israel | Judah |

Jerusalem

| Assyria & the Nations | Ezra | Babylon |

Did We Miss the Reunion?

Have the two houses been reunited since that time? The answer is: "Yes and no."

Yes, in that all who are truly of Messiah's Body are Israelites. But no, in that all Israel has not fully manifested that unity.

Yes, in that Yeshua has made us into "one new man." Our oneness in spirit is presently ascribed in Him (Ephesians 2:14-16). But no, in that all Israel has not fully applied that oneness. Most Believers walk in a partial application. Our unity is imputed and is presently available, but we have not fully implemented our oneness. Both houses of Israel have thus far failed to walk as the completely repentant, reunited, and restored people of Ezekiel 37:15-28.

Similarly, Yeshua is now sitting on the throne of His father David, yet His is a Kingdom still to come in its fullness. Additionally, although there was a specific day when Yeshua was sacrificed as our Passover Lamb, He is nevertheless called "the Lamb slain from the foundation of the world" (Revelation 13:8, KJV). [175]

Until *all Israel* meets certain criteria, they continue to walk as separate houses. Only when they enter fully into their New Covenant will they once more be a reunited Israel.

Israel will only be fully restored when both have the Father's laws written in their minds and on their hearts—by the Spirit of Messiah Yeshua.

Only when it can be said that man is no longer teaching his neighbor, or his brother, saying, "Know the LORD," because they all know Him, from the least of them to the greatest (Hebrews 8:8-12, NIV; Jeremiah 31:31-33)—only then—can it be said that all Israel has entered fully into its New Covenant and that it is fully reunited.

We conclude that Judah does not represent all Israel.

---

175 That He already has "sat down" indicates that He now rules (Luke 1:32; Heb 1:3; 10:12; 12:2; Rev 3:21); and yet, His is a Kingdom yet to come: Matt 6:10; Luke 11:2; also see Isa 27:9; 55:3; 59:21; Jer 31:31-34; 32:38-40; Heb 8:8-12; 10:16. Passover Lamb: 1 Cor 5:7; John 1:29; 1 Pet 1:19; Mark 15:34.

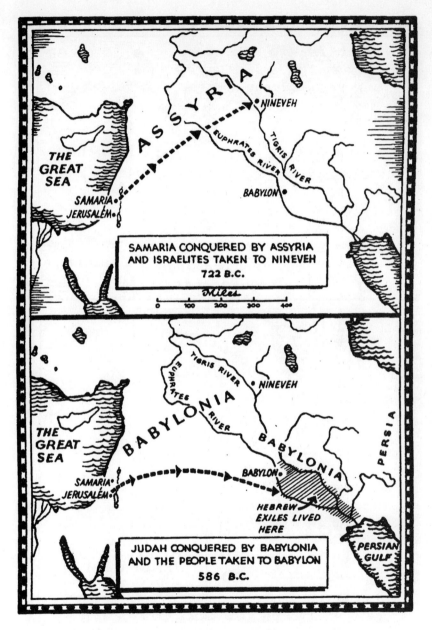

From *A Map Book For Bible Students* by Frederick L. Fay, pg 18,
Old Tappan, NJ: Fleming H. Revell. Used by permission.

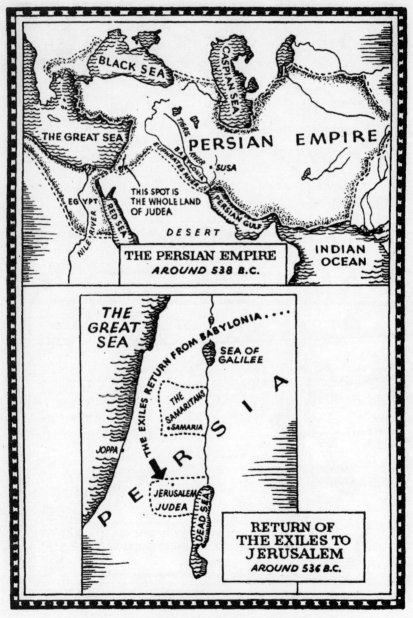

From *A Map Book For Bible Students* by Frederick L. Fay, pg 20,
Old Tappan, NJ: Fleming H. Revell. Used by permission.

16

Hallmarks of Restored Israel

Despite past failures, our Father promises to fully reunite Israel in the last days. He even describes certain attributes of both of the participants, as well as their victorious reunion:

"Then the jealousy of Ephraim will depart, and those who are hostile to Judah will be cut off; Ephraim will not be envious of Judah, nor will Judah [vex and] harass Ephraim. Together will they invade the western borders of the Philistines [the Palestinians]; side by side shall they plunder the tribes of the east; in union will they possess Edom and Moab and make the sons of Ammon [Jordan] their subjects" (Isaiah 11:11-14, TNKH).

Ephraim's Jealousy Will Depart

As Ephraim's jealousy of Judah departs, he will cease to either idolize or despise the Jewish people. The Father will likewise lift the veil of Romans 11:25 from Ephraim's blinded eyes. He will then see the truth of his own Israelite identity and will cease to be jealous. He will realize that he is no more or less chosen than Judah.

With this revelation comes a key that will open a door to healing and change in Ephraim. When he understands who he is, he will feel more secure as part of the people of Israel, and will better understand his divine call.

A Repentant Ephraim

The Father says of a formerly wayward Ephraim, "I have surely heard Ephraim grieving."

In repentance, Ephraim responds:

"Thou hast chastised me, and I was chastised, like an untrained calf; bring me back that I may be restored, for Thou art the LORD *my God. 'For after I turned back, I repented; and after I was instructed [The Emphasized Bible says: "after I came to know myself" [176]], I smote on my thigh; I was ashamed, and also humiliated, because I bore the reproach of my youth'"* (Jeremiah 31:18,19).

After he comes to know himself—after he is instructed about his own Israelite roots—Ephraim will be ashamed of the sins of his youth. In his repentance he will turn from his pagan practices. Then "he will be like a mighty man." Then YHVH "will whistle for them, to gather them together [with Judah]" and, "Ephraim will come trembling from the west." At that time the people of Ephraim will return in great numbers, "Until no room can be found for them" (Zechariah 10:7,8,10; Hosea 11:10).

Those Hostile to Judah Will Be Cut Off

This change will result in Judah's enemies being cut off because Ephraim will stand with Judah. Ephraim's stand will make a difference because he stands as a mighty man. As a fully repentant and truly changed Israel, he stands as a powerful prince.

We see in this plan a certain principle at work. As Yeshua said: "Any kingdom divided against itself is laid

---

176 *The Emphasized Bible* by J. B. Rotherham, *26 Translations of the Holy Bible*, Zondervan, 1985, Mathis.

waste; a house divided against itself falls" (Luke 11:17).

The opposite is also true: A united kingdom cannot be laid waste; a united house will not fall. When Ephraim and Judah stand together, Judah's enemies will be cut off.

Judah Will Cease to Vex Ephraim

When Judah sees change in Ephraim, he will cease to vex[177] him. No more will he refuse to recognize Ephraim as a legitimate, equal heir. Judah will do so because Ephraim will begin to behave like an Israelite. Together they will become an invincible army that overcomes an old enemy.

The Ancient War Between Ishmael and Isaac

When the two houses overcome their internal conflict, they also will settle the ancient war between Ishmael and Isaac. We see this in that the Arab peoples are primarily descended from Ishmael, whereas Ephraim and Judah are principally descended from Isaac and Jacob.

Surely we have seen the three great religions, Judaism, Christianity, and Islam, do battle in the past.

In addition, when the two houses of Israel unite, "The House of Jacob [Judah] shall be fire, and the House of Joseph [Ephraim] flame, and the House of Esau shall be straw." For YHVH has sworn, "I will bend Judah as My bow, I will fill the bow with Ephraim...and I will make you like a warrior's sword" (Obadiah 1:18, TNKH; Zechariah 9:13; 1 Samuel 17:45; Isaiah 11:13-14).

A Cleansed, Whole Israel

"'The sons of Israel will come, both they and the sons of Judah as well; they will go along weeping as they go, and it

---

177 Vex: Strong's word # H 6887, *tsarar* (צרר): to cramp, afflict, besiege, bind, distress, be an adversary/enemy, oppress, vex. *Tsarar* can speak of "being restricted," or of "strong emotional response," as in the case of "controversial decisions" (see TWOT, word # 1973, p 778). Thus Paul says those of Judah are "*enemies* of the gospel for your sake" (Rom 11:28).

will be YHVH their God they will seek. They will ask for the way to Zion, turning their faces in its direction; they will come that they may join themselves to YHVH in an ever-lasting covenant..." "At that time...search will be made for the iniquity of Israel, but there will be none; and for the sins of Judah, but they will not be found'" (Jeremiah 50:4-5,20).

Forgetting the Ark and the Exodus

Those once called "faithless Israel and treacherous Judah" will yet return to Zion:

"I will give you shepherds after My own heart, who will feed you on knowledge and understanding. And...when you are multiplied in the Land...they shall say no more, 'The ark of the covenant of the LORD.' It shall not come to mind, nor shall they remember it, nor shall they miss it, nor shall it be made again. At that time they shall call Jerusalem, The Throne of YHVH...[and] will not walk anymore after the stubbornness of their evil heart. In those days the house of Judah will walk with the house of Israel, and they will come together from the land of the north" (Jeremiah 3:14-18). [178]

"Days are coming...when it will no longer be said, 'As YHVH lives, who brought up the sons of Israel out of the land of Egypt,' but, 'As YHVH lives, who brought up the sons of Israel from the land of the north and from all the countries where He had banished them.' For I will restore them to their own land which I gave to their fathers" (Jeremiah 16:11-16).

The Holy One will save the house of Judah and the house of Israel from the east and the west. He will return to Zion, and thereafter Judah and Ephraim will call Zion "The City of Truth" (Zechariah 8:3,7,13).

---

178 North, *tsaphon* (צָפוֹן): a compass direction; to conceal something for a definite purpose; the place of the meeting of the Gods; where judgment of sin is stored. Strong's # H 6828; TWOT # 1953. Stems from # 6845: *tsaphan* (צָפַן), a primal root meaning to hide by covering over, to reserve, protect, esteem, hide, keep secret. See Psa 91; 17; 27:5; 31:20; Isa 26:20-21; Zeph 2:3.

A Pure Israel

Finally, we look to Ezekiel's description of reunited Israel:

"Take one stick for Judah, then take another stick for Ephraim," for thus says the LORD God of Israel, "I will make them one stick in My hand. And, I will make them one nation in the land. One king will be king for all of them. They will no longer be two nations, and they will no longer be divided into two kingdoms. And they will no longer defile themselves with their idols, or with their detestable things, or with any of their transgressions...I will be their God and they shall be My people...and they will all have one shepherd; and they will walk in my ordinances...And they shall live on the land I gave to Jacob...forever...and I will set My sanctuary in their midst forever" (Ezekiel 37:22-26).

Judah and Ephraim Have Not Yet Been Reunited

It is not as taught. We have not missed the reunion.

- After Judah's partial return from Babylon, they left the Land again. But once YHVH reunites the two, they will live on the Land forever. They will no longer give away portions of the Promised Land for peace.
- Scripture describes a reunited Israel that does not even remember the Ark. Instead, they remember their Deliverer in terms of a glorious Exodus yet to come. Until we see a people who exhibit those characteristics, Israel's reunion is not yet fully manifested.
- Ephraim and Judah have yet to experience the complete destruction of their enemies: the Philistines and Babylon.
- Once YHVH reunites Israel, they do not defile themselves with any of their transgressions. There is no iniquity in Israel, nor sin in Judah: "This will be the full price of the pardoning of [Jacob's] sin: When he makes all the altar stones like pulverized chalk stones; when Asherim and incense altars will not stand"

(Isaiah 27:9). Neither Christianity nor Judaism is entirely pure in practice. In their present states, neither qualifies as Ezekiel's fully reunited house.

- When YHVH reunites all Israel, they will have one King. Since He is the last King the world will have, He is none other than the King of kings and LORD of lords—Yeshua—the Shepherd King of Israel.
- Never, since their scattering, have Judah and Ephraim fulfilled these Scriptures. Since their dispersion, the two houses have not been one nation in the land, with control over all their inheritance. Nor have they had a Davidic king over them.[179] Nor have they become a people who do not defile themselves with any of their sins and transgressions.[180]

Fulfillment of these prophecies demands there be no iniquity—no manifested sin—not in either house. These verses speak of a united, pure, righteous, holy Israel. They speak of a future time when Yeshua will reign as King over the City of Truth. Until that happens, the Father is still dealing with both Judah and Ephraim.

The Rabbis and the Ancient Writings Agree

Over the years, many rabbis have taught that the two houses have not yet been reunited. For example, the *ArtScroll Tanach Series* says of the noted *Rambam* (Moshe Ben Nachman), in his comments on Ezra:

"*Rambam* maintains that the Ten Tribes did not return to the Land...The Jewish settlers in Jerusalem consisted only of members of the tribes of Judah and Benjamin and a few representatives of other tribes." [181]

John Hulley, Israeli author of *Comets, Jews & Christians* (Root & Branch, Jerusalem, 1996), writes:

---

179 "God...has given the kingship of Israel to David and his descendants forever" (2 Chr 13:5). Herod was a non-Jew and the Hasmonean kings were from Levi. So neither fulfilled this scripture (NIV Study Bible footnote, Matt 2:1).

180 Also see Eze 11:15-20; 14:4; Isa 27:6-9.

181 *Ezra*, Mesorah, 1984, p 151.

"Belief in the continued existence of the ten tribes was regarded as an incontrovertible fact during the whole period of the Second Temple and of the Talmud." [182]

Many rabbis have long believed that great will be the day when the exiles of Israel are reassembled. They believe that The Ten Tribes shall return and have a share in the "World-to-Come" [183]

Numerous Jewish writings claim that those of Joseph/Ephraim were, and still are, lost in the Diaspora as "Gentiles." They believe Joseph is very much alive.

We find such quotes in the writings of Israeli scholar, Yair Davidy, who recites many Rabbinical commentators to prove his points about Ephraim's dispersion.

Davidy writes, "Taken at face value most [Jewish Commentators] easily lend themselves to a 'Lost Ten Tribes In Western Europe' interpretation." [184]

In the ancient book, *Second Esdras*, we read,

"The ten tribes which were led away from their own land into captivity in the days of King Hoshea"—"They were taken into a strange country. But then they resolved to leave the country populated by the Gentiles and go to a distant land never yet inhabited by man." "They have lived there ever since..." (vss 13:40-46).[185]

Israel is not yet fully reunited.
Ancient writings confirm it.
Many Jewish rabbis know it.
Yeshua's people need to know it also.

---

182 *Encyclopaedia Judaica*, s.v. *Ten Lost Tribes*, p 1004.
183 See: Rev. Dr. A. Cohen, *Everyman's Talmud, New American Edition*, Dutton, N.Y., 1949, p. 354; Rabbi Rafael Eisenberg, *A Matter of Return*, Feldheim, Jerusalem & New York, 1980, p 130; and *House of David Herald*, Restored Ephraim: Key To Israel's Victory, Vol 12, Book 3; *Do The Rabbis Expect To See the Lost Tribes*, John Hulley, Jerusalem, 2000.
184 *Ephraim*, chapter eight, Yair Davidy, Israel, 1995. Also see *Lost Israelite Identity* by Davidy, Jerusalem, 1996.
185 *The New English Bible With the Apocrypha*, Oxford, 1970. The *Apocrypha* is an ancient writing that offers an early view of this matter.

Scripture	Restored Israel Hallmark
Isaiah 11:13	Ephraim's jealousy departs
Jeremiah 31:18,19	Ephraim repents of his paganism
Isaiah 11:13	Those hostile to Judah are cut off
Isaiah 11:13	Judah ceases to vex Ephraim
Zechariah 10:7	Ephraim becomes like a mighty man
Hosea 11:10	Ephraim comes trembling from the West
Zechariah 10:8,10	Ephraim returns in great numbers
Obadiah 1:18	Jacob becomes a fire, Joseph a flame
Zechariah 9:13	Judah is like a bow, Ephraim the arrow
Jeremiah 3:14; 50:5	Repentant Israel asks for the way to Zion
Jeremiah 50:20	No more iniquity found in Israel
Jeremiah 3:17;16:14	Both forget the Ark and the Exodus
Zechariah 8:3,7,13	They call Zion The City of Truth
Ezekiel 37:15-28	Two sticks become one nation in the land
Ezekiel 37:24	Ephraim and Judah have one king over them
Ezekiel 37:23-24	They are not defiled with any transgressions
Ezekiel 37:26-27	YHVH sets His sanctuary in their midst forever

17

Leaving Elementary Things Behind

The author of the Book of Hebrews says he has "much to say" about Yeshua, but he has a problem, in that his audience has "become dull of hearing."

He therefore chastens them:

"Though by this time you ought to be teachers, you need someone to teach you the elementary truths of God's word all over again. You need milk, not solid food! Anyone who lives on milk, being still an infant, is not acquainted with the teaching about righteousness. But solid food is for the mature, who by constant use have trained themselves to distinguish good from evil" (Hebrews 5:10-14, NIV).

The author wants the people to "leave the elementary teaching about the Messiah," and to "press on to maturity."

He encourages them not to lay "again a foundation of repentance from dead works and of faith toward God, of instruction about washings and laying on of hands, and the resurrection of the dead and eternal judgment. And this we will do," he says, "if God permits" (Hebrews 6:1-3).

Elementary principles are absolute essentials. They are

fundamental to any good foundation. Thus fundamentals are taught to every child in elementary school. If a child does not learn 2+2=4, he will never be able to move on to advanced math. If he does not learn his ABC's, he will not be able to read or write.

On the other hand, if we only teach the basics of 2+2 and ABC, due to the endless repetition, out of sheer boredom the child will probably drop out of school, and then stumble through life incapable of fulfilling his true destiny.

The Beginning Essentials

Scripture lists the fundamental principles, the essentials, of our faith:

- Repentance from dead works
- Faith toward God
- Baptisms
- Laying on of hands
- Resurrection of the dead
- Eternal judgment

Beware the Sluggishness Pit

After making the above list, the writer of Hebrews turns our attention to those who "have tasted the good word of God" but "have fallen away." He is concerned about this problem and gives encouragement to those who have been faithful "in ministering to the saints," saying he hopes they will "show...diligence...until the end" (Hebrews 6:5-11).

A certain pitfall that we want to avoid is then revealed. This pit is defined by connecting verses 6:1 and 12:

"Therefore leaving the elementary teaching about the Messiah, let us press on to maturity, not laying again a foundation of repentance from dead works and of faith toward God....So that you may not be *sluggish*, but imitators of those who through faith and patience inherit the promises."

The pit is one of sluggishness, *nothros*, (νοθρος),[186] meaning to be sluggish, lazy, stupid, dull, and/or slothful.

The warning to "press on" (vs 6:1) comes on a two-edged sword. It cuts two ways. When we hear the gospel of the kingdom, we must be diligent to press on and not stumble due to laziness or lack of self discipline.[187] But he who preaches the gospel also needs to move beyond the basics.

If the preacher only preaches the elementary principles of the faith, he encourages laziness in his hearers. People feel no need to press on if they think they already know the basics. They are not inspired or challenged. Like our hypothetical child who is bored with endless ABC's, they may fall away due to utter boredom and never fulfill their divine destiny.

But the Book of Hebrews offers hope...

Believer's Boredom and its Cure

Those who become sluggish run the risk of getting sick with a case of "Believer's Boredom." The author of Hebrews describes this sickness, and prescribes a cure, beginning with a reference to Abraham's blessing:

"When YHVH made his promise to Abraham, since there was no one greater for him to swear by, he swore by himself, saying, 'I will surely bless you and give you many descendants.' And so after waiting patiently, Abraham received what was promised."

The writer next explains that "men swear by someone greater than themselves...[thus confirming] what is said."

However, "Because God wanted to make the unchanging nature of his purpose very clear to the heirs of what was promised, he confirmed it with an oath. He did this so that, by two unchangeable things in which it is impossible for God to lie, we who have fled to take hold of the hope offered to us may be greatly encouraged" (Hebrews 6:13-19, NIV).

---

186 Strong's # G 3576; from # G 3541 (# 3541 is used in Heb 12:8 to speak of "illegitimate" children who are "without discipline").
187 Hos 6:3; Mat 24:14; Phil 3:12-14; 2 Pet 1:10.

Those who feel sluggish are told to take hold of a certain hope. "Here," the writer of Hebrews offers, "Take this hope pill. It will chase away your despondency."

What Is the Hope and Who Are the Heirs?

"Faith is the assurance of things hoped for, the conviction of things not seen" (Hebrews 11:1).

The author of Hebrews wants to boost our faith by showing us something we can hope in. Hope encourages the weary soul, and so he wants us to see that:

- "Because God wanted to make the unchanging nature of his purpose very clear to the heirs of what was promised, he confirmed it with an oath" (Hebrews 6:17, NIV).
- His "desire...[is] to show to the heirs of the promise the unchangeableness of His purpose" (Hebrews 6:17, NASB)
- He is "willing more abundantly to show unto the heirs of promise the immutability of his counsel" (Hebrew 6:17, KJV).

Our God wants us to clearly see His unchangeable, immutable, unswerving determination to keep the promise He made to our forefather Abraham. [188]

Who does He want to see the truth about His promise to Abraham?

"The heirs of the promise."

And who are the heirs of the promise?

"If you belong to Messiah, then *you* are Abraham's offspring, heirs according to the promise" (Galatians 3:29).

A Different View of Certain Verses...

The Father wants us to see, to be filled with hope by, His unchangeable determination to keep His promised word to bless and multiply Abraham's seed.

---

188 Strong's # G 4055, 276, 1012 respectively.

Concerning His immutable word, He warns:

"You shall not add to the word which I am commanding you, nor take away from it..." (Deuteronomy 4:2; 12:32).

We are not to add to, nor take away from, the inspired words of Scripture. Yet we might say that most people unwittingly add words to Galatians 3:29. They feel the verse says, "If you belong to Messiah, you *become* Abraham's *spiritual* seed."

However, the verse is actually written, "If you belong to Messiah, then you *are* Abraham's seed." If we take the verse at face value, we see that it can be interpreted to mean that, belonging to Messiah serves to prove that we *are* Abraham's seed.

Another example of possibly adding meaning is found with Galatians 4:28: "You brethren, like Isaac, are children of promise."

To actually be "like Isaac," one would have to be a physical heir who is filled with hope in the God of Abraham. That is what it means to actually be "like Isaac."

We say this not to deny the truth that we are to be Abraham's heirs in spirit, nor to deny any Believers who might not be related to him—but to show that the verses also can be taken as confirmation of the Father's promise to greatly multiply Abraham's biological seed.

Making the Heart of the Righteous Sad

Again, biological descent from Abraham cannot be proven and therefore it cannot be established as any sort of requirement. Period. We further note that Abraham is "the father of *all* who believe" (Romans 4:11).

But on the other hand, we must not try to rob someone of their hope if they believe they *are* of Abraham's biological seed. If they believe they are physically part of the people of promise, then we should not try to divest them of that hope.

The Father warns that He is against those who "dishearten the righteous with falsehood when YHVH did not cause him that grief" (Ezekiel 13:22).

If it brings joy to the heart of a Believer to believe that he is a biological heir of Abraham the Believer—and since it cannot be proven otherwise—then we had best beware of telling him otherwise. Again, YHVH warns about "making the heart of the righteous sad" when He has not made them sad (Ezekiel 13:22, KJV).

We must not discourage Believers and thereby cause them to be "like Esau" and likewise deny their birthright (Hebrews 12:15-17). Let us not be found guilty of his sin, nor of leading others into similar error, for it was a sin of terrible consequence.

Take Hold of the Hope

After explaining our need to press on, the writer of Hebrews says we have been given "Strong encouragement to take hold of the hope set before us [which]...hope we have as an anchor of the soul, a hope both sure and steadfast..." (Hebrews 6:18-19).

Let us determine in our hearts that we will move beyond our elementary milk diet and take hold of this strong hope. Let us be greatly encouraged and press on to become true teachers of righteousness.

Take hold of the hope!

18

From Orphans To Heirs

In the past, many non-Jewish Believers have shrouded themselves in the tattered theories outlined in the previous chapters. These theoretical rags have made them feel like unworthy "Gentile Believers." They have felt like adopted, second-class citizens when they were in the presence of Jewish Believers, as though they were not quite as chosen as the Jewish people. They often felt like tolerated step-children, or an unimportant parenthesis in a statement God is making about the Jewish people. [189]

Such feelings of inferiority can cause a distinct limp in a person's spiritual walk, or affect how he feels he is perceived. But now is the time for Ephraim to be delivered—because the God of Israel has a job for him to do. He needs to provoke Judah, to make him want what Ephraim has.

To have the nourishment necessary for the job, we are instructed to change our diet of milk to one of meat (Hebrews 5:12-14).

---

189 This is not to ignore the anti-Jewishness of the "Church," but to change Ephraim and begin restoration (Isa 11:13; Rom 11:18-21; Joel 2:32-3:2; Obad 1:12; Zech 2:12).

Yeshua explains what it means to partake of meat when He says, "My meat is to do the will of Him that sent Me" (John 4:34, KJV).

To partake of meat is to do the will of the One who sent us. Meat is doing. And YHVH sent forth Abraham's seed and commanded them to *do* a job: be fruitful, multiply, increase, be great, excel, exceedingly, be in positions of authority.

This is the job assignment of the seed of Abraham. His children are to be like Isaac —the faith-filled child of promise who does the will of his father (Galatians 4:28; Hebrews 11:13-20; James 2:21).

But until Ephraim "comes to know himself," he will continue to be jealous of Judah. He will not be up to doing his job (Jeremiah 31:18-19; Isaiah 11:13; Romans 11).

In the past, Ephraim has often felt a bit like Little Orphan Annie, but he would do better to see himself as the returning prodigal...

The Return of the Prodigal

In the parable of the prodigal, Yeshua tells the story of a man who had two sons, the younger of whom asked for his inheritance, then went to a distant country where he squandered it on loose living. When famine came, the son had to take a job feeding swine. Hungry, he wished he could even eat of the pig's pods, but he was given nothing.

Coming to his senses, he said, "How many of my father's hired men have more than enough bread, but I am dying here with hunger!" So he determined to return to his father's house to confess his sin and renounce his disobedience. Feeling unworthy to be called his son, he would ask to become one of his father's hired men.

The son's father, having long yearned for the boy's return, saw him coming and ran to embrace and kiss him.

He said to one of his slaves, "Quickly bring out the best

robe and put it on him, and put a ring on his hand and sandals on his feet; and bring the fattened calf, kill it, and let us eat and celebrate; for this son of mine was dead and has come to life again; he was lost and has been found."

The older son, who had been out in the field, upon approaching the house, heard music and dancing. After inquiring, he was told, "Your brother has come, and your father has killed the fattened calf because he has received him back safe and sound."

Unwilling to go in and join the celebration, the older brother became angry. So his father came out and began pleading with him. But he said to his father, "For many years I have been serving you and I have never neglected a command of yours; and yet you have never given me a young goat, so that I might celebrate with my friends; but when this son of yours came, who has devoured your wealth with prostitutes, you killed the fattened calf for him."

To this the father responded, "Son, you have always been with me, and all that is mine is yours. But we had to celebrate and rejoice, for this brother of yours was dead and has begun to live, and was lost and has been found" (see Luke 15:11-32).

The Prodigal Portrays Ephraim

This story can be seen as a depiction of Ephraim's return home to his Heavenly Father:

♦ The prodigal went to a foreign land:
✓ "Israel [Ephraim] will certainly go from its land into exile" (Amos 7:11).
♦ The prodigal lived loosely:
✓ Father says, "Ephraim is a trained heifer that loves to thresh, but I will come over her fair neck with a yoke; I will harness Ephraim..." (Hosea 10:11).
♦ The prodigal was hungry:
✓ "'Behold, days are coming,' declares YHVH Elohim, 'when I will send a famine on the land, not a famine

for bread or a thirst for water, but rather for hearing the words of YHVH" (Amos 8:11). Today, Ephraim feels he is wasting away in gatherings that offer only the elementary milk of the Word when he needs the filling protein of meat. He craves the excitement of *doing* the Father's will (John 4:34).

♦ Pig's pods:

✓ Being close to pigs describes the younger Ephraim and not Judah. Judah does not touch pork, while Ephraim celebrates his supposed "freedom" by eating pork and Easter hams. Though he has been out wallowing in the pig's mire, Ephraim will repent and return home, and the Father will welcome him.

♦ The prodigal came to his senses and began to repent of his youthful sins:

✓ The Father says, "I have surely heard Ephraim grieving." Repentant Ephraim cries, "'Thou hast chastised me, and I was chastised, like an untrained calf; bring me back that I may be restored, for Thou art YHVH my Elohim. For after I turned back, I repented; after I was instructed, I smote on my thigh; I was ashamed, and humiliated, because I bore the reproach of my youth" (Jeremiah 31:18-19).

♦ The father of the prodigal yearned for his son:

✓ Our Heavenly Father says, "Is Ephraim My dear son? Is he a delightful child? Indeed, as often as I have spoken against him, I certainly still remember him; therefore My heart yearns for him; I will surely have mercy on him" (Jeremiah 31:19-20).

♦ When the prodigal returned, the older son was not pleased with his reappearance. He was even angry.

✓ Like the older son, First Century Jewish leaders were not happy about the return of those once lost among the nations. They accused Paul of bringing Greeks into their Temple and defiling their holy place. Some were even angry enough to kill (Acts 21:27-31). Sadly, they walked in the same spirit as some of their fathers: "The inhabitants of Jerusalem...said [of scattered Ephraim], 'Go far from the LORD; this land has been given us as a possession'" (Ezekiel 11:15). Today, some Jewish Believers are likewise unhappy about Ephraim's re-emergence; they reject the idea that the non-Jews might be equal heirs in Israel. Some want non-Jewish Believers to be in their synagogues for the wrong reasons. Paul says of this type, "They make much of you, but for no good purpose; they want to exclude you, so that you may make much of them" (Galatians 4:17, NRSV). In other words, they want to appear superior, that you might look to them for acceptance.

Bringing Judah Into the Party

At the time of the younger son's return, the older son was "out in the field." In the parable of the tares and the wheat, Yeshua says, "The field is the world..." (Matthew 13:38). The older son was not inside the father's house, but was "approaching" it. He was "drawing nigh" (KJV).

Let all who are jealous of Judah see that it was the prodigal who was *in* the house making merry with his father. The older son was *outside*.

Let us also acknowledge that the father went out to meet the older son. He even pleaded with him. Such is the Father's heart toward Judah. For He has sworn and will keep His promise to again possess Judah:

"YHVH will possess Judah as His portion in the holy land, and will **again** choose Jerusalem" (Zechariah 2:12).

Our Father wants Judah to join the party. He would have those of Ephraim behave in a way that would make Judah want to join the celebration. Yes, that is the job long ago assigned to Ephraim: Make Judah want what you have!

To Make Jealous—Make Merry!

The secret to Israel's reunion is for Ephraim to make

Judah jealous. And the older brother was provoked because he saw that his younger brother was in the house celebrating and rejoicing, or making merry, with the father.

Making merry is translated from *euphraino, euphraino* (εὐφραίνω *yoo-frah'ee-no*), meaning to be in a good frame of mind, to make glad, to be or to make merry, to rejoice.[190]

We must realize that legalism and religion will not provoke Judah to jealousy—but celebration will.

One reason so many non-Jews now feel an overwhelming urge to celebrate the feasts of Israel is because celebration is the key to provoking Judah to jealousy. Having others see us in a good frame of mind is the Father's plan of evangelism. When others see that knowing Yeshua makes us glad and causes us to rejoice, they will want to join in. This is the secret to our reunion.

For celebration suggestions especially for Messianic Israelites, we recommend the liberating book, *Israel's Feasts and their Fullness.* [191]

The Many Shades of Jealousy

The Father speaks of a day when "the envy and jealousy of Ephraim shall depart...and Judah shall not vex and harass Ephraim" (Isaiah 11:13, TAB).

These ancient traits characterize current Christian and Jewish relationships. Ephraim is envious, or jealous, of Judah. The Hebrew word is *kanah* (קנא), and jealous is a good translation, because both words cover a wide range of emotions. *Kanah* can be used in a favorable sense to speak of consuming zeal focused on a loved one, as in: "*Kanah* for Thy house has consumed me" (Psalm 69:9). It also is used to describe our Father when He says: "I, YHVH your God, am a [*kanah*]jealous God" of (Exodus 20:5; 34:14).

The positive, protective aspect *kanah* is seen when Believers speak of the "unexplainable love they feel for the Jew."

---

190 Strong's # G 2165.
191 *Israel's Feasts and their Fullness* by Batya Wootten, Key of David, St. Cloud, FL.

Even with little Biblical knowledge, some people have a desire to protect their Jewish brothers and sisters.

However, jealousy can grow into violent wrath and anger when it is distorted and left unchecked.

Just as Ephraim's fierce anger once burned against Judah (2 Chronicles 25:10), such destructive anger is evident in Church history. The result of this anger is seen in the shameful anti-Semitic violence perpetrated against the Jewish people. Church history is replete with anti-Jewish actions and doctrines: The tyranny of the Crusades, the torture of the Spanish Inquisitions, the burning and pillaging of the Pogroms, plus the indescribable horror of six million Jewish lives annihilated in the Holocaust.

The record of the Church is tarnished by jealousy, marred by hatred. Her wedding gown is stained with Jewish blood. It is a stain that must be washed away—can only be washed away—with true tears of repentance.

Now is the time for Ephraim to humbly repent and seek forgiveness from her sister Judah.

A Close Relative?

Judah's problem is that he "vexes" Ephraim. The word is *tsarar* (צרר), which means to cramp, afflict, besiege, bind, distress, oppress, to be an adversary, or enemy.[192] *Tsarar* speaks of restricting, tying up, or having strong emotional response to controversial decisions. This word is used in Isaiah 8:16: "*Bind* up the testimony."

"Binding" through legalism is one way that Judah vexes Ephraim.[193] Legalistic misrepresentation of Torah hinders Ephraim, because it keeps him from seeing and embracing its many truths.

---

192 Those of Judah are "*enemies* of the gospel for your sake" (Rom 11:28).
193 *Strong's* # H 6887; TWOT #1973. Restrict: see Isa 49:19; 2 Sam 20:3. Note: Hosea describes Ephraim's sin as being "bound up" (vs 13:12).

Judah has also long distressed Ephraim by refusing to acknowledge him as an equal heir in Israel, though Judah has obviously had legitimate complaints and justifications for his actions.

The Second Book of Samuel describes an incident between Israel's two houses that illustrates these traits.

King David was being escorted across the Jordan, principally by the people of Judah. But they did not wait for *all* Israel to assemble and escort the king, so Ephraim became angry when he was left out of the procession.

"All the men of Israel [Ephraim] came to the king and said to the king, 'Why had our brothers the men of Judah stolen you away, and brought the king and his household and all David's men with him over the Jordan?'

"Then all the men of Judah answered the men of Israel, 'Because the king is a close relative to us. Why are you angry about this matter? Have we eaten at the king's expense, or has anything been taken for us?'

"But the men of Israel answered the men of Judah and said, 'We have ten parts in the king, therefore we also have more claim on David than you. Why then do you treat us with contempt? Was it not our advice first to bring back our king?'" (2 Samuel 19:41-43).

Harsh, Fierce Words

The Father's comment sums up His opinion of this matter: "Yet the words of the men of Judah were harsher than the words of the men of Israel."

"The king is a close relative to us" are harsh, fierce (KJV) words. To claim the king was "closer" to them due to biological relationship was cruel, since the Ephraimites could not change how they were born.

King David was a type of King Messiah, and a similar scenario is being played out today.

For centuries, vast numbers of Ephraimite Believers have implored people everywhere to follow King Jesus (Yeshua). Yet many Jewish Believers are now claiming

Messiah Yeshua is *their* close brother, and those of Ephraim are once again feeling wounded, left out, treated with contempt.

In this state, they tend to respond with an inexcusable explosion of anger.

In opposition to the "one hope of...calling" declared in Ephesians 4:4, this type of hurtful behavior is often dismissed under the errant guise of Jewish Believers having "a different calling." The truth is that the non-Jewish Believer may in reality be a descendant of one of Yeshua's apostles, and the supposed "Jewish" Believer could descend from one who converted to Judaism. As stated in Esther 8:17: "Many among the peoples of the land became Jews, for the dread of the Jews had fallen on them."

More important is the fact that Yeshua frowns on any who would pridefully "lord it over" another by claiming such a special relationship. He explicitly said, "Whoever does the will of My Father who is in heaven, he is My brother..." (Matthew 12:48-50).

Judah and the Family Album

Historically, Judah has vexed Ephraim. Jewish leaders put First Century followers of the Messiah out of the synagogue.[194] Judah also began reciting a curse over the Jewish Believers in their daily prayers.[195] Even today, Messiah's followers find it difficult to obtain citizenship in Israel.

In allowing this to happen, it is as though the Father gave Judah control over the "family photo album," yet Judah will not allow Ephraim's picture to be in that album.

Let those of us who see the truth of the situation rise above the fray and become people of solution.

---

194 John 9:22; 12:43; 16:2; Acts 26:9-11.
195 *The Feasts of Israel*, Victor Buksbazen, W. Collingswood, NJ: Gospel Ministry, Inc, 1976, chapter 7, "Seventh Day or First Day." p 60-61.

Who Is Israel? Past, Present, and Future

19

Jeremiah's Olive Tree

In Scripture, the first use of a word or theme sets the standard for further interpretation. And Jeremiah was the first to use an olive tree to symbolically describe the people of Israel when he said of them:

"They have turned back to the iniquities of their ancestors who refused to hear My words, and they have gone after other gods to serve them; the house of Israel and the house of Judah have broken My covenant which I made with their fathers" (Jeremiah 11:10).

Jeremiah said this to both "the house of Israel and the house of Judah." He also said of them, "YHVH called your name, 'A green olive tree, beautiful in fruit and form;' with the noise of a great tumult He has kindled fire on it, and its branches are worthless" (Jeremiah 11:16).

YHVH called both Ephraim *and* Judah "a green olive tree," meaning they were to be one, they were to be a singular olive tree, because it was, and still is, His plan to have *one* people. They also were to be a green tree, as in full of life, fruitful.

However, division came to Israel, and with it came two branches in the tree.

To see this tree in all its fullness, let us briefly review some historical background that will help us understand these two branches of Israel.

Abraham, the first Hebrew, fathered Isaac, who fathered Jacob (Israel), who in turn fathered twelve sons who became known as "the twelve tribes of Israel." [196]

Judah was the fourth-born of those twelve sons. Those of the house of Judah were the first to be called *Jews*, a name that is a diminutive of Judah.

You cannot have a "Jew" before you have the first one named Judah, and Judah, a son of Israel, was the first person to be so named. Thus we cannot say that all Israel is Jewish, because Jacob/Israel existed before Judah.

Jacob was not Jewish, meaning of Judah. Instead, he was the *father* of Judah. From Judah, from this *son* of Israel, came the Jews.

Judah's brother, Joseph, was the eleventh-born son of Jacob/Israel, but the firstborn of Jacob and Rachel.

Joseph did not descend from Judah, but was his brother. Joseph's firstborn heir was Ephraim, who likewise was not Jewish. Instead, Ephraim had an uncle named Judah.

Abraham — Isaac — Jacob

1) Reuben	2) Simeon	3) Levi	4) Judah	5) Dan	6) Naphtali
7) Gad	8) Asher	9) Issachar	10) Zebulun	11) Joseph	12) Benjamin

The Twelve Sons of Jacob in their Birth Order

---

196 Gen 14:13; 32:28; 35:22; 49:28.

Two Branches— Called to be One

Metaphors are often used in Scripture to describe reality. For example, the Father likens His people to horticultural analogies, such as trees and vines (Matthew 7:15-20; John 15:5-8).

As we know, some time after entering into the promised Land, Israel divided into the two houses of Ephraim/Israel and Judah. Then, after the Father scattered Ephraim among the nations, He called both houses an olive tree.

The first thing we note about the olive tree of Israel is that it has two major branches: Ephraim and Judah.

The First Branches to be Broken Off

Both "chosen families" were branches in the olive tree, but because the Ephraimites had a penchant for paganism and served the gods of the heathen, they were the first to be broken off the tree (Jeremiah 33:23-26; 11:10,16; 2:18,21). This happened because they had become *roa,* or worthless, their condition below par (Jeremiah 11:16).[197] So Father scattered them in Assyria.

Ephraim was sent to Assyria, Judah to Babylon. First the olive tree was stripped of most of its Ephraimite branches, later it was stripped of most of its Judahite branches.

When Jeremiah uses horticultural analogy to speak of those "on the road to Assyria," he speaks of Ephraim.

Of those wanderers, YHVH asks:

---

197 TWOT, Vol. 1, Moody, 1981, word # 2191; BDBL word # H5237.

"I planted you a choice vine, a completely faithful seed. How then have you turned yourself before Me into the degenerate shoots of a foreign vine?" (Jeremiah 2:18,21).

To become *degenerate* is to turn aside. *Foreign*, or *nokri*, means to be a stranger, as in foreign to Israel's God. (In modern Hebrew, *Nokri* means Gentile.) [198] With trees, to become *degenerate* is to become *wild*...

The Wild Ones

The Ephraimites became wild because they delighted in debauchery. They were therefore scattered among the nations—there to languish "like a vessel in which no one delights" (Hosea 8:8; 2:23; Romans 9:21-22).

The Ephraimites left their native homeland, the Land of the Cultivator, and they became foreign. They stumbled down an Assyrian road—because they did not revere their "Vinedresser." While in His Land, they did not allow His Word to "break up their fallow ground." So the Father pruned and scattered them, in hopes that one day they might bear fruit (Hosea 10:12; John 15:1-7).

In the graphics that follow, we see pictures of Jeremiah's olive tree and how that tree was pruned. First it was pruned of the Ephraimite branches, then of the Judahite branches, and finally, we see how a few branches from Judah were returned from Babylon.

When we examine these stages in the life of this tree, with the final stage, we will see Israel's olive tree as it was at the time the apostle Paul wrote about it.

---

198 TWOT, Vol. 1, Moody, 1981, pp 620-621,580; also see Judges 19:12; 1 K 8:41, and the *House of David Herald*, The Notzrim, Vol 9, Book 6.

Jeremiah's Olive Tree With Both Branches:
Ephraim and Judah

Ephraim
is Dispersed
⇨

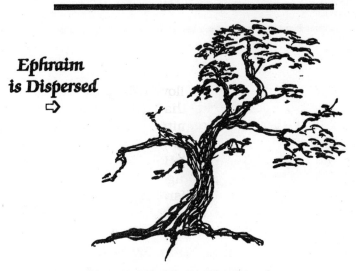

The Olive Tree after Ephraim's Dispersion
Judah Continues to Live in the Land
722 B.C.

Judah
is Dispersed
⇐

**The Olive Tree After Judah's Dispersion
Both Houses Have Been Dispersed
586 B.C.**

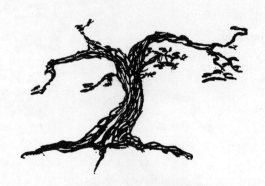

**The Olive Tree After Some From Judah Return
and During the Times of
Yeshua and Paul
30 A.D.**

Paul's Olive Tree

I do not want you, brethren, to be uninformed of this mystery—so that you will not be wise in your own estimation—that a partial hardening has happened to Israel until the fullness of the Gentiles has come in"

(Romans 11:25).

When Paul the apostle penned these enigmatic words, the tree of which he spoke looked much like the final olive tree depicted in the last chapter.

Both Ephraim and Judah had been scattered. Then a remnant from Judah had returned from Babylon. Along with the descendants of the farmers and fishermen left behind long ago by their conquerors, these comprised the people who collectively become known as "the Jews."

This severely pruned tree, cut back by the Cultivator Himself, its branches scattered by His Holy hand, is the substance of the mysterious tree of Romans Eleven.

Many non-Jewish Believers associate themselves with Israel through their understanding of this olive tree, and many believe they are "grafted into a Jewish olive tree."

What is the real truth about this tree?

In his metaphor, Paul was not grafting *pears* into a *peach* tree, but "wild *olive* branches" back into an "*olive* tree."

- Between the "wild olive branches" and "natural olive branches" the common denominator is that both are "olive branches."
- If we search the Scriptures, and allow them to interpret themselves, we see that in the First (Old) Covenant (which sets the standard), "Gentiles" were never once called an "olive tree." But Israel certainly was.
- Paul spoke of olive into olive—*Israel back into Israel.*
- In speaking of "wild olive branches," Paul cryptically spoke of *Ephraim*—of fruit of the same species.

The Mystery...

The *New Revised Standard Version* translates Romans 11:25: "So that you may not claim to be wiser than you are, brothers and sisters, I want you to understand this mystery: a hardening has come upon part of Israel, until the full number of the Gentiles has come in."

After telling us about the Father's plan for His natural and wild olive branches, Paul tells us:

- He is addressing a *mystery*
- A hardening, or *blindness* in part has occurred
- That blindness happened to *Israel*
- It would last *until*...
- Israel was destined to enter into a certain *fullness*

As previously stated, there is no mystery in having those

from the nations join the people of Israel. So there must be something more to the story.

Both Houses Are Blinded—Both Stumble

The King James translates this important verse, "For I would not, brethren, that ye should be ignorant of this mystery, lest ye should be wise in your own conceits; that blindness in part is happened to Israel, until the fulness of the Gentiles be come in" (Romans 11:25, KJV).

As prophesied, all twelve tribes of Israel were given "a spirit of stupor, eyes to see not and ears to hear not" (Romans 11:8; Deuteronomy 29:4).

Paul spoke of a "partial hardening," a stupidity, or callousness in part,[199] that happened to both Ephraim and Judah. He spoke of a mystery that would not be understood until a certain point in time.

Until then, a certain blinding would cause both Judah and Ephraim to be tripped up, to "stumble" over the Messiah (Romans 11:11). Both would misunderstand Him.

That both houses of Israel would stumble was foretold by Isaiah: "It is the LORD of hosts whom you should regard as holy," he said.

The LORD of hosts is *YHVH Tsavaot*, and Isaiah said of Him: "He shall be your fear and He shall be your dread. Then He shall become a sanctuary; but *to both the houses of Israel*, a stone to strike and a rock to stumble over..." (Isaiah 8:13-14).

Scripture foretold that the LORD of hosts would become a Sanctuary, and thereafter, "both the houses of Israel" would stumble over Him.

When some asked Yeshua for a sign, He said, "Destroy this temple [sanctuary], and in three days I will raise it up." (He was speaking of the temple of His body.) And, "when He was raised from the dead, His disciples remembered that He said this; and they believed *the Scripture*" (John 2:18-22).

---

199 Strong's words # G4457, 4456, 3313.

The Scripture the disciples remembered and believed was Isaiah 8:14—the verse that spoke of the LORD of hosts becoming a sanctuary over whom both the houses of Israel would then begin to stumble.

The people of Israel did not realize that through His son, YHVH wanted to build a temple made with living stones.[200] And in different ways, both houses began to trip over Yeshua. To this day, both stumble over Him—because both were partially blinded. YHVH poured out a veil over their eyes, so both see darkly, as if looking in a faded, faulty mirror (1 Corinthians 13:12).

Blinded in Different Ways

Ephraim and Judah were blinded in different ways: Ephraim can see Messiah, but not his Israelite roots. Judah can see his roots, but cannot see the Divine Messiah.

Ephraim and Judah
Blinded in Different Eyes
Blinded in Different Ways

Further, due to the consequences of his punishment of "rootlessness," of not knowing the truth about his own Israelite roots,[201] Ephraim often feels inadequate in the presence of Judah, who has what appears to be long, beautiful, meaningful roots.

Jealousy is the problem. Ephraim does not see the role he has played as the other house of Israel. He does not truly see the olive tree in which he abides.

For some, jealousy of Judah's roots is even causing them to forget that they are rooted in the most important Root of all—Yeshua!

---

200 1 Pet 2:5; 1 Cor 6:19; Eph 2:21.
201 To understand Ephraim's punishment, see Eze 4:5; Lev 26:18,21; Hosea 1-2; and *Restoring Israel's Kingdom*, Angus Wootten.

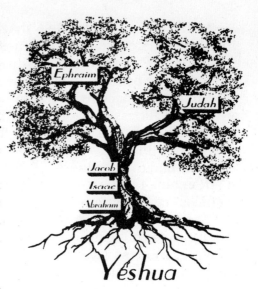

- Looking at this symbolic tree, we see that Yeshua is the Root.
- Moving upward, we see a trunk comprised of Abraham, Isaac and Jacob.
- Springing from that trunk are two main branches, Judah and Ephraim.

The Root of the Tree

Yeshua said, "I am the root and the offspring of David" (Revelation 22:16).

Of what tree is Yeshua the Root?

King David said, "As for me, I am like a green olive tree in the house of Elohim." And that those who fear YHVH will have "children like olive plants" (Psalm 52:8; 128:3).

David definitely was/is in Israel's olive tree, and Yeshua, the Branch of Isaiah 11:1, is David's offspring. Yeshua is both a Branch in Israel's olive tree and He is its Root.

Just as a root gives life to the tree, so Yeshua is the life-source for all, including our patriarchs.[202]

Until...We Enter Into Our Fullness

Both Ephraim and Judah have stumbled over the Sanctuary. To date, both houses have only seen in part.[203] The veil that once shrouded their Israelite eyes was to remain "until..."

We are living in the days of that *until.*

---

202 John 11:25; 14:6; 1 John 5:12; Luke 1:72: John 6:49-50.
203 Isa 8:13-14; Jer 33:24; John 2:18-22; Rom 11:25-26.

Many are now realizing that a certain fullness was promised to Israel in the end times, specifically to Ephraim and Judah. Completion is destined to come to Israel. She is destined to be filled to over-flowing.

Ephraim especially needs to be filled with hope in this promised fullness. He needs to be inspired to fulfill his divine call and thus help usher those of Judah into their promised fullness.

Paul told of a "fullness" of the Gentiles that is to "come in" (Romans 11:25). Those of Ephraim were to become a "fullness" of the nations (Genesis 48:19).

Some believe Paul spoke of a specific number of Gentiles coming to faith. That could be one meaning of the verse. However, fullness (*pleroma*) means repletion, completion, what fills. It comes from a word that means to finish (a period or task), to verify (a prediction).[204] Moreover, the words come in mean to enter.[205] This verse indicates that the Father has a last day's job for Ephraim to do. He wants him to verify something to Judah.

The "fullness of Gentiles" that is Ephraim (whatever the number) is now being called to enter into a new era. It is an era of celebrating the feasts of Israel as they have never been celebrated before.

Romans 11:25 seems to have more to do with completion of a task rather than a certain number of non-Jews being saved. It appears to have to do with Ephraim's maturation; telling of a time when he presses on beyond the elementary (but necessary) points of the gospel (Hebrews 6:1-3).

This important chapter also alludes to the end of Ephraim's punishment.[206] It speaks of the time when he responds to Jezreel: "The sons of Judah and the sons of Israel will be gathered together, and...great will be the day of Jezreel" (Hosea 1:11).

---

204 Strong's #'s G 4138 and 4137 respectively.
205 Strong's # G 1525.
206 Ephraim's punishment: see Eze 4:5; Lev 26:18,21; Hosea 1-2; and *Restoring Israel's Kingdom*, Angus Wootten, 2000, Key of David.

Judah's Fullness

Judah too is destined to come to fullness: "Now if their transgression is riches for the world and their failure is riches for the Gentiles, how much more will their fulfillment be! (Romans 11:12).

Micah spoke of a time when Judah will "return to the sons of Israel" (Micah 5:3). Moses said the Father will "bring him unto his people [Israel]..." (Deuteronomy 33:7).

Judah enters into fullness when he hears the Word of Messiah Yeshua, and the divine plan is for him to hear that word through the mouth of his long-lost brother Ephraim.

Judah also needs to be returned to the sons of Israel, because his branches were broken off the olive tree of Israel (Romans 11:17).

The Mandate

Despite their formerly wild state, YHVH planned to use Ephraim and companions: Salvation came to them to make Judah jealous (Romans 11; Ezekiel 37:16,19).

YHVH gave Wild-Branch-Ephraim a Divine Mandate:

Make Judah want what you have.
Excite him to rivalry.
Stimulate him.
Make him want to be like you!

Judah

There Are Two Main Branches In The Olive Tree of Israel: Ephraim and Judah

When the Father first called "Israel" an "*olive tree.*"
He specifically said He was speaking to:
"The house of Israel *and* the house of Judah" (Jeremiah 11:10).
Yeshua said, "*I am the root* and *the offspring* of David"
(Revelation 22:16).

21

Honoring Both Branches

We must realize that both branches of the olive tree are Israel and that both have been used by the Father.

For example:

Romans 9:4 speaks of "the Israelites, to whom belongs...the covenants."

Though Judah wrote the book, history records that it is a remnant of the formerly wild olive branches that the Father has chosen to be His New Covenant keepers (Deuteronomy 18:18-19; John 17:8, 20,21;12:49-50).

YHVH has used Ephraim to proclaim to the world that He has a Son (Proverbs 30:4). If not for the continuing efforts of these primarily non-Jewish ones, how would we know about the Anointed One, or His New Covenant? [207]

Father did not use those of Rabbinic Judaism to preserve Israel's promised New Covenant. He placed it in Ephraim's hands for safekeeping.[208]

---

207 Messiah and Christ mean "Anointed" (see Strong's word #'s H4899; G5547).
208 Ephraim has made mistakes in presenting the New Covenant. However, by placing its record in Ephraim's hands, the Father may have been repressing

(continued...)

Thus, Romans 9:4 takes on new meaning. Paul says it is the "Israelites, to whom belongs the adoption as sons, and the glory and the covenants and the giving of the Law and the temple service and the promises."

The situation that existed during Paul's time has changed. Today we see Ephraim as the one whom the Father appointed as the keeper of Israel's New Covenant. [209]

This means that if we teach about "indebtedness to the Jew," to be fair, we should teach the same about Ephraim.

In Ezekiel's two sticks reunion, the prophet uses the word *etz* (עץ), which means *tree*. Since paper comes from trees, we can see two paper Bibles—one kept by Judah, the other by Ephraim. Two Books of Covenant, each serving as a good witness about the God of Israel, each needing the other to be complete.[210]

The Plan of Salvation for All Israel

Both Judah and Ephraim have been used by the Father to tell of His two-fold message: He has a Law, but for all law-breakers He offers Grace. Two witnesses: Law and Grace. [211]

In His plan to preserve all Israel, the Father has used Judah as a witness to His Law, which "is our tutor that brings us to Messiah" (Galatians 3:24).

This standard must be upheld in the earth, because "where there is no law, there is no transgression" (Romans 4:15, NIV). Judah has tried to uphold this standard since their return from Babylon. [212]

---

208 (...continued)
"nationalistic pride." (See Eze 34:11-15; Isa 56:8; Hos 8:8; Amos 9:9; John 10:16,27; 11:52; Matt 15:24; Acts 15:16).

209 This is not to say that either house fully complies with or fully understands the particular "Covenant Book" the Father has placed in their hands.

210 Strong's # H 6086.

211 Neither house teaches these truths "exclusively." They are not mutually exclusive principles.

212 They sometimes distort the truth about YHVH's "Law." See the *House of*
(continued...)

The Father has also used Ephraim, who has been giving witness that we are redeemed by Messiah's precious blood.

Ephraim has been proclaiming for almost 2000 years the truth that "by grace are we saved" (1 Peter 1:18,19; Romans 4:16).[213] In making this vital proclamation about our redemption, Ephraim, the firstborn son of the double portion, is being a type of redeemer to all Israel.

In our day, the Father desires to fully reunite His divided house. He wants His two witness peoples to serve their ultimate purpose—to confirm to the world the entirety of His Word, from Genesis to Revelation.

Unfortunately, as we seek to reunite both the houses of Israel, we find some people who continually try to exalt one house over the other.

Jewish Roots?

Today, many encourage Believers to return to their "Jewish roots." However, this tree is "Jewish" only to the extent that He Who is the Root of David also is "the Lion from the Tribe of Judah" (Revelation 5:5). [214]

As to Yeshua being crowned as King, we must realize that it is not Rabbinic Judaism that has been working these past two thousand years to honor Him.

Paul said, "Branches were broken off... for unbelief" (Romans 11:20). Those who did not believe in "the Root" (the "Branch"

---

212 (...continued)
David Herald, Vol. 6, Book 10, Good Laws—Bad Attitudes.
213 Ephraim often distorts the truth about "Grace." See *Mama's Torah*, "Good Laws—Bad Attitudes," by Batya Wootten, Key of David, 2003, Saint Cloud, FL.
214 The scepter, which is a symbol of leadership, was to be with Judah only until Shiloh's coming, then unto Him would be the gathering of the peoples (Genesis 49:10). This is a Messianic prophecy, and Messiah has come. He now sits, scepter in hand, at the right hand of the Father. From there He rules in the hearts of all who accept Him as their own (Psa 110:1-2; Heb 10:12; Rev 3:20-21).
Hebrew letters are also used as numbers, and "Shiloh" = 358, which is the same number for the title "Messiah." The Targums (Aramaic paraphrase) in this passage translates "Shiloh" as "Messiah," which fits with the Talmud, where Shiloh is said to be one of the names for the Messiah.

sent to restore all Israel) were broken off the olive tree. If one was of faith and not conceited about their position, but stood in fear of Him who would not spare them if they did not "continue in His kindness"—those remained attached to Israel's source of eternal life (Romans 11; John 15:5).

Of these broken Jewish branches, Paul said, "If they do not continue in their unbelief, they will be grafted in; for God is able to graft them in again" (Romans 11:17-23).

When Judah is grafted in again, he is grafted into an olive tree that has primarily been kept alive, though admittedly rather wild, for multiplied hundreds of years by the non-Jews long ago grafted into it.

On Being Grafted In

Once grafted into a natural tree, a branch is then part of the cultivated tree—as are its shoots. So it is for those long ago grafted into Israel's tree, and for their offspring.

Therefore, to teach that non-Jewish Believers are now being grafted into a "Jewish" olive tree—when in fact it is an "Israelite" olive tree, is to intimate that they are something less than who they are in truth. They are a people who, despite their mistakes, have been trying to tell the world about "The Root" for the past two thousand years.

Natural Branches?

Romans 11:21: Paul called the Jewish brethren of his day, "natural branches," or *"kata phusis klados."* [215]

Paul's primary point was about how one responds to the Father.

Defining the Greek words Paul used will help explain how we should view his statement.

- *Klados* (κλαδων) speaks of a twig or bough.
- *Kata* (κατα) has to do with being "in accord with," or "joined to" something or someone.

---

215 *Kata phusin kadown* (κατα φυσιν κλαδων): These words are contingent on the relationship of the sentence to the parties being addressed.

For example, "Let it be done to you *kata* your faith" (Matthew 9:29).

- *Phusis* (φυσις) speaks of our *natural response.*
  This word is used in the following verses:
  Women who go against *phusis* (Romans 1:26).
  Unregenerated Gentiles who do by *phusis* the things of the law (Romans 2:14-15).
  By faith we become partakers of the *Divine phusis* (2 Peter 1:4) [216]

These words speak of a branch that is joined to, has a proper response to, the Cultivator. It has to do with our *nature*, meaning, how we *naturally* relate to our Father, the Cultivator of the vine. The emphasis is not on genetics, but on a heart response; on being joined to, and in one accord with, Him.

As for Gentiles, it was not their *phusis* to do the things of the Law. They were heathen, and had not been taught the Word. Remember, it is the hearing of the Word that leads one to naturally do the things of the Word. [217]

We all need to have a nature that is joined to, and in one accord with, the Holy One of Israel and His Messiah. To remain in His olive tree, one must have a *phusis* that is joined to His purposes.

The Jews of Paul's day were the keepers of YHVH's Word. That Word included the promise that He would bring forth a Righteous Branch from their formerly cut-down tree. This righteous Branch would preserve all Israel.[218]

All Israel is called to be in one accord with this plan. Yeshua is the life source of the olive tree, the One through Whom Israel gains eternal life—the One in Whom we must abide (Romans 11:24; John 15:4-11). Regardless of background, our *nature* must be in one accord with Yeshua.

---

216 *Klados:* Strong's # G2798. *Kata:*, # G2596, also frequently denotes *intensity.*
Phusis: Strong's # G5449. See Rom 1:26; 2:14-15; 2 Pet 1:4.
217 *Heathen/Gentile:* Strong's # G1484: "Specifically a *foreign* (*non-Jewish*) one (usually by implication *pagan*):—Gentile, heathen, nation, people."
218 Isa 4:2; 11; Jer 23:5.

As stated in 1 Corinthians 2:14, "A natural man does not accept the things of the Spirit of God, for they are foolishness to him; and he cannot understand them, because they are spiritually appraised." Likewise, the truth about Israel's olive tree must be spiritually appraised.

Calling All Non-Jewish Believers "Ephraim"

Should we call all non-Jewish Believers "Ephraim"?

If we use this title, does that mean we believe there are no "Gentiles" who are *not* biologically related to Abraham among the non-Jewish Believers in Messiah?

No, it does not. To believe that the Father is primarily gathering Israelite branches does not mean we deny salvation to those who are *not* physically related to Israel, because—*both houses include converts.*

Judah has had converts to their faith and we call them "Jews." Therefore, we would be using a double standard if we denied the title of "Ephraimites" to olive branches who once became wild.

Moreover, the Father uses these titles when speaking of joining the "two sticks" (Ezekiel 37:15-28). If He uses them, yet does not deny salvation to those not related to Abraham, then we should feel free to use them without incrimination.

It is not valid to argue that the two house teaching withholds the Gospel from those not related to Abraham, because no one can know for sure from whom any of us descend.

No one can honestly withhold the Good News from any man, regardless of race, color, or creed.

We conclude that the olive tree, its branches and leaves, are often used to symbolize peace, prosperity, new life, strength, beauty, friendship, divine blessing, and...*Israel.*

May our understanding of this tree be used to bring these blessings to the whole house of Israel.[219]

---

219 To better understand "biological Israel," please read the *Addendum, Genetic Confirmation,* by Michele Libin, page 243. The latest research is now confirming that, by this time in history, on at least some elementary level, everyone is probably related to Abraham.

22

New Kingdom—New Rules

A re Believers in Messiah who might not descend from the patriarchs also part of Israel?

Yes.

In ancient Israel, once foreigners joined His people they were natives of the Land. [220] Again, the three citizenship requirements were circumcision, observing Passover, and sojourning. These same three essentials continued to be requirements for citizenship in New Covenant Israel— although the rules were given different emphasis. [221]

We must realize that Yeshua was and is the King over New Covenant Israel. His is an eternal Kingdom that is not of this world.

With Yeshua's advent, the Kingdom of Israel, and the emphasis on Israel's Kingdom rules were both changed.

New Covenant Israel's eternal Kingdom was placed in the hands of the apostles (1 Peter 1:1; 2:9). Determining membership in that Kingdom likewise was in their hands.

---

220 See Chapter 12, *Israel: A Mystery Until...*

221 Lev 19:34; Num 9:14; 15:15,16; Deut 18:15-19; Heb 3:3; 5:6; 7:12; Luke 22:8,15,19, 20; 1 Pet 1:19; 1 Cor 5:7; 11:26; Rev 3:20; Rom 2:29; Col 2:11,12; Phil 3:3; Eph 2:11-19.

- Yeshua said to Israel's chief priests: "I say to you, the kingdom of God will be taken away from you, and be given to a nation producing the fruit of it."
- And He said to His disciples: "Do not be afraid, little flock, for your Father has chosen gladly to give you the kingdom" (Matthew 21:43; also see Luke 12:32; 22:30; Daniel 7:9-22; Acts 1:6).
- In New Covenant Israel, the Priesthood was changed from that of Aaron to that of Melchizedek.[222]
- And "when the priesthood is changed, of necessity there takes place a change of law also" (Hebrews 7:12).

From a Lamb to The Lamb

Israel's Passover law was changed with Messiah's Sacrifice. The Lamb of God became our sacrifice (John 1:29; 1 Corinthians 5:7). That Lamb, Yeshua, "stands at the door" of our hearts and knocks. If we will open to Him, if we will apply His blood to our heart's doorway,[223] then He will come in and dine with us (Revelation 3:20). [224]

Messiah Yeshua moved the *primary emphasis* of circumcision from the flesh to the heart.[225] Circumcision and Passover were redefined for those of New Covenant Israel in and through Him and His sacrifice.

Just as Abraham was first circumcised of heart, then the flesh, so New Covenant Israelites are called to first emphasize circumcision of the heart.

Concerning Passover: the emphasis is no longer to be on a lamb that was sacrificed yearly, but on The Lamb of God who was sacrificed once and for all (Jeremiah 4:4; Hebrews 7:27; 9:12; 10:10).

Thus the first two citizenship rules of circumcision and Passover were redefined for New Covenant Israel.

---

222 Heb 7; 9:7,16; 2:17; 3:1; 5:10; 8:1,3; 1 Cor 5:7.
223 If *you* have not yet asked Messiah Yeshua into your heart, repent of your sins and ask Him in now. To know Him is to know a Glory that will last for an eternity!
224 NC Passover: Mark 14:22; Luke 12:37; 22:19; 1 Cor 5:7; 11:24; Rev 19:9.
225 Deut 10:16; 30:6; Jer 4:4; 1 Chr 29:17; Mt 23:25-28; Rom 2:28-29; Acts 10:47; John 4:23; Col 2:11.

The Apostolic Hinge

After Yeshua's Ascension, the third condition of *sojourn-ing* remained undefined. Thus we see the Council of Acts Fifteen in essence asking, "How is this third requirement met"?

At this meeting the apostles reached a conclusion. They attached four basic convert requirements to a *hinge* statement. Endorsement of converts hung on this pivotal point. They established a "sojourning" condition (Acts 15:21).

In essence, the Apostolic decision was:

"With these minimal *sojourning* requirements, we can accept these Believers who have been circumcised by *Ruach HaKodesh* (the Holy Spirit), *because* there is something we can count on. We have seen them partake of the bread of the New Covenant Passover,[226] and so, *if* they meet this one third condition, we can accept them. *For,* there is something we know to be true."

James basically said, "Brethren, it is not necessary that these new followers of The Way begin to *immediately* observe, understand, and follow all the ordinances of Israel. We should not suddenly put Torah teachings before them as a stumbling block. Rather, let us write to them outlining certain minimal standards for them to follow. If they agree to abide by these minimal behavior modification standards we can receive these people into our sect of Judaism—*for*— in every town, ever since the earliest times, there have been those who teach the Law of Moses" (see Acts 15:1-21).

The apostles agreed. These new people would become part of "The Way." [227] They would go to the synagogue and Temple as the apostles did. There they would learn of the principles of wisdom found in the Torah of Moses. [228]

"Amen," they all said. And the matter was settled.

---

226 Luke 22:1-19; John 6:35,58; 1 Cor 5:7-8.

227 Acts 9:2; 19:9,23; 24:14,22; John 14:6.

228 We speak of YHVH's eternal Torah truths, of His "Living Torah" (John 1:1-5). We do not uphold man-made laws or errant interpretations of Torah that cause people to stumble. See Deut 4:5-6; 11:8-9; 1 Ki 2:3; Psa 119:1-6; Lev 18:5; Eze 20:11; Matt 19:17; 5:17-18; 5:20-24; 22:36-40; 23:13; 10:25-28; 16:17; 11:52.

So Much to Hang On One Little Word...

Upon one little word hung acceptance of converts by the apostles: the word "*For.*"

This is significant in that the Greek word used, *gar*, speaks of a *cause and effect relationship.* [229]

The presiding elders of the Jerusalem council believed that the newcomers who were claiming faith in the Messiah of the New Covenant would hear about the Law of Moses, and that the effect would be that the Holy Spirit would write the essence of the Law on their hearts.

They believed this because it was the very heart of Israel's promised New Covenant, and because that was how Israel's divided kingdom would be restored. [230] They would hear the Torah taught, and the Spirit, the *Ruach,* would do a work in their hearts. As YHVH declared, "I will put My law within them and on their heart I will write" (Jeremiah 31:33).

Everyone in the faith would abide by His three rules, and so would no longer be "Gentiles" (Ephesians 2:12-19).[231]

Only Twelve Gates—No Other Way

Whatever their presumed genetic backgrounds, most Believers would surely agree that ultimately they will be united with all the "Believing" people of Israel.

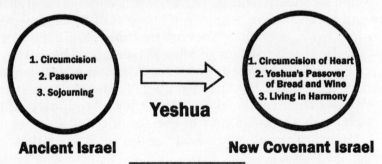

1. Circumcision
2. Passover
3. Sojourning

Yeshua

1. Circumcision of Heart
2. Yeshua's Passover of Bread and Wine
3. Living in Harmony

Ancient Israel   **New Covenant Israel**

---

229 *Strongs* # G1063. Gar: assigning a reason, as, because (that), but, even, for, indeed, no doubt, seeing then. *The word speaks of grammatical connection.*
230 Acts 15:14-17; Amos 9:9-11; Jer 3:12-18; 12:14-15; 31:18-19; 31:31-33; Hosea 3:5; 4:6; 5:3-4,11,15; 8:1,8,11-12; Isa 11:11-14; Oba 1:18; Zec 8:13; 9:13-17.
231 Being born into a religious system is not enough—not in Israel or the Church. We must truly be "of the faith" (Rom 9:6; Matt 7:22-23; Rev 2:9; 3:9; 2 Cor 13:5).

Further, all Believers will enter the New Jerusalem through one of the City's twelve gates, named after Israel's tribes. For there are no other entrances (Revelation 21:12; Ezekiel 48:30-34).

All Believers will ultimately belong to one of Israel's eternal tribes, because the One God has but one people. [232]

All of YHVH's people can be called "Israel." This is true whether they are being obedient or disobedient.

A disobedient Israelite can of course be put outside the believing Israelite camp. In the eyes of those in the camp, he would thus no longer be "of Israel." But he would still be a physical descendant of Israel. As such, he and his descendants would continue to have an eternal call on their lives even though he was being disobedient to that call.

Dividing the Camp

Almost two thousand years ago, Paul said the "former" Gentiles had been excluded from the commonwealth of Israel. "But now, in Messiah Yeshua you are no more strangers and aliens," but are "fellow citizens" (Ephesians 2:11-19). In other words, Paul told the non-Jewish Believers of his day that they were no longer outsiders, exiles, migrants, and aliens. They were no longer excluded from the rights of citizens, but they "shared citizenship with ...God's own people" (Ephesians 2:19).

Restated, they were no longer heathen, but were *of Israel.* If an individual had a Gentile background, once he was "in Messiah Yeshua," he became a "fellow citizen of the commonwealth of Israel." Moreover, his children would also be children of Israel. Through faith in Yeshua's Passover sacrifice, heart circumcision, and sojourning, the converts Paul spoke of were long ago given full citizenship in Israel.

---

232 Ezekiel says: "You are to distribute this land among yourselves according to the tribes of Israel. You are to allot it as an inheritance for yourselves and for the aliens who have settled among you and who have children. You are to consider them as native-born Israelites; along with you they are to be allotted an inheritance among the tribes of Israel. In whatever tribe the alien settles, there you are to give him his inheritance,' declares the Sovereign LORD" (Eze 47:21-22).

A Chosen People

Peter wrote his first letter to, "Those who reside as *aliens.*"[233] He called those aliens *chosen.*

"You are a *chosen* people, a royal priesthood, a holy nation, a people belonging to God, that you may declare the praises of him who called you out of darkness into his wonderful light. Once you were not a people, but now you are the people of God; once you had not received mercy, but now you have received mercy" (1 Peter 1:1; 2:9-10, NIV).

The *New International Version Study Bible* says of these aliens who once were not a people: "In Hosea it is Israel who is not God's people; in Romans it is the Gentiles to whom Paul applies Hosea's words; in 1 Peter the words are applied to both." [234]

These words are applied to *both.* Could it be that they are one and the same people?

They could well be, because "When the most High gave the nations their inheritance, when He separated the sons of man, He set the boundaries of the peoples according to the number of the sons of Israel" (Deuteronomy 32:8).

Time to Arise

Again we ask, what difference does it make whether or not we are part of the people of Israel?

The difference? Esau versus Jacob.

The conflict? Are we orphans or true heirs?

The difficulty? Discerning the players in the game.

The importance: It is time for Ephraim to arise—that all Israel might be fully restored!

---

233 Strangers and aliens: "Moses...became an *alien* in the land of Midian," and Abraham's descendants were "*aliens* in a foreign land" (Acts 7:6,29). These words speak of an acquaintance, a guest; of one who lives elsewhere. Sojourners make their home with Israel (see Strong's #'s G 3581, 3941, and Foreigner [Stranger]: *Interpreter's Dictionary of the Bible*, Vol. 2, Abingdon, 1962, pg. 310).
234 NIV Study Bible 1 Peter 2:10 footnote, p 1890.

Part Three

Israel's Future—
Challenges and Destiny

23

The Two Witnesses and Their Fullness

Before Israel entered the Promised Land, Moses sent twelve men, one from each of the twelve tribes, to spy out the Promised Land. Only two returned with a good report: Caleb, from the tribe of Judah; and Joshua, from the tribe of Ephraim (Numbers 13:2,6,8).

The first example of two who gave a good report about YHVH's promises were a Judahite and an Ephraimite.

Yeshua says of His two witnesses: "I will grant the power of prophecy to My two witnesses" (Revelation 11:3, TAB).

These two witnesses are anointed to speak for the Holy One of Israel. Yeshua describes them as "The two olive trees ...that stand before the LORD of the earth" (Revelation 11:4).

After seeing *two olive trees* (or branches), Zechariah asked the Holy One about them, and He answered:

"These are the two who are anointed to serve the LORD of all the earth" (Zechariah 4:11,14, NIV).

- These two trees poured forth oil, which is a source for light.
- Yeshua's two witnesses are called "two lampstands."
- Lampstands are churches, or *ekklesias*. *Ekklesias* are assemblies, or congregations, of "called out ones" (Revelation 11:3,4; 1:20).
- Lampstands give light, and Yeshua says of those who follow Him: "You are the light of the world" (Matthew 5:14).
- Scripture describes two witnesses who are called to give forth light and who are depicted as two congregations of peoples.
- Our Father is now calling forth these two congregations. They are the "two sticks" or "trees," [235] that are presently being made "one in His hand" (Ezekiel 37:15-28). They are Judah and Ephraim.

Metaphorically, the two witnesses are two anointed olive trees who speak for the God of Israel. Judaism and Christianity are the only two religions that give testimony about Him.

Although the people of Islam claim to follow Abraham's God, YHVH calls Himself "The God of Abraham, Isaac and Jacob" (Exodus 3:16; Acts 3:13). Islam denies that Isaac and Jacob are Abraham's heirs. Islam instead claims that Ishmael is Abraham's true heir, so their god, *Allah,* and the GOD of Abraham cannot be one and the same.

Two Individual Witnesses

Many teach that there will be two *individuals* who will arise as "two witnesses." If beyond the two companies of

---

235 Eze 37:20: Strong's # H 6086: 'ets, ates (עץ); from H 6095; a tree.

Ephraim and Judah there are to be two *individual witnesses* (and there well may be two men who do arise), Scriptural precedent suggests that one will be an Ephraimite and the other a Judahite.

Further, if there are to be two individual witnesses, they probably will lead the two houses of Israel in a war against the beast. The fact that the beast makes war with the two witnesses suggests a *company* of two peoples, because a head of state would not likely make war with two individuals (Revelation 13:7,10).

If ever there were a beast that would devour both Christians and Jews, it is the radical beast that uses the sword of Islam against them. [236] Nonetheless, the *Amplified Bible* says of Ephraim and Judah:

"But [with united forces] Ephraim and Judah will swoop down upon the shoulder of the Philistine's land sloping toward the west; together they will strip the people on the east [the Arabs]. They will lay their hand upon Edom and Moab, and the Ammonites shall obey them" (Isaiah 11:14).

A Witness Even Unto Death

As Israelites we are to be witnesses for the God of Israel. The Greek word for "witness" comes from *martus* (μαρτυς), which is where we get the English word "martyr." Many of Israel's latter-day witnesses will be martyrs in the fullest sense of the word, because they will testify even to the peril of their own lives. They will overcome "because of the blood of the Lamb and because of the word of their testimony, and they did not love their life even to death" (Revelation 12:11).[237]

Wanting to Escape with Our Lives

Instead of focusing on being a living witness for the Father, some Christians look for an escape in a Pre-Tribulation Rapture. However, we gain patient endurance by not

---

236 See, *Is Fanatic Islam A Global Threat?* by Victor Mordecai, Jerusalem, 2002. Fifth Edition. Also see *Christian Revival for Israel's Survival*, Jerusalem, 1999.
237 Strong's # G 3144.

loving our lives even on pain of death (Revelation 13:10). [238]

The late Corrie Ten Boom, a Christian woman who lost most of her family in the Holocaust because they supported the Jewish people, cautioned Believers: "*The rapture-before-tribulation doctrine is now an exclusively American message.*" This woman of truly tested faith repeatedly warned all who had ears to hear, "*Don't listen to those false prophets...*" [239]

Those who teach this theory separate the Church and Israel, and we have demonstrated that this theory is flawed. They fail to recognize that there awaits a glorious prize for all who show unfailing allegiance during the end times. Those "beheaded because of the testimony of Yeshua and because of the word of God...will be priests of God and of Messiah and will reign with Him" (Revelation 20:4-6).

We must not focus on avoiding momentary earthly affliction, but on transcendent eternal reward. [240]

First They Believe—Then They See

Christians who believe in a Pre-tribulation Rapture think they will be snatched away, that the Jewish people will be left to go through the tribulation, and that in the end, the Jewish people will come to believe as they do. [241]

Whether realized or not, this view purports that "wrath brings conversion." But Scripture tells us that it is *kindness* that leads us to repentance (Romans 2:4).

The people of Judah do not need more wrath. They need to see Messiah's kindness in His people.

In addition, the idea that Judah will look on Yeshua and *then* believe opposes Scripture: "O Jerusalem, Jerusalem," Yeshua said, "who kills the prophets and stones those sent to her! How often I wanted to gather your children together, the way a hen gathers her chicks under her wings, and you

---

238 Luke 21:19; 2 Cor 6:4; Heb 10:36; 12:1; James 1:3-4; 5:11.
239 Corrie Ten Boom, late author of *The Hiding Place*, Chosen Books.
240 Rev 20:4,6; 22:12; John 15:13; Luke 6:23.
241 Jewish people are offended by the idea of being left behind for slaughter while Christians fly away for a "Wedding Feast." It is heartless to think of one group of Father's people eating wedding cake while the other is being severely afflicted.

were unwilling. 'Behold, your house is left to you desolate! "For I say to you, from now on you will not see me until you say, 'Blessed is He who comes in the name of the LORD'" (Matthew 23:37-39).

Judah will not see Yeshua *until* he first acknowledges Him as the Blessed One. First Judah believes, then he sees. *And he will not believe until Ephraim makes him jealous!*

Some people base their "see then believe" concept on Zechariah 12:10: "They will look on Me whom they have pierced; and they will mourn." But John applies this verse to Yeshua's crucifixion, saying, "They will look on the one they have pierced" (John 19:37; Psalm 22:16-17).

When our King returns in glory and we look on His nail-pierced hands, this verse will again be fulfilled. We too will mourn, knowing He was pierced for *our* transgressions. [242]

Putting On Immortality

The Rapture theory, which speaks of Christians being snatched away, is largely based on 1 Corinthians 15:52-54: "We will all be changed, in a moment, at the last trumpet." This change specifically speaks of believing mortals "putting on immortality."

Believers will be changed. We will become immortal. The only question is: When?

In the Book of Revelation, seven angels sound seven trumpets. When the seventh angel sounds the last trumpet, then the mystery of God is finished. It is done. The kingdoms of the world have become the kingdom of our LORD. At that time, the LORD God Almighty "has begun to reign" (Revelation 8:2; 10:7; 11:15-17; 16:17).

If another angel were to sound another trumpet after this *last* trumpet, then all was not finished. Thus the trumpet of the seventh angel must be the *uttermost* trumpet.[243]

We will be here to see the lawless one revealed, because

---

242 Isa 53:5,10; 1 Pet 2:24; Heb 12:2; John 19:34; 1:29; Rev 6:15-16; Mat 24:30-31.
243 Last/uttermost: Strong's # G 2078. See *Rapture or Transformation*, by Batya Wootten, 2003, Key of David, Saint Cloud, FL.

2 Thessalonians 2:1-4 warns: "Let no one in any way deceive you, for it will not come unless the apostasy comes first, and the man of lawlessness is revealed."

We must look for transformation, not Rapture. We must look for victory, not escape. And it will help us to be transformed as a people when we see that....

There are Two

YHVH is dealing with two houses of Israel. He has:

- Two Houses (Isaiah 8:14; Jeremiah 31:31-33; Hebrews 8:8-10)
- Two Nations (Ezekiel 35:10)
- Two Chosen Families (Jeremiah 33:24)
- Two Sisters (Ezekiel 23:2-4)
- Two Olive Branches (Zechariah 4:11-14; Jeremiah 11:10, 16-17; 2:18,21; Romans 11; Revelation 11:4)
- Two Sticks (Ezekiel 37:15-28)
- Two Witnesses (Revelation 11:3-4)
- Two Lampstands (Revelation 11:3-4)
- Two Silver Trumpets (Numbers 10:2-3)
- Two Leavened Loaves (Hebrews 9:28)
- Two Cherubim (Exodus 25:18-20)

The Significance of the Twos

- *Two leavened loaves* were waved before the Almighty (Leviticus 23:17). Leaven often is used to symbolize *imperfection*, and like Ephraim and Judah, although the two loaves were imperfect, they were nonetheless the prescribed wave offering.
- *Two hammered silver trumpets* were to be blown to summon all Israel (Numbers 10:2-3). The silver first had to be purified, then hammered into shape. Only then could their *unified* sound be used to summon the congregation.

    When Judah and Ephraim are both hammered into shape their purified voices will sound like ancient trumpets. With that unified sound, all Israel will again be gathered together (Numbers 10:2-3).

- *Two cherubim of gold:* The Presence of the Holy One was found over the Mercy Seat of the Ark between the two cherubim of gold (purity) made of "hammered work." It was in the embrace of these two that one found mercy (Exodus 25:18; 37:9). It is in the embrace of a unified Judah and Ephraim that we will again find mercy and see YHVH's manifest Presence. In that embrace we will find revival.

The Perfected Fullness of Ephraim

Romans 11:25 tells us that a "fullness" of the Gentiles is destined to "come in." Fullness speaks of completion, of what fills. The same Greek word is used in 1 Corinthians 10:26 to quote Psalm 24:1: "The earth is the LORD's, and the fullness thereof."

Ephraim was to become a *fullness* of the nations. Since there is nothing on Earth that does not "belong to the LORD," many feel the promise speaks of *great numbers*. However, we also note that, in Romans 11:25 "come in" is translated from a word that means "to enter." [244]

Yeshua tells us, "Jerusalem will be trampled under foot by the Gentiles until the times of the Gentiles be *fulfilled"* (Luke 21:24).

When combined, Luke 21:24 and Romans 11:25 provide a cryptic picture of latter-day formerly Gentile Ephraim. It is a portrait of his numbers *entering into a new era.*

After essentially finishing his task of fully preaching the message of salvation by Grace among the Nations—after telling his brothers of the Father's great mercy—after pressing on beyond the elementary things—Ephraim comes to a place of perfection and maturity. [245]

---

244 Strong's # G 1525.

245 *Pleroma* means repletion, completion, what fills (used in Rom 11:25). It comes from *pleroo*, which means to make replete, to finish (a period or task), to verify a prediction (used in Luke 21:24). Strong's #'s G4138 and 4137 respectively.

Like the cherubim over the Ark, and the Menorah that gave forth light, like the silver trumpets used to gather all Israel, Ephraim will also be hammered/*miqshah,* into an attractive, well-set state.[246] Then his primary focus will turn to the restoration and reunion of all Israel.

Judah's Fullness

Judah also will come to completion: "Now if their transgression is riches for the world and their failure is riches for the Gentiles, how much more will their fulfillment be! (Romans 11:12).

Judah will "return to the sons of Israel" (Micah 5:3). Father will "bring him unto his people" and "help him from his enemies" (Deuteronomy 33:7). Judah will also acknowledge Ephraim, and the ten tribes will take hold of him:

"In those days ten men from all languages and nations will take firm hold of one Jew by the hem of his robe and say, 'Let us go with you, for we have heard that God is with you'" (Zechariah 8:23, NIV).

Like the lion that he is, Judah will once again roar!

The Fullness of Messiah

Riches will come forth when Judah comes into the fold, and fullness is surely coming.

Judah and Ephraim will serve and bring to pass a victory in the Earth for *YHVH Tsavaot,* the LORD of Hosts.[247] In "the fullness of time," all things will be "summed up in Messiah." The good news is that we are part of that fullness.

Yeshua is the fullness of Him who fills all in all. All the fullness of Deity dwells in bodily form in Him. [248]

The fullness, the completion, the perfection for which all Israel longs, is only found in our Divine Messiah—in Him Who is truly the Israel of GOD.

---

246 Strong's #'s H 4749, 4748; TWOT # 2086. See Exo 25:18,31; Num 10:2.
247 Like their Master, some may find "victory" in death (Rev 11:8-13).
248 Gal 4:4; Eph 1:10-11,23; 4:13; 3:19; Col 1:19; 2:9.

24

Called To Be Watchmen

osea said "Ephraim was a watchman with my God" (Hosea 9:8).

Ephraim will yet return to his divinely appointed watchman's post. As Jeremiah prophesied, "There shall be a day when watchmen on the hills of Ephraim shall call out, 'Arise and let us go up to Zion, to our God'" (Jeremiah 31:6).

We live in that day. Now is the set time for the Father's watchmen to arise. Now is the time for those of Ephraim to fulfill their call to be His watchmen.

The Notzrim

In Israel, Christians are called *Notzrim* (נוצרים), a word that stems from a Hebrew root that is the source for:

- *Notzrim* (*notesreem*)—watchmen, or guardsmen.
- *Netzer* (*natsiyr*)—preserved.
- *Natz'ra*—Nazareth, home of the Nazarene (Yeshua).
- *Netzer*—branch
- All stem from *n tz r* (נצר), which essentially means to watch, keep, preserve. [249]

---

249 Strong's s # H 5341 and 5336.

Isaiah said that from a "cut-down tree" a "shoot of Jesse" would appear. From this green growth would come a *netzer*, a branch (Isaiah 11:1). [250]

A new branch preserves a tree, and Yeshua is the Branch Who brought renewed life to Israel's olive tree. He is the Servant appointed to "raise up the tribes of Jacob, and to restore the preserved *[netzer]* ones of Israel" (Isaiah 49:1-6).

Ephraim is being delivered and preserved in Yeshua. [251]

Seeing and Declaring the Truth

Our God says of His watchmen, "There will be a day when watchmen/*notzrim* on the hills of Ephraim will call out, 'Arise, and let us go up to Zion, to YHVH our God'" (Jeremiah 31:6).

YHVH is imparting a vision to His watchmen in these latter days. He is allowing us to see into the night so we can foretell what is coming. He wants us to see His plan, and to be faithful to declare that plan to all Israel.

He wants us to work to preserve all Israel, to be like Manasseh, Reuben, and Gad, who had their own inheritance but would not rest until their brethren also had their inheritance (Joshua 1:12-15).

The Father's Secret-Hidden Ones

"I proclaim to you new things...even hidden/*netzer* things which you have not known," says YHVH (Isaiah 48:6) With this sense of *netzer* in mind, Israeli citizens Ephraim and Rimona Frank write:

The history of the "hidden ones" of Ephraim has been deleted from the chronicles of mankind, as was prophesied in the Word. Today, it takes a process of unearthing, from the layers of dust and ashes of forgetfulness, to bring forth the truth which has been buried for centuries and longer

---

250 "A branch out of his roots shall bear fruit" Soncino *Isaiah* (Soncino, 1985) p 56.
251 See, Jer 31:2; Eze 20:15,17,35; Hosea 2:14; the *House of David Heralds*, Vol. 6 Book 1, The Wilderness Experience; and, Vol. 8 Book 5, The Lord, He Is God; Vol. 10 Book 7, The Restoration of All Things, by Ephraim and Rimona Frank.

—the truth of a covenant promise made long ago over Ephraim, son of Joseph. [252]

We are Messiah's "hidden ones." The truth of who we are as the other house of Israel has been hidden from our eyes for many, many years. We were punished with a blindness that is now coming to an end. [253]

Manning Our Post

Another Hebrew word associated with watchmen is *shamar* (שומר). It means to guard, protect, attend to, take heed, keep, mark, look narrowly, observe, preserve, be circumspect, regard, save, be a watchman.

- The word describes YHVH's followers: "On your walls, O Jerusalem, I have set *shomrim*/watchmen; all day and all night they will never keep silent. You who remind YHVH, take no rest for yourselves; and give Him no rest until He establishes and makes Jerusalem a praise in the earth" (Isaiah 62:6).

Another important Hebrew word is *tsaphah* (צפה,), or the plural *tsophim*. This word speaks of leaning forward to peer into the distance, to observe, wait, behold, espy, look up, to keep watch. [254]

- "Listen! Your watchmen/*tsophim* lift up their voices, they shout joyfully together; they will see with their own eyes when YHVH restores Zion" (Isaiah 52:8).

These watchmen foretell the good that is coming to the chosen ones of Zion.

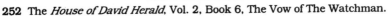

---

252 The *House of David Herald*, Vol. 2, Book 6, The Vow of The Watchman.
253 See Col 3:3; Isa 8:14; Rom 11:25; Psa 31:20; 83:3; Mat 13:35; Luke 18:34; Eze 4:5; Lev 26:18,21; Hos 1-2.
254 *Shamar:* Strong's # H 8104. *Tsaphah:* Strong's # H 6822. For more info see *The Wilderness Experience*, Batya Wootten, 2003.

The Trumpets of Teruah

The Holy One said to our fore-fathers, "I set watchmen/ *tsophim* over you, saying, 'Listen to the sound of the trumpet!'" (Jeremiah 6:17).

In this last day we are being called to sound two unified trumpets, for Israel was instructed to blow two trumpets on *Yom Teruah*, the *Day of Trumpets* (Numbers 10:2). [255]

Let us be serious about our call to sound an alarm. For Hosea said that although Ephraim was called to be a watchman/ *tsopheh*, still "the snare of a bird catcher was in all his ways." For this reason he went "deep into depravity" and was "devoted to shame." Thus YHVH said of them: "As for Ephraim, their glory will fly away like a bird—no birth, no pregnancy and no conception" (Hosea 9:8-11).

In the past, Ephraim has been a flighty people, capable of giving birth to little more than wind. But now is the time for them to give birth to the Sons of the Living God. It is time for them to arise, and to begin to truly *watch* over the house of YHVH, to be sentries who take charge, preserve, and safeguard the people. [256] It is time for Ephraim to become a mighty man (Isaiah 26:18; 66:7-10; 2 Kings 11:7).

The Duties of a Watchman

Habakkuk 2:1 explains the duty of the watchman:

"I will stand upon my watch [sentry post], and set me upon the tower [stronghold], and will watch [peer into the distance to keep watch] to see what He will say unto me, and what I shall answer when I am reproved."

A watchman watches his own actions, and takes it for granted that he will be corrected. He watches his ways and his heart. He prays that he not enter into temptation, and

---

255 Yom Teruah: *Israel's Feasts and their Fullness* by Batya Ruth Wootten.
256 Watch: Strong's # H 4931.

he meditates on the Word (Matthew 26:41; Luke 11:35; Proverbs 4:26,23; 2 John 1:8; Psalm 119:148).

He also watches out for Judah. For YHVH has sworn: "In that day...I will strike every horse with bewilderment and his rider with madness. But I will watch over the house of Judah, while I strike every horse of the peoples with blindness" (Zechariah 12:4).

The watchman prays for Israel's remnant, because "the effective, fervent prayer of a righteous man availeth much" (James 5:16, KJV): [257]

- *Effective*—he sees the problem.
- *Fervent*—he cares about solving it.
- *Righteous*—he is covered by Messiah's blood.

Watching Over the Promised Land

The Father swore concerning Ephraim: "In the place where it was said to them, 'You are not My people,' there it will be said to them, 'You are the sons of the living God'" (Hosea 1:9,10).

This declaration was made on the hills of Ephraim, and it is to those hills that Ephraim will yet return:

"The ransomed...will return, and come with joyful shouting to Zion, with everlasting joy upon their heads. They will find gladness and joy, and sorrow and sighing will flee away" (Isaiah 35:10).

"The sons of Israel will return and seek YHVH their God and David their king [in his Son]; and they will come trembling to YHVH and to His goodness in the last days" (Hosea 3:5; also see verse 11:10).

We must pray without ceasing for the full restoration of the Chosen City, Jerusalem (Psalm 122:6). We must cry out for her to become the City of our Great King. For the Holy One of Israel has sworn:

"On your walls, O Jerusalem, I have appointed watchmen; all day and all night they will never keep silent. You

---

257 Remnant: Jer 31:7; Psa 5:3.

who remind YHVH, take no rest for yourselves. And give Him no rest until He establishes and makes Jerusalem a praise in the earth" (Isaiah 62:6-7).

It has been decreed from of old that watchmen *will* go forth, but will we be numbered among them? Will we call out like watchman of long ago? "Day after day, my Lord, I stand on the watchtower; every night I stay at my post" (Isaiah 21:8, NIV).

Taking the Watchman's Vow

Habakkuk 2:1 outlines the watchman's vow:

"I will stand on my guard post and...keep watch to see what He will speak to me."

Whereas there is a collective call for watchmen, the call to be a watchman is given on an individual basis—because the Father has a different post for each of us.

Each *Notzrim* has a position, a place to occupy, a job to do. If any one of us fails to watch over our given post, then there is a hole in the collective wall that guards Israel.

Each post is important to the well-being of the whole community: Each has a chosen position, and each should walk in it as unto the Father. Each *Notzrim* must also listen for the voice of the Holy One. Each must cry out:

"O Elohim, what would you say to me?"

Let us therefore take the watchmen's vow, knowing that all who call on Him in truth will hear His voice behind them, saying, "This is the way, walk ye in it" (Isaiah 30:21, KJV).[258]

---

258 Thanks to long time friends, Ephraim Frank, Botanist, and Rimona Frank, Hebrew Editor, for declaring this truth, and for help with this chapter. Thanks also to the late Rabbi Isidor Zwirn, "The Rabbi From Burbank," who likewise often taught about the Isaiah 11 prophecy and the restored "Notzrim."

25

Return, O Virgin Israel!

Set up for yourself roadmarks, place for yourself guideposts; direct your mind to the highway, the way by which you went. Return, O virgin of Israel, return to these your cities (Jeremiah 31:21).

YHVH is calling for Ephraim's return. It is a call to repent and return in righteousness. It is a call for a returning *virgin* (Ezekiel 37:23; Jeremiah 3:14-18).

Hosea said, "Gray hairs are sprinkled on him [Ephraim], yet he does not know it" (Hosea 7:9). Restated, Ephraim is from Israel of old, but does not realize it. He will have been around for a long time before he finally sees that his age-old problem is his penchant for paganism. And he will have to repent of his youthful sins before he returns home (Jeremiah 31:18-19).

Ephraim has been under a corporate punishment and has been unable to see the truth about his heritage until now. He was given a three hundred and ninety year-long punishment (Ezekiel 4:4-6). The penalty was that he would be "*LoAmmi*" (Hosea 1-2). When he did not repent of his youthful paganism, his punishment of *namelessness* was increased seven-fold (Leviticus 26:18-28).

Consequently, Ephraim has been *"Not-a-People"* for the last two thousand seven hundred years. [259] But the end of his punishment is at hand. It is time for obscure Ephraim to come forth. Just as Yeshua called Lazarus forth from the grave, formerly wayward Ephraim must now come forth. However, to be fully resurrected, to truly escape from the grave of his dispersion, he must leave behind the tattered shrouds he has been wrapped in for so long.

To restore what was lost, Ephraim must find himself, realize certain truths, and come forth in righteousness.

Finding the Lost

To find the "lost" tribes, we do not need to search for an as-yet-uncharted island. Though some from Judah have found a few lost ones huddled in remote areas,[260] we must realize that what the people of Ephraim have been lost to is their *identity*. They are lost to the truth of *who they are* (Hosea 1-2). They are lost to their call to be part of a set-apart people.

Lost to the Father's Truth

While wandering among the nations for centuries, Ephraim has also been lost to the wisdom of the Father's commands, or Torah. Thus his children are *forgotten ones*.

"My people are destroyed for lack of knowledge. Because you have rejected knowledge, I also will reject you from being My priests. Since you have forgotten the law of your God, I also will forget your children" (Hosea 4:1,6).[261]

Ephraim has always had a problem with Torah. The Father said of him: "Though I wrote for him ten thousand precepts of My law [Torah], they are regarded as a strange thing" (Hosea 8:12).

Torah is thought to be strange by most Christians. Because they believe Torah is "for the Jews," and that they

---

259 See *Restoring Israel's Kingdom*, Angus Wootten.
260 "Quest For The Lost Tribes," Simcha Jacobovici A&E TV: www.biography.com.
261 YHVH says Ephraim will not be forgotten forever (Jer 31:20; Hos 11:9).

are "Gentiles." They think of the Torah as *strange*, or *foreign*. *Foreign Gentiles = Foreign to Torah.*

To teach Torah to emerging Ephraimites we would do well to first teach them about their Israelite heritage. When they realize that truth, they will then be better equipped to properly see the truths of Torah—as Israelites

Losing Our Balance

Many Believers are now discovering their Hebraic roots, but in their search, some have become overly enamored with Judaism. They have become so "pro-Jewish" that their judgments are out of balance. They rightly condemn the errors of the Church, but overlook the fact that it was the Jewish hierarchy that first threw the followers of The Way out of the synagogues. [262] They cry out against the many errors of the Roman Emperor, Constantine, but are silent when it comes to the false Messiahs of Judaism.[263]

The truth is that our roots are Hebraic or Israelite, not Jewish. Ephraim is not called to embrace "all things Jewish," for there are many things taught in Judaism that are the flawed ideas of man.

As Ephraim begins to embrace the principles of Torah and return to Israel's feasts, he is destined to question what has been taught about these things for many centuries.

He will then be used by the Father to help bring the whole house of Israel into greater understanding of its collective call. Ephraim is to encourage his brethren to return to the simple faith of Abraham, and to base that faith on the truth of Scripture.

Similarly, Jewish Believers are destined to question the errant teachings of Christianity. Because of their heritage, they often have special insights into Torah that the Father would have them share, with the ultimate purpose of building the faith of the whole house.

---

262 John 9:22; 12:42; 16:2; Acts 9:2; 26:9-11.
263 See *Rabbi Akiba's Messiah: The Origins of Rabbinic Authority*, Daniel Gruber, 1999, Elijah Publishing, Hanover, NH.

The Sins of Jeroboam

Many of Ephraim are presently leaving behind the sins once encouraged by Jeroboam, Ephraim's first king.

Jeroboam led Israel into sin after its division. He began to fear what would happen if his people should "go up to Jerusalem." He feared for his position, should Ephraim be reunited with Judah. So he encouraged idol worship to keep them at home. He said, "It is too much for you to go up to Jerusalem; behold your gods, O Israel..."

He "made houses [of harlotry] on high places," and he "made priests from among all the people who were not of the sons of Levi." This errant king also instituted a feast in the eighth month on the fifteenth day of the month, like the feast...in Judah...Then he went up to the altar which he had made...even in the month which he had devised in his own heart; and he instituted a feast for the sons of Israel" (1 Kings 12:27-33).

Jeroboam tried to keep Ephraim away from the true faith—from going up to Jerusalem—because he feared losing his "ministry position." He thus encouraged another type of spiritual harlotry by gathering people unto himself. He made for himself priests. He gathered a group of "yes men." He surrounded himself with those who would do it his way. But his way was not the Father's way.

The Similar Sins of "the Church"

This deviant king created his own feast days. He spoke against the plan of the Most High and sought to "make alterations in set times and in law." He disdained YHVH's prescribed feasts and created replacement celebrations (Exodus 31:16-17; Daniel 7:25; 1 Kings 12:27-33).

Worse yet, his actions foreshadowed those of the Church. For she too has made her own proclamations, changed the Sabbath, and changed the feast days.

We must repent of these sins. We are called to be a royal priesthood and to proclaim restoration to all Israel. The feasts help us to do that. Each feast should be to us as "a holy assembly, a holy *miqra* (מקרא), meaning, a rehearsal" (Exodus 12:16).[264]

In celebrating or commemorating them we depict the Father's three-phase plan of redemption:
- Passover (personal redemption)
- *Shavuot,* Pentecost (infilling of the Spirit)
- Tabernacles (full restoration of the divided kingdom).

The feasts are a "shadow" of the glory found in Yeshua (Colossians 2:17; Hebrews 10:1). Moreover, our Father makes a promise to those whose hearts are being drawn to them: "I will gather those who grieve about the appointed feasts—they came from you, O Zion; the reproach of exile is a burden on them" (Zephaniah 3:18).

Those who are grieving in their hearts about the loss of these things will be gathered to the Father's bosom.

Just as shadows are attached to substance, so annual rehearsals of YHVH's feasts should be attached to His people. Let us therefore celebrate in Yeshua, freely rejoicing in the Father's Holy *miqra's,* guided by His Holy Spirit. But let us not be legalistic about it (James 2:10), because it is impossible to keep the feasts exactly.

Returning to the Tents of Tabernacles

The Father says of Ephraim: "I have been YHVH your God since the land of Egypt; I will make you live in tents again, as in the days of the appointed festival" (Hosea 12:9).

Not dwelling in the tents of Tabernacles describes Ephraim well, for he has long said to Judah: "I do not need your feasts nor festivals." Although Ephraim rightly does not need man-made traditions, he is wrong to turn from "the feasts of YHVH" (2 Chronicles 2:4). The Father now wants to correct Ephraim in this regard. He wants to teach him how to celebrate anew Israel's ancient traditions. [265]

---

264 Strong's # H 4744: called out, rehearsal; assembly, convocation, reading.
265 See *Israel's Feasts and their Fullness* by Batya Ruth Wootten, 2003, Key of David Publishing, Saint Cloud, FL.

More Changing of Feast Days

Judah is also guilty of changing the feasts. They erroneously call the Day of Blowing *(Yom Teruah) Rosh Hashanah* (Head of the Year). But YHVH says: "This month [Aviv] shall be the beginning of months for you; it is to be the first month of the year to you" (Exodus 12:2).

The rabbis say it is a *civil* new year celebration, but at this time of year they begin anew their yearly cycle of Torah readings instead of at the actual beginning of the year. For this and other reasons, Judah also stands guilty. [266]

Israel is to have a constitution, the Torah, that is based on YHVH's Instructions. They are not to try to govern their nation based on the imperfect interpretations and decrees of man.

Returning to Jerusalem

Today, many are responding to the Holy Spirit's call to "go up to Jerusalem." They are joining in Israel's annual Tabernacles celebration, where Believers from around the world come to show support for the people of Judah.

Ephraim is also leaving behind those who gather people unto themselves. He is refusing to drink of the muddied waters of errant shepherds. He instead looks for those who seek after the Father's heart and who feed the flock on knowledge and understanding. He is drinking of the "living water" that flows from Yeshua, who is the Shepherd King (Ezekiel 34; Jeremiah 3:15).

Although Jeroboam created his own feast day and tried to change the set times, today Ephraimite saints are repenting of the paganism of their forefathers. They are instead celebrating the Father's Sabbath and rejoicing in His feasts (Leviticus 23:44; Isaiah 42:21). [267]

But refusing to continue in errant traditions is resulting in many being drawn into a wilderness experience...

---

266 *Ibid.*
267 *Ibid.*

The Wilderness Experience

The Father said of those of Ephraim:

"Behold, I will allure her, bring her into the wilderness and speak kindly to her. Then I will give her vineyards from there, and the valley of Achor as a door of hope. And she will sing there as in the days of her youth, as in the day when she came up from the land of Egypt. It will come about in that day, declares YHVH, That you will call Me Ishi and will no longer call Me Baali. For I will remove the names of the Baals from her mouth, so that they will be mentioned by their names no more" (Hosea 2:14-17).

He also says, "I will bring you into the wilderness of the peoples, and there I will enter into judgment with you face to face" (Ezekiel 20:35). And that He would allure Israel into a "wilderness of the peoples," and there, enter into judgment with her "face to face" (Ezekiel 20:11-44).

Many who have been drawn into this desert have felt lost, alone, alienated. But Israel is brought to this place for a reason. It is as the *Soncino Books of the Bible* says:

"As in the wilderness of Egypt they were constituted the people of God, so in this desert, cut off from intercourse with heathen nations, they will be made again into His people. There God will *plead* with them *face to face* with none to distract their attention from Him" (Ezekiel 20:35).

During our desert experience the Father gives us "the valley of Achor as a door of hope" (Hosea 2:15). *Achor* means "trouble." After a season of trouble, Ephraim will be restored.

At Achor, Achan and his conspirator family was stoned to death for his dishonesty. His actions brought curse and defeat to all Israel. Victory was withheld until they dealt with the sin in the camp. Achor was regarded as being key to Israel's victory, and dealing with sin in the camp is key to our victory (Joshua 7:24-26; Isaiah 65:10). [268]

Repentance of the sins that drove Israel into exile will prove to be a door of hope. While in the desert, the names

---

[268] See Strong's # H5911; Deut 8:2, and the book, *The Wilderness Experience* by Batya Wootten, 2003, Key of David, Saint Cloud, FL.

of the Baals are removed from her, and she is fully betrothed to Messiah. Once she enters through that door, she
"will sing there as in the days of her youth" (Hosea 2:14-20).

Repairing the Breach

Those of us who understand these things must seek to
repair the breach in Israel. We must work to break every yoke
so the oppressed can be set free. We must help "raise up
the age-old foundations," then we will be called "a repairer
of the breach, a restorer of the streets in which to dwell."

As we learn to call the Sabbath a delight, and to delight
in YHVH, then He "will make us ride on the heights of the
earth; and He will feed us with the heritage of Jacob our
father" (Isaiah 58:1-14; Hebrews 4:1,9).

Feasting On Our Inheritance

We who desire to sit at the Master's table must be
properly dressed for the occasion. We must discard our sin-
stained rags and clothe ourselves in the change Yeshua
would bring at this time. He whose mercies are new every
morning would now do a new thing in and through us
(Lamentations 3:22-23; Jeremiah 31:22; Revelation 2:17).

To walk in this way let us follow YHVH's instructions:

"Look to Abraham your father and to Sarah who gave
birth to you in pain; when he was but one I called him, then
I blessed him and multiplied him" (Isaiah 51:2).

Let us now repent, and seek to become the nation our
Father ordained from the beginning.

"Through this Jacob's iniquity will be forgiven; this will
be the full price of the pardoning of his sin: when he makes
all the altar stones like pulverized chalk stones; when
Asherim and incense altars will not stand" (Isaiah 27:9).

Let us feed on the heritage of Jacob.

Let us walk in the simple, life-changing faith of our
forefather Abraham.

26

The Heart of the Matter

The Holy One is calling us to return to Him. But what are we to return to?

Some stress that Ephraim must return to Torah, that he must become "Torah observant."

While the truth of Torah is to be written on our hearts, we must note that many who have followed this path have become so infatuated with study of Torah and Judaism that they have denied their faith in Messiah Yeshua and converted to Judaism. [269]

In his return, it is imperative that Ephraim take a fresh look at some ancient truths. For example, he needs to understand that "the Ten Commandments" are the Father's "covenant" (Exodus 34:28; Deuteronomy 4:13).

He needs to see that the *book of the Law,* also called the Torah, the five books written by Moses, was placed *"beside* the ark of the covenant." And that it was to remain there as a "witness" (Deuteronomy 31:26-27). In other words, the Torah is a "reference" book that is always either for, or against, the actions of the people of Israel.

---

269 See the Messianic Israel Herald article, "The Other Side of Evangelism," http://www.mim.net/Heralds/Heralds.shtml#HeraldMagazineList.

The "book of the Law" was placed *beside* the Ark, but the Tablets of the Covenant were *in* it (Exodus 25:21; Deuteronomy 10:2-5).

Restated, the essence of the Law was inside the Ark, whereas the "amplified version," meaning the Torah, was on the outside.

Believers are like the Ark. They are to have the *essence* of the Torah inside themselves. *The heart of the matter, the essence of Torah, is to be written on our hearts.* And the heart, or spirit, of Torah is the Ten Commandments.

When we do not understand the *spirit* of the Law, we tend to stumble over the minutia of the *letter* of the Law. Then the letter of the law becomes "a testimony against us," meaning that it will explain where we went astray.

Ten Commandments—Two Commandments

Messiah Yeshua gave a simple explanation of the Father's commands. One might say that He consolidated the Torah, even the Ten Commandments, into Two Commandments.

When being tested by a lawyer, Yeshua was asked, "Teacher, which is the greatest commandment in the Law?"

The Messiah answered him, "You shall love the LORD your God with all your heart, and with all your soul, and with all your mind. This is the greatest and foremost commandment. The second is like it, 'You shall love your neighbor as yourself. *On these two commandments depend the whole Law and the Prophets"* (Matthew 22:36-40).

Torah Summed up in a Word

In saying this, Yeshua was not denying any part of Torah, but was simplifying its message, or giving an outline for the whole Torah. He was speaking of its pure essence, which is *love:* We must *love* YHVH with all our hearts and we must *love* our neighbor as ourselves. That is the essence of the Torah and the prophets.

The essence of the Ten Commandments was brought down to Two Commandments, and those Two Commandments have a common command, they can be distilled down to one word: Love. [270]

As John the apostle says, "The one who does not love does not know God, for *God is love"* (1 John 4:8).

The Book of the Law was written by Moses to help Israel understand how to actually walk in that love. The *Sefer Torah*, the Book of Torah, serves as a witness about how we are walking our walk. It is a Book that testifies *against* us when we fall short of its high call, and it testifies *for* us when we fulfill its commands.

The Essence of the Essence

The Ten Commandments are the *essence*, or the *spirit*, of the God-inspired five books written by Moses.

Of these books of the Covenant, Moses said, *"Keep and do them, for that is your wisdom and your understanding in the sight of the peoples who will hear all these statutes and say, 'Surely this great nation is a wise and understanding people.' For what great nation is there that has a god so near to it as is YHVH our God whenever we call on Him? Or what great nation is there that has statutes and judgments as righteous as this whole law which I am setting before you today? Only give heed to yourself and keep your soul diligently, so that you do not forget the things which your eyes have seen and they do not depart from your heart all the days of your life; but make them known to your sons and your grandsons"* (Deuteronomy 4:6-9).

Torah came forth from a heart filled with love. Its Holy Words might rightly be called *Loving Instructions*. They serve as defined parameters given to the children of a Father who wants to protect them, to keep them safe.

---

270 The first four of the Ten Commandments were essentially summed up in Yeshua's greatest commandment, which is to love YHVH with all your heart. He then summed up the following six commandments in His second commandment, which is to love your neighbor (see Deu 6:5; 30:6; Lev 19:18).

Yeshua brought out the *essence* of the *essence* of the Law. The many words of Torah can be summed up in one word. The spirit, the essence of Torah's essence, is realized in the word *love*.

If we do not have love, as Paul the apostle says, our words about Torah will only sound like a "clanging cymbal" (1 Corinthians 13:1).

The world will see Messiah Yeshua in us when they see us truly walking in love. All that we do, all that we are, all that we live and teach and preach of the Father's truths, must be done from a heart of love.

We who wish to bring restoration to the whole house of Israel must understand the heart of the matter. We must understand the overcoming power of love.

27

Mama's Torah

My son, hear the instruction of thy father, and forsake not the torah/law of thy mother: Indeed, they are a graceful wreath to your head and ornaments about your neck....

Keep thy father's commandment, and forsake not the torah/law of thy mother: Bind them continually on your heart; Tie them around your neck. When you walk about, they will guide you; when you sleep, they will watch over you; and when you awake, they will talk to you
(Proverbs 1:8-9, KJV; 6:20-22, NASB).

Our God is doing a new thing in the earth today. He is bringing forth a renewed, reunited, and fully restored people of Israel—Judahites who know and love His Divine Son, Yeshua, as well as Ephraimites who know and love the wisdom of Torah.

In teaching the principles of Torah to restored Israel, for a moment let us think of them as being like newborn babes. And in the natural, babies are first given to their *mothers*...

In the "Mama's Torah" commands quoted above, we see a principle that will teach us how to convey the truths of Torah to all Israel.

Sibling rivalry is deeply rooted in both the houses of Israel, and there are many obstacles to overcome. Thus they now desperately need motherly types who will remind them of the Father's elementary principle of loving one another as brothers.

Those who would minister to Israel at this time, be they male or female, would do well to envision themselves as a "mother" who is dealing with two sons who have bad attitudes toward each other.

A Tale of Two Brothers

To describe past and present problems with the two houses, we listen to a story about two little boys, "Johnny and Joey":

Johnny and Joey were brothers, and Johnny was the type who would pinch his little brother when Mama wasn't looking. He also would tell little Joey that he was "adopted."

"I know," he would say, "they found you under a rock! I was there when they brought you home!!"

This of course would bring Joey to tears. It made him question whether he really "belonged" to the family. It also made him very, very angry. And Joey had a real problem with anger. So when Johnny taunted him, Joey would in turn hit him really hard with his plastic bat.

One day, while playing in their bedroom, and after going through their usual verbal routine, Johnny jumped on Joey for hitting him.

Fists flying, the two boys fell on the bed. In the fray, Joey's arm got tangled in the cord that went to the lamp sitting on the night table.

This sent the lamp crashing to the floor and the sound coincided with the breaking of the bed frame.

The commotion caused their mother to come running...

The challenge for our imaginary mother is that when she comes into the room she must make a judgment as to what happened. If for one minute she blames Joey for something that Johnny did, Johnny will think his mother is a *schnook*, and Joey will think she is *unfair*.

To fully settle the dispute, Mama must judge with absolute equity. Anything less will only fuel their ever-smoldering flame.

This same principle holds true for Ephraim and Judah.

As we seek to put an end to their ancient family rift, we must use equal weights and measures. For it is written:

"You shall not have in your bag differing weights, a large and a small. You shall not have in your house differing measures, a large and a small. You shall have a full and just weight... a full and just measure, that your days may be prolonged in the land which YHVH your God gives you. For everyone who does these things, everyone who acts unjustly is an abomination to YHVH your God" (Deuteronomy 25:13-16; also see Proverbs 20:10).

Like Johnny and Joey's mother, we must fairly judge past actions of the siblings. Anything less will perpetuate their hostility. [271]

We must understand this vital truth.

Children are First Trained by their Mothers

Scripture speaks of our "Mother's Torah," but there is no mention of a "Father's Torah." We are told of our Heavenly Father's Torah, which He gave to our forefathers (2 Kings 17:13)—and we read of "Mama's Torah."

Why so?

Because mothers establish the *heart* of the home.

This explains why YHVH is against Israel having "foreign wives," because foreign wives establish foreign ways in the hearts of His children (Ezra 10:10).

---

271 *House of David Herald*, Vol. 7 Book 11, Just Weights and Measures.

Children are trained early in life, which explains why they first need "godly mothers." That is how we develop *natural*, or *cultivated*, vines (Romans 11), meaning children nurtured and trained in the ways of the Holy One.

The Holy One uses the mothers of Israel to help Him write the elementary principles of Torah-love on the hearts of the children of Israel.

Once babies are weaned from their mother's milk, they are turned over to their fathers for a different type of training. He teaches the child about the commandments. Traditionally, he prepares his son to become "Bar Mitzvah," or "Son of the Commandments."

Thus the Biblical principle is:

• First Mama mothers them.
• Then they are ready to hear Papa's principles.

Different Types of Training

Mothers and fathers give different types of training. The female expression of mankind is often said to be intuitive, whereas the male expression tends to be logical.

Scripture tells us that our mother's godly instructions are to be as a graceful wreath to our head and ornaments about our necks. We are to bind them on our hearts. As we walk about they will guide us; when we sleep, they will watch over us, and when we awake, they will talk to us.

The intuitive truths taught to us by our mothers will be with us in prayer, they will complain to us when we are disobedient, and will even declare and confirm truth to us.

This same principle holds true for the Body of Messiah.

Nurturing Truth

Restored Israel is being called to embrace the necessity of teaching Torah in a way that *nurtures* members of the Body, much like the mother nurtures her baby.

Our first encounter with the truths of Torah should be as delightful as mother's milk. It should be warm, soothing.

It should help build up our immune system and make our bodies strong.

Mother's milk might be likened to the elementary principles of grace and mercy. Although these truths are basic, if we do not first learn to suckle at the breast of mercy, to nurse at the bosom of grace, we will never grow up to be a people imbued with the Father's power. We will never become sons and daughters of the commandments.

We must teach truth in a way that nurtures the hearer. We must value this idea of mother's milk as much as we value the elementary teachings of our faith (Hebrews 6:1-3).

What is "Mama's Torah"?

Scripture does not define "the torah of thy mother." However, our Heavenly Father apparently placed great importance on its role in our lives.

Why?

Again, woman is intuitive, she tends to be a "spirit-led" creature. From this we see that the Father intended Torah *to first be understood in the spirit.*

In the natural, mothers deal with their child's *heart attitude.* They are more inclined to handle the intuitive, spiritual matters of the heart, because they tend to focus on the child's *character.*

They also watch over their children's relationships with their siblings.

Some relationship commands given by our mothers might have been:

"You watch out for your little brother now!"
"You take each others hand, and don't let go!"
"You all kiss and make up."
"You children play nice together."

Such commands are abstract in that they do not tell you exactly how to "play nice." However, they are clearly understood even by children, because they are matters of the heart.

Becoming Bar Mitzvah—
Sons of the Commandments

What does it mean to be a true "Son of the Commandments"?

We must first be trained in the spirit.

We must begin by honoring "the spirit of Torah."

Torah is a feminine word. It is derived from another word that speaks of flowing as water, of an arrow, of pointing out, and thus, instruction.[272]

Torah teachings are meant to flow as water. They are meant to cleanse, to refresh, and to restore the heart. And they are always to be given *in the Spirit.*

To try to train a son in the commandments without first training him in his mother's teaching—meaning to be led by the Spirit of Torah—is like trying to send your son to high school before he ever goes to kindergarten.

Elementary things must come first.

We must first learn to appreciate the spirit of Torah (Mama), before we will be equipped to appreciate the details of Torah (Papa).

Walking in this principle will empower Ephraim to become the "watchmen" our Father intended him to be.

It will empower him to send forth Torah-arrows that go straight to the heart of the matter.

---

272 Strong's words # H 8451; 3384.

28

Misunderstandings and the Law

Many have suggested that Paul did not keep the Law, and that he instructed New Covenant Believers not to keep it. But Paul followed Yeshua, who told us to keep the commandments. Moreover, John said that the way we express our love for the Father is by keeping His commandments. However, we must realize that in the last days, the dragon makes war with those who seek to do so (Matthew 19:17; 1 John 5:2-3; Revelation 12:17; 14:12).

Like the Messiah and His disciples, Paul honored the eternal principles of Torah, but he did not pursue the Law after the flesh. He honored its principles from his heart, which is how we should honor it.

As we seek to understand the Law, the first thing we must realize is that we cannot fully keep it. We must also realize that if we look to the Law for our salvation, we are deceived. If we try to establish our righteousness by keeping the Law, then we must keep the *whole Law* and return to the Mosaic system of sacrifice, but we cannot do that. The Father allowed the Temple to be destroyed after His Son paid the price for us (1 Peter 1:18-19). We cannot offer animal sacrifices as the Law demands.

Nonetheless, we are called to walk as our Messiah walked. We are to emulate Him, and He kept every commandment. He even said of the Law: "Do not think that I came to abolish the Law or the Prophets; I did not come to abolish but to fulfill" (Matthew 5:17).

Yeshua came to *fulfill*, to satisfy, the sacrificial requirements of the Law—and He satisfied them once and for all. He came to fulfill the Law, to fully preach, to perfect it. In other words, He came to personify how the Law is to be walked out by mankind. [273]

"The one who says he abides in Him ought himself to walk in the same manner as He walked" (1 John 2:6).

Wisdom is Still Wisdom

Although Yeshua satisfied the sacrificial requirements of the Law, that awesome act did not annul or abolish the wisdom found in Torah. Wisdom continues to be wisdom. The Father's commandments continue to bring soundness to our lives: "Keep and do them, for that is your wisdom and your understanding in the sight of the peoples. .... "Keep every commandment...so that you may be strong and go in and possess the land" (Deuteronomy 4:6; 11:8).

We want to be wise. We want to be strong. And we look to the standards of Torah for wisdom.

To know how to honor Torah—we look to Yeshua. He kept the law, yet He is the epitome of grace and mercy. Again, He summed up the essences of Torah in one word: *Love* (Matthew 22:36-40).

Love is the foundation of God's Law because God *is love*.

Dead Men Walking

If we faithfully followed the Law we would all be dead men. Apart from the grace and mercy of Messiah Yeshua we would all be dead in our trespasses—because the wages of sin is death. That is why Paul said we were "made to die to

---

273 Fulfill: Strong's # G4134. Rom 6:10; Heb 7:27; 9:12; 10:10;1 Pet 3:18; Jude 1:3.

the Law through the body of Messiah, so that we might be joined to another, to Him who was raised from the dead, in order that we might bear fruit for God" (Romans 6:23; 7:4).

We must approach the laws of Torah as if we were dead men. We are as people who have already been tried, found guilty, and put to death for our infractions.

That is the bad news.

The good news is that in the Messiah we are raised in the newness of life. Because of Him we live again. And in our new life, we *choose* to serve with all our hearts the One who found us guilty in the first place.

Robots versus Choice

As born-again Believers, we are called to walk in the *wisdom* of Torah, because the essence of the New Covenant is that the Father will write His law of love on our hearts (Jeremiah 31:31-33; Hebrews 8:10; 10:16).

However, we must realize that the Father does not want us to be obedient because we feel it is "mandated" that we do so. He is not looking for puppets or robots. He wants all obedience to be born from a heart of love for Him. He wants us to love Him and His ways. He wants us to *choose* Him. And He wants us to realize that His Laws better our lives.

He also wants us to realize that His many children can be in various stages of learning about His ways. And we must never try to force on others the truths the Holy One is graciously revealing to us—because different people realize different things at different times.

We must not be condescending with those who do not yet see what we see. Yeshua did not treat us that way, yet He surely knows far more than we do. Instead, Yeshua always comes in mercy. He lifts us up. He nurtures us. And we must do the same.

It is the job of the Holy Spirit to convict people of sin. We must walk in what we know to be truth, and at the same time show lovingkindness to others. That is the example our Messiah set for us and we must follow it.

Rabbi Paul

The apostle Paul understood these things. He walked in grace and mercy, yet he did not do as many have taught: he did not speak against the Father's Law.

We see this in that:

- Rabbi Paul acted as a *mohel* and circumcised Timothy before they went to the Jews (Acts 16:1-3).
- To disprove the claim that he was teaching Believers to "forsake Moses," Paul kept his Nazarite vow and even paid the fee so that those with him could keep their vows (Acts 18:18; 21:21-26). [274]
- Paul's detractors put up false witnesses to try to prove that he spoke against Moses (Acts 6:13).
- "But this I admit to you," said Paul, "that according to the Way which they call a sect I do serve the God of our fathers, believing everything that is in accordance with the Law and that is written in the Prophets" (Acts 24:14)
- Paul said, "In my inner being I delight in God's law" (Romans 7:22).
- "I have committed no offense either against the Law of the Jews or against the temple or against Caesar," the apostle declared (Acts 25:8; also see 28:17-18).

Paul committed no offence against the Law because he honored Torah. He said in his letter to Timothy, "The Law is good, if one uses it lawfully" (1 Timothy 1:8).

"Good," or *kalos*, means beautiful, valuable, virtuous, honest, well, worthy. "Lawfully," or *nomimos*, means legitimately, agreeable to the rules. [275]

The Law is beautiful when it is presented in a manner that is agreeable to the Father's rule of love.

Paul did not speak against the Father's Law, but against the errant laws of men. He even said that those who obey the Fathers' Law will be declared righteous:

---

274 Nazarite vow: Num 6:2,5,9,18.
275 Strong's # G2570.

"The Law is holy...righteous...good...spiritual," he wrote. "It is not the hearers of the Law who are just before God, it is those who obey the law who will be declared righteous" (Romans 7:12,14; 2:13).

Paul said he served God the way his forefathers did, and that he believed everything that is in accordance with the Law. He spoke reverently of Torah, saying, "All Scripture is inspired by God and profitable for teaching, for reproof, for correction, for training in righteousness; that the man of God may be adequate, equipped for every good work" (2 Timothy 3:16-17).[276]

The Scriptures Paul referred to were the Old (First) Covenant Scriptures, because the texts of the New Covenant was not yet regarded as Canon.[277]

This Apostle to the Nations taught that our Messiah was our Passover sacrifice. He even refused to spend time in Asia because he was "hastening" to be at Jerusalem for the day of Pentecost, or *Shavuot* (1 Corinthians 5:7; Acts 20:16).

Galatians 4:8-11

"When you did not know God, you were slaves to those which by nature are no gods. But now that you have come to know God, or rather to be known by God, how is it that you turn back again to the weak and worthless elemental things, to which you desire to be enslaved all over again? You observe days and months and seasons and years. I fear for you, that perhaps I have labored over you in vain."

In the Book of Galatians, Paul addressed the problem of Judaizers who wanted to impose legalistic interpretations of the Torah onto the non-Jewish Believers. [278]

---

276 See Acts 24:14; Rom 2:13-16.

277 Torah declared that Israel must listen to the coming One who would speak the words of the Father. Yeshua is that promised One, and He prayed for those who would believe in Him through the words of His disciples (Deu 18:18-19; Jn 5:46-47; 8:28; 12:49-50; 17:8,17). Thus Torah validates the New Covenant. See *Has Torah Failed Us?* www.messianicisrael.com.

278 Judaizers: Those who try to bring people into conformity with Judaism, especially to adopt rabbinic interpretations of Torah and oral law.

The Judaizers thought that obeying the laws of circumcision would bring them salvation. Thus Paul feared for them. He argued that legalistic compliance with the Law would not bring eternal salvation—*that only comes through being born anew through faith in Messiah Yeshua.*

Messianic Jewish commentator David Stern says of these verses, "When Gentiles observe these Jewish holidays...out of fear induced by Judaizers...they are not obeying Torah but subjecting themselves to legalism; and legalism is just another species of those *weak and miserable elemental demonic* spirits no better than the idols left behind." [279]

Stern also suggests the "days, months, seasons and years" may refer to pagan traditions. He says this because Paul was speaking to non-Jews when he said, "You were slaves to those which by nature are no gods."

Of these non-Jews he asked, "How is it that you turn back again to the weak and worthless elemental things?"

In the same letter, Paul warned of the "elemental things of the world" (Galatians 4:3). And he warned the Believers of Colosse, "See to it that no one takes you captive... according to the elementary principles of the world, rather than according to Messiah" (Colossians 2:8).

This does not describe the principles of Torah or the feasts. Scripture defines them as "YHVH's appointed times" (Leviticus 23:2). The feasts are not worldly, nor weak and miserable times. Those words define pagan practices.

Colossians 2:16-17

"Let no one act as your judge in regard to food or drink or in respect to a festival or a new moon or a Sabbath day— things which are a mere shadow of what is to come; but the substance belongs to Messiah."

These verses emphasize that the feasts outline, depict, and portray our Messiah. Stern says they should be rendered: "These are *definitely* a shadow of things to come."

---

279 *Jewish New Testament Commentary* by David H. Stern, Clarksville, MD: Messianic Jewish Publications, 1995, p 557.

And, "The festivals do *indeed* have value." [280]

We agree with Stern, because "shadows cannot rightly be separated from their substance." [281] They are divine hints at coming heavenly realities.

Paul said to let no one "act as your judge" in these matters. This could mean that the Colossians were not to let the *heathen* judge them for honoring the Father's feasts, dietary laws, new moon festivals, and Sabbaths (vs 2:16).

Again, the Jerusalem Council had ruled that new converts were to obey certain minimal requirements, and go to the synagogue to hear the words of Torah (Acts 15:21).

New Believers were accepted into the fellowships with minimal behavior requirements, *because* it was assumed that they would soon begin to hear and obey the eternal truths taught by Moses and the prophets.

If we view matters from this perspective, we see that Paul was saying that true meaning and fulfillment of the feasts are found in the Messiah. We see that these verses were meant to encourage us to celebrate the feasts— because they depict our faith to the world.

These verses also could be about Judaizers judging the people for not following their rabbinic teachings, or for not following Torah soon enough. Either way, concerning such deception, Paul warned:

"See to it that no one takes you captive through philosophy and empty deception, according to the tradition of men, according to the elementary principles of the world, rather than according to Messiah" (Colossians 2:8).

Paul condemned the traditions of men, but he did not speak against the Father's traditions.

Romans 14:1-6

"Now accept the one who is weak in faith, but not for the purpose of passing judgment on his opinions. One person has faith that he may eat all things, but he who is

---

280 *Jewish New Testament Commentary*, p 611.
281 *Israel's Feasts and their Fullness*, Chapter 2, Where Do We Go For Answers?

weak eats vegetables only. The one who eats is not to regard with contempt the one who does not eat, and the one who does not eat is not to judge the one who eats, for God has accepted him. Who are you to judge the servant of another? To his own master he stands or falls; and he will stand, for the Lord is able to make him stand. One person regards one day above another, another regards every day alike. Each person must be fully convinced in his own mind. He who observes the day, observes it for the Lord, and he who eats, does so for the Lord, for he gives thanks to God; and he who eats not, for the Lord he does not eat, and gives thanks to God" (Romans 14:5-6).

Some believe these verses teach that those who live by the dietary laws of Torah are "weak" in their faith, and that the "strong" ones are those who pay no attention to such laws, believing they were annulled by Messiah Yeshua.

Most importantly, these verses have to do with *how* we are to relate to those who are in a different place in their walk of faith. For instance, Paul said, "One person regards one day above another, another regards every day alike. Each person must be fully convinced in his own mind." Paul's point is that we cannot legislate observance of the feasts. We must not try to force others to believe what we believe when we believe it, because the Father allows each of His children to make their own decisions when *they* are ready.

Handling Those With Strong Convictions

In their book, *Take Hold*, Ariel and D'vorah Berkowitz teach that Romans 14 and 15 describes "the right behavior in handling an individual who has strong convictions over a disputable matter." They define "weak" as "delicate," and say the word means to treat a person "delicately" when they have strong convictions on a matter in which Scripture is not clear. They suggest being gracious so long as his convictions are not causing a serious problem in the body.[282]

---

282 Berkowitz, *Take Hold*. Chicago: First Fruits of Zion, 1999, p 218.

These verses cannot mean that all days are equal in the sight of the Almighty, or that it is not important whether or not we honor His Sabbath or feast days.

Paul is not suggesting that people celebrate the Sabbath any time they want, nor is he encouraging replacement holidays for the Father's appointed times. Instead, he is addressing *our attitudes* toward those who are in a different place in their faith walk.

Paul tells us to "accept the one who is weak in faith, but not for the purpose of passing judgment on his opinions."

Stern says some have "strong" and some have "weak" trust, and both types are found among Jewish and non-Jewish Believers. Paul is not speaking of "weak Jewish faith" as some suggest, but is talking about weak Believers in general. He is instructing those who are strong to help the weak grow in their faith.

Wanting You for the Wrong Reasons

Paul also dealt with some who were causing another problem among the new Believers: "They eagerly seek you, not commendably, but they wish to shut you out so that you will seek them" (Galatians 4:17).

Judaizers try to put people in bondage to themselves and to their own man-made rules. Their actions are not commendable, because they try to get you to seek approval from them, so they can feel important by "shutting you out."

In other words, they make you feel unworthy and excluded so they can feel good about themselves.

We must flee from such attitudes. They only bring bondage to the hearer.

The Most Misunderstood Man in History

The Hebrew man, Shaul of Tarsus, may well be the most misunderstood man in all of history.

Peter even wrote of him:

"Our beloved brother Paul, according to the wisdom given him, wrote to you, as also in all his letters, speaking

in them of these things, in which are some things hard to understand, which the untaught and unstable distort, as they do also the rest of the Scriptures, to their own destruction" (2 Peter 3:16).

Such was the case in the time of the apostles, and such is still the case in our day.

Paul's teachings about women have also been misunderstood. For instance, we read that, "Women are to keep silent in the churches; for they are not permitted to speak, but are to subject themselves, just as the Law also says" (1 Corinthians 14:34).

This verse changes dramatically when we legitimately translate the word speak, as "chatter." We can then see that women were not to *chatter* endlessly in congregational meetings. They were not to talk about babies and recipes, as though they were not called to learn the principles of Torah. They were to instead sit quietly and learn.

The faith of Abraham needs to be restored to us, as does the Torah that our Patriarchs faithfully followed.

The truth about women also needs to be restored to us, so half of our spiritual army can be freed to fight the good fight of faith.

In addition, a true understanding of the Scriptural role of women will help pave the way for a proper understanding of the role of the Ruach HaKodesh in our lives. [283]

We who desire a full restoration of all things would do well to reexamine Paul's letters in light of the truths our Father is revealing to us at this time.

We desperately need to better understand this most misunderstood of men.

---

283 See *Mama's Torah* by Batya Wootten, 2003, Key of David, Saint Cloud, FL; *Beyond Sex Roles* by Gilbert Bilezekian, 1985, Baker; and, *I Suffer Not A Woman: Rethinking 1 Timothy 2:11-15 In Light of Ancient Evidence* by R &C Kroger, 1992, Baker. For more books about the Scriptural role of women, we suggest the site: http://www.cbeinternational.org/shopsite_sc/store/html/page3.html

29

Yeshua:
Epitome of All That Is Israel

As we seek to have Scriptural truths restored to us, and to reunite the two house of Israel, let us never let go of the truth of who our Messiah is to us.

Let us also remember that Jacob told his sons: "The blessings of thy father...shall be on the head of Joseph" (Genesis 49:26, KJV).

However, this blessing was next given to Ephraim, yet it is written that Judah *prevailed.* The firstborn blessing was given to Ephraim, and it included the right to the ruling position in the family. Yet we read that Judah "prevailed over his brothers" (1 Chronicles 5:2).

This seeming mystery is unveiled when we see that Judah's blessing was *conditional.* Jacob said Judah would be pre-eminent "until Shiloh comes, and to him shall be the obedience of the peoples" (Genesis 49:10).

Shiloh is the High Priest, the Prince, the Lion of Judah. He is Yeshua, the Man with many names.[284]

---

284 Given to Ephraim: Gen 48:19; Eze 37:19. Judah prevailed: 1 Chr 5:2;
(continued...)

Through this blessing, Jacob blessed Judah with a role to play in helping to bring forth the True Firstborn. The tribe of Judah is truly privileged to have such a One descend from them. The Holy One of Israel came to this earth as a man. He came as a Jew.

In accord with the Law of Moses, Yeshua was presented in the Temple as a firstborn son of the tribe of Judah (Luke 2:21-24). Because of this, the tribe of Judah was honored above all the peoples on the face of the earth. This privilege by itself makes Judah preeminent among the nations. No other tribe of peoples will ever be so honored as Judah.

However, "though Judah was the strongest of his brothers and a ruler came from him, the rights of the first-born belonged to Joseph" (1 Chronicles 5:2, NIV).

How can this be explained?

Jacob did not give his firstborn inheritance to fourth-born son Judah, nor to Joseph's son Ephraim, nor to any of their descendants. Instead, Jacob made the benefits of the Firstborn blessing available to all the sons of Israel.

How this was accomplished becomes clear through a study of two of Yeshua's titles: The *Only* Begotten Son, and The Firstborn of *Many*.

The Only Begotten Son

Yeshua came to this earth as a particular type of man. He came as "the only begotten from the Father" (John 1:14). To us the Father "gave His only begotten Son" (John 3:16).

The Greek word for "only begotten" is *monogenes*, meaning sole, single, unique, only-born.[285] Yeshua is the unique, only begotten Son of God. However, He was not begotten in the sense of being *created*. YHVH said of Yeshua, "Thou art My Son, today I have *begotten* Thee" (Psalm 2:7).

---

284 (...continued)
Prevailed: Strong's, # H1396: *gabar*, have strength, be powerful, mighty. Shiloh: Isa 9:6,7; 11:1-4; Eze 21:27; Dan 7:14; Luke 1:31-33.
285 Strong's # G 3439; *Thayer's Greek-English Lexicon*, Baker, 1983, # 3439.

The Hebrew word for "begotten" is *yalad.* It is used here to depict a father helping a baby to be born.[286] It is not used in the sense of being *created,* because Yeshua is the One "who is and who was and who is to come, the Almighty" (Revelation 1:8). He is the "I AM" (John 8:58).[287]

The Father uses the term *yalad* because He helped bring Yeshua forth as a human child. [288] In this role, Yeshua is His only begotten Son. He is the only "human" ever to be brought forth in this way.

As this only begotten Son, Yeshua came as the fulfillment of the promise given to Judah. He came as *Shiloh* and was given Judah's scepter. As prophesied, the people of New Covenant Israel began to be gathered unto Him. [289]

The King of the Jews then offered Himself as a Sacrifice. As foretold in Psalm 22, the only Begotten Son of God died on the cross, or tree. [290]

But this Lion from the tribe of Judah has overcome (Revelation 5:5). Through His sacrifice, He overcame sin and death. Then He rose again! However, Yeshua rose again as a different type of man.

The Firstborn of Many Brethren

When Yeshua was resurrected, He arose from the grave

---

286 As interpreted by the late Hebrew scholar, Rev. Robert Lindsey, author, *Jesus, Rabbi, and Lord* (Cornerstone, 1990). Also see Strong's # H 3205.

287 Yeshua is a "God-man." He "shared" in humanity (Heb 2:14, NIV). *Metecho*, μετεχω, *shared* (Strong's G 3348). Used in 1 Cor 9:10 and translated as "sharing" the crops—meaning, to "take only part." Yeshua "took part" of humanity; He took upon Himself a form of human *flesh*—that He might redeem His creation, but He did *not* "partake" of Adam's sin-filled blood. His bloodline came from His Heavenly Father and is "sinless" blood. The *Amplified Bible* (Zondervan), says, "Great and important and weighty, we confess, is the hidden truth—the mystic secret—of godliness. He (God) was made visible in human flesh" (1 Tim 3:16).

288 Phil 2:5-12.

289 This is a prophecy like those concerning the Kingdom: it is and yet it also is yet to come. Though the scepter has been passed to Messiah Yeshua, Judah continues to be YHVH's "lawgiver" (see Psalms 60:7; 108:7; Gen 49:10; 2 Chr 13:5; Lk 1:33; Heb 1:3; 10:12.

290 Died: We speak of passing from this life to the next, and not of one "ceasing to exist" (as some errantly think of death). As Deity, Yeshua could not cease to exist. But He could pass through the same door that mortals must go through.

as Ephraim the Firstborn—son of the double portion—the first man to have life in this world and life in the world to come. And He arose as the Firstborn of *many* brethren.

"He is the image of the invisible God, *the firstborn of all creation*." "He is also head of the body, the church; and He is the beginning, *the firstborn from the dead*, so that He Himself will come to have first place in everything."

"When the Father brought His firstborn into the world, He said, 'Let all the angels of God worship Him.'" [291]

As stated earlier, in the case of Isaac and Jacob, it took an act of divine intervention to bring them forth as the firstborn. While Scripture records no such action in the birth of the physical Ephraim, Joseph's son, there was divine intervention in the bringing forth of YHVH's Firstborn Ephraim. And in this role, Yeshua, the Man with many names, is *Firstborn Ephraim*.

There Can Be But One...

The Father says, "Israel is My firstborn." And, "Ephraim is My firstborn." And it is written that, "His beloved Son.... is the...firstborn of all creation" (Exodus 4:22; Jeremiah 31:9; Colossians 1:13-15).

YHVH calls Israel Ephraim, and Yeshua His firstborn. However, there can only be *one* firstborn. Thus, it must be that it is in the spirit of Messianic prophecy that the Father says, "Ephraim is My firstborn" (Jeremiah 31:9).

Yeshua is both "Israel" and "Ephraim." When He arose from the grave, He came forth as Ephraim the Firstborn —The Son of the double portion—The first Man to have life in this world and life in the world to come.

Ephraim: The First Immortal Man

When Yeshua was conceived as a man-child, the Father Himself opened His mother Mary's womb. After He was offered as a sacrifice, again it was through another great act

---

291 Firstborn of many: Rom 8:29. Worship Him: Col 1:15,18; Heb 1:6.

of divine intervention that He was brought forth. This time, however, the Father opened the womb of the grave!

Thus began fulfillment of YHVH's promise to those of Firstborn Ephraim: "I will ransom them from the power of the grave; I will redeem them from death. Where, O death, are your plagues? Where, O grave, is your destruction?" (Hosea 13:14, NIV).

The plague of death was removed when Yeshua was resurrected. For He was resurrected as "Ephraim," The First Immortal Man!

This resurrection was foretold by David, through whom YHVH declared, "I also shall make Him My firstborn" (Psalm 89:27). *Make* in Hebrew is *natan*, and means to set, put, give, make, lift up, bring forth, ordain, appoint.[292] By His Spirit the Father lifted Yeshua up on the third day, He brought Him forth from the grave, and appointed Him as the Firstborn—the One ordained to be given to the Nations.

In this role, we see Yeshua is Ephraim, the Firstborn of many brethren. He is calling all Israel into His "ekklesia of the Firstborn," into His renewed covenant Kingdom of Israel (Hebrews 12:22-24).

Yeshua is the Firstborn of many, for since He opened the gates of glory, many have followed Him as eternal brethren and thus share in His double portion.

Through these two separate roles Yeshua fulfilled the promises to both Judah and Ephraim: The only begotten Son is a fulfillment of Judah's blessing; the firstborn among many brethren is a fulfillment of Ephraim's blessing.

Ephraim: The Maoz

In Hebrew, *maoz* (מעוז) means a place or means of safety, protection, refuge, stronghold.[293] Scripture tells us, "God is my *[maoz]* strong fortress" (2 Samuel 22:33). Also, King David said of YHVH: "Thou art my *[maoz]* strength" the "God [Who] is our refuge and strength, a very present help in

---

292 Strong's, BDBL, # H 5414.
293 BDBL word # H4581.

trouble" (Psalm 31:4; 46:1). However, we also are told: "God hath spoken in his holiness....*Ephraim* also is the strength *[maoz]* of mine head" (Psalm 108:7-8, KJV).

YHVH, Yeshua, Ephraim: All are the *maoz*—the ever present strength; the very present refuge that is Salvation.

Fulfilled in Yeshua

Jacob's blessing is truly fulfilled in Messiah Yeshua. For "He Himself is our peace, who made both groups into one" (Ephesians 2:14). YHVH planned that through Yeshua, "He might make the two into one [re]new[ed] man, thus establishing peace" (Ephesians 2:15).

In Him the barrier of the dividing wall, the enmity, between Jew and Gentile (Ephraim)—is ended (Ephesians 2:14).

It is the Father's desire that there be manifested peace in New Covenant Israel. Thus He did not exalt one people over another. Although each house has been allowed to play a special role—the primary heir is still Yeshua.

Jacob Knew...

Jacob did not give his precious blessing to mortal men only. He knew no mere mortal could in himself fulfill the high calling of *Yisrael*. He knew it could only be fulfilled when a person encounters and is truly transformed into the image of the Firstborn.

Jacob knew. For "The prophets who prophesied... made careful search and inquiry, seeking to know what person or time the Spirit of Messiah within them was indicating....It was revealed to them that they were not serving themselves, but you, in these things which now have been announced to you through...the Holy Spirit..." (1 Peter 1:10-12).

Yes, Jacob knew that when your soul and character become like that of Yeshua, then you become Yisrael.

Preserving the Righteous

Yeshua was sent to restore Israel's preserved ones, and

those who take refuge in Him are forever preserved. They are "the righteous [who] will inherit the land and dwell in it forever." [294]

In turn, these preserved ones must "preserve justice and do righteousness." They are to pray for one another to "be preserved complete, without blame at the coming of our Lord Messiah Yeshua." [295]

Yeshua's Imperishable Seed

Our Father swore regarding His Firstborn: "My covenant shall be confirmed to him. So I will establish his seed forever" (Psalm 89:28-29).

In fulfillment of this promise, Yeshua has myriads of *seed* who will live eternally. He has given birth to children for whom He travailed in labor—a hard, painful labor on the cross. His was a labor that was to give birth to a new creation. He died to give birth to sons of righteousness.

Through faith in His sacrifice on our behalf, we become sons of God. For, to "as many as received Him, to them He gave the right to become children of God, even to those who believe in His name" (John 1:12).

When one believes in the Name of Yeshua, Yahveh's "seed abides in him...because he is born of God" (1 John 3:9). As His children, we are "born again not of seed which is perishable, but imperishable, that is, through the living and abiding word of God" (1 Peter 1:23).

These reborn ones are the eternal descendants promised to Firstborn Israel They have the imperishable seed of the Holy One of Israel abiding in them and are "the Israel of God" (Galatians 6:16).

The Father wants them to become conformed to Yeshua's image: "For whom He foreknew, He predestined to become conformed to the image of His Son, that He might be the firstborn among many brethren" (Romans 8:29).

---

294 Psa16:1; 37:28.
295 Isa 56:1; Luke 17:30-33; John 10:28-29; 1 Thes 5:23; Heb 12:23,24.

The Firstborn's Double Portion

These heirs share in the double portion of the Firstborn, which is given by YHVH's Anointed. [296] Yeshua declared Himself to be that Anointed One when He stood in the synagogue and read from Isaiah:

"The Spirit of the LORD is upon Me, because He anointed Me to preach the gospel...to proclaim release to the captives ....to set free those who are down-trodden" (Luke 4:17-21).

Isaiah said Messiah would "comfort all who mourn... giving them...the oil of gladness....the mantle of praise....so they will be called....the priests of the LORD....Instead of shame you will have a *double portion*...they will shout for joy over their portion...they will possess a *double portion* in their land, everlasting joy will be theirs" (Isaiah 61:2-7).

This double portion is reserved for all who receive Messiah's Good News, for those who mourn over their sins. They are anointed with the oil of Yeshua's forgiveness. Instead of shame, they have a double blessing, or portion: Life in this world and eternal life in the world to come.

The Congregation of Firstborn Ones

These same children are called "to the general assembly and *ekklesia* of the firstborn who are enrolled in heaven...to Yeshua, the mediator of a new covenant" (Hebrews 12:22-24).

In this verse, the Greek word translated *firstborn* does not refer to Messiah, but is used in the plural. Thus Jay P. Green, in *The Interlinear Bible*, translates it: We have come to "a church of firstborn *ones.*" The *New International Version Bible* translates it: "To the *ekklesia* of the firstborn whose *names* are written in heaven."

These firstborn ones have become one with *The* First-born—Messiah Yeshua. For He is the "head of the body, the *ekklesia;* he is the beginning and the firstborn from among the dead, so that in everything he might have the supremacy" (Colossians 1:18, NIV).

---

296 The "Anointed One" speaks of the Messiah, of YHVH's King. TWOT # 1255.

In Israel, Yeshua has firstborn supremacy and the double portion. He is the High Priest and the King of kings. Only He fulfills all the requirements to be Jacob's heir.

Yeshua is both Israel the Firstborn, and Ephraim the Firstborn. Both titles are His because He is the epitome of the Powerful Prevailing Prince of Israel—He is the only One truly capable of ruling with YHVH Elohim. Only He could have paid the price!

Blessed Be His Righteous Name Forever!

30

An Israel Yet To Come

Just as King David ruled over all Israel, so too will Messiah Yeshua one day be King over all Israel.

"'At that time,' declares YHVH, 'I will be the God of all the families of Israel, and they shall be My people'" (Jeremiah 31:1).

Our Father declared a latter day plan to reunite His "two chosen families." Thus says YHVH of hosts, "'In those days ten men from all the nations will grasp the garment of a Jew saying, 'Let us go with you, for we have heard that God is with you'" (Jeremiah 33:24; Zechariah 8:23).

Ten to one.

These were the numbers the Father used when He said to Jeroboam: "I...give you ten tribes....but to his [David's] son I will give one tribe" (1 Kings 11:31,36). Ephraim outnumbered Judah ten to one: "The sons of Israel were 300,000, and the men of Judah 30,000" (1 Samuel 11:8).

When the Father fully reunites both the houses of Israel, "In those days the house of Judah will walk with the house of Israel, and they will come together from the land of the north to the land that I gave your fathers as an inheritance" (Jeremiah 3:18).

Ephraim and Judah will come together. Ten will grab the garment of the Jew, and the Jew will begin to "walk with Israel." The two will reach out and join with one another.

"It will come about in that day that the nations will resort to the root of Jesse....then it will happen on that day that the LORD will again recover the second time with His hand the remnant of His people....And He will lift up a standard for the nations, and will assemble the banished ones of Israel, and will gather the dispersed of Judah from the four corners of the earth" (Isaiah 11:10-12).

In that glorious day, "at that time, they shall call Jerusalem 'The Throne of YHVH'" (Jeremiah 3:17).

Our Father will gather Judah and Israel. [297] Together they will yet call Jerusalem the "Throne of YHVH." Formerly divided brothers will begin to honor one another for the godly things each has been used to accomplish on the earth (Romans 13:7).

A Trembling Ephraim Will Yet Be Gathered

We have already begun to see the miracle of the re-gathering of Judah, but we have not yet seen the fulfillment of YHVH's glorious plan to re-gather scattered Ephraim:

"How can I give you up, O Ephraim? How can I surrender you, O Israel?....All My compassions are kindled ....I will not destroy Ephraim again ....They will walk after YHVH, He will roar like a lion; indeed He will roar, and His sons will come trembling from the west" (Hosea 11:8-10).

While in the West, Ephraim will be instructed. There, he will come to full repentance and begin to see the glorious truth about his heritage and call in Messiah Yeshua (Jeremiah 31:18-19).

When he sees this truth he will tremble, and then the Father will whistle for him (Zechariah 10:8).

Ephraim will begin to understand the awesomeness of

---

297 In their Jeremiah 3:18 footnote, the NIV Study Bible, Zondervan, 1995, says: "In the Messianic age God's divided people will again be united (see e.g., Isa 11:12; Eze 37:15-23; Hos 1:11)," p 1119.

the God he serves. He will tremble at the glory of His plan for His restored people. At this time Ephraim will become a "vessel fit for honorable use." [298] He will at last be made ready to walk in the footsteps of his father Joseph, for Ephraim too will become a source of protection and provision for his family.

Where Did They All Come From?

Isaiah speaks cryptically of Israel's coming reunion. He says to those who are being obedient to the Holy One:

"Shout for joy, O heavens! And rejoice, O earth! Break forth into joyful shouting, O mountains! For YHVH has comforted His people and will have compassion on His afflicted" (Isaiah 49:14).

In response, a latter-day, troubled Zion (Judah) says, "The LORD forsaken me, and *Adonai* [299] has forgotten me."

The Father answers Judah's complaint saying, *"Can a woman forget her nursing child and have no compassion on the son of her womb? Even these may forget, but I will not forget you. 'Behold, I have inscribed you on the palms of My hands; your walls are continually before Me. Your builders hurry; your destroyers and devastators will depart from you.*

"'Lift up your eyes and look around; all of them gather together, they come to you. As I live,' declares YHVH, 'You will surely put on all of them as jewels and bind them on as a bride. For your waste and desolate places and your destroyed land—surely now you will be too cramped for the inhabitants, and those who swallowed you will be far away.

The children of whom you [a formerly glorious Zion and capital of a united Israel] were bereaved [the scattered ones of Israel] will yet say in your ears, 'The place is too cramped for me; make room for me that I may live here.'"

"Then you [Judah] will say in your heart, 'Who has begotten these for me, since I have been bereaved of my

---

298 Hos 8:8; Rom 9:21-23.
299 Strong's #136. Form of H113; (used as a proper name of God). *My Lord,* especially used by the house of Judah to speak of the Almighty One.

children and am barren, an exile and a wanderer? And who has reared these? Behold, I was left alone; from where did these come?"

To which the Father responds:

"Behold, I will lift up My hand to the nations and set up My standard to the peoples; and they will bring your sons in their bosom, and your daughters will be carried on their shoulders..." (Isaiah 49:13-23).

Yes, Ephraim will yet return to his homeland, and he will happily bring those of Judah with him.

The Two Sticks

The Father speaks of uniting the two families through the uniting of the "two sticks" that represent them.

Speaking of that day, the Holy One said to Ezekiel:

"'Son of man, take for yourself one stick and write on it, 'For Judah and for the sons of Israel, his companions;' then take another stick and write on it, 'For Joseph, the stick of Ephraim and all the house of Israel, his companions.' Then join them for yourself one to another into one stick, that they may become one in your hand.

"And when the sons of your people speak to you saying; 'Will you not declare to us what you mean by these?' say to them, 'Thus says the LORD God,' 'Behold, I will take the stick of Joseph, which is in the hand of Ephraim, and the tribes of Israel, his companions; and I will put them with it, with the stick of Judah, and make them one stick, and they will be one in My hand....I will take the sons of Israel from among the nations where they have gone, and I will gather them from every side and bring them into their own land; and I will make them one nation in the land, on the mountains of Israel; and one king will be king for all of them; and they will no longer be two nations, and they will no longer be divided into two kingdoms.

"And they will no longer defile themselves with their idols, or with their detestable things, or with any of their transgressions....And they will be My people, and I will be

their God....They will all have one shepherd....and I will...
set My sanctuary in their midst forever. My dwelling place
also will be with them; and I will be their God, and they will
be My people'" (Ezekiel 37:16-27).

An Invincible Army

When Ephraim and Judah are united in YHVH Elohim,
when their reunion is fully manifested, they become an
invincible army—an army of powerful, prevailing princes
capable of fighting the battles of the God of Israel.

The *Amplified Bible* says of this coming army:

*"But [with united forces] Ephraim and Judah will swoop
down upon the shoulder of the Philistines land sloping
toward the west; together they will strip the people on the
east [the Arabs]. They will lay their hand upon Edom and
Moab, and the Ammonites shall obey them" (Isaiah 11:14).*

Of that day, YHVH says:

*"I will bend Judah as My bow, I will fill the bow with
Ephraim....Then YHVH will appear over them...and YHVH
will blow the trumpet....YHVH Tsavaot will defend them....
and YHVH their God will save them in that day as the flock
of His people; for they are as the stones of a crown,
sparkling in His land....For YHVH of hosts has visited His
flock, the house of Judah, and will make them like His
majestic horse in battle....and they will be as mighty men,
treading down the enemy in the mire of the streets in battle;
and they will fight, for YHVH will be with them; and the
riders on horses will be put to shame.*

*"And I shall strengthen the house of Judah, and I shall
save the house of Joseph....Ephraim will be like a mighty
man, and their heart will be glad as if from wine; indeed,
their children will see it and be glad, their heart will rejoice
in YHVH.*

*"I will whistle for them to gather them together, for I have
redeemed them; and they will be as numerous as they were
before...They will remember Me in far countries, and they with
their children will live and come back. I will bring them*

back from the land of Egypt, and gather them from Assyria;
and I will bring them into the land of Gilead and Lebanon,
until no room can be found for them" (Zechariah 9:13-10:10).

Yes, "The sons of Judah and the sons of Israel will be
gathered together." Their reunion will be glorious, "for great
will be the day of Jezreel" (Hosea 1:11).

A Day of Holiness

Great and holy will be the day when the Father fully
reunites His chosen people. It will be a holy day because
the Holy One has sworn: "All the sinners of my people will
die by the sword" (Amos 9:10). "'It will come about in that
day,' declares YHVH of hosts, 'that I will cut off the names
of the idols from the land, and they will no longer be
remembered; and I will also remove the prophets and the
unclean spirit from the land'" (Zechariah 13:2).

Yes, the Almighty has decreed, "I will remove from your
midst your proud, exulting ones. And you will never again
be haughty on My holy mountain. But I will leave among
you a humble and lowly people, and they will take refuge in
the name of YHVH. The remnant of Israel will do no wrong
and tell no lies, nor will a deceitful tongue be found in their
mouths" (Zephaniah 3:11-13).

The Father will yet have His way. He will have an
obedient, united House of Israel. He will have a House of
Israel that loves Him, His people, and His Messiah.

The Answer to the Question

One day soon, the sky will part and a glorious Messiah
Yeshua will be revealed. Seated on a white horse, the Prince
Who is *Yisrael* will sit tall in His saddle.

In that day, Yeshua will be clothed in a robe dipped in
blood and will have written on His thigh a title: *King of
kings and LORD of lords.*

He also will have in His hand a scepter of two sticks that
have been made one in His hand.

In that moment the whole world will behold His glory. He will then nudge His stead to move toward the Earth, and in that instant all who are His will be changed. The mortals who love Him will instantly become immortal.

In the twinkling of an eye, a redeemed people will find themselves suddenly seated on white horses. For they have been made ready to forever serve their Master—they are ready to return and reign with their King. In that awesome moment, the answer to the *Who Is Israel* question will be answered.

May we, by His grace, prove to be part of that answer.
May we prove to be part of His redeemed people.

Finish

Study Helps

and More...

The Different Dispersions And Times of Ephraim and Judah

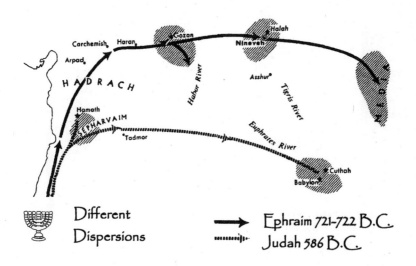

🕎 Different Dispersions

➡ Ephraim 721-722 B.C.
⋯⋯▸ Judah 586 B.C.

To understand Israel, we must see that
Ephraim and Judah were dispersed at different times,
and that they were sent to different locations.
There were more than 135 years between the times of their
dispersions, and as much as 500 miles difference in the
locations to which they were each dispersed.

Fall And Restoration of Israel's Kingdom

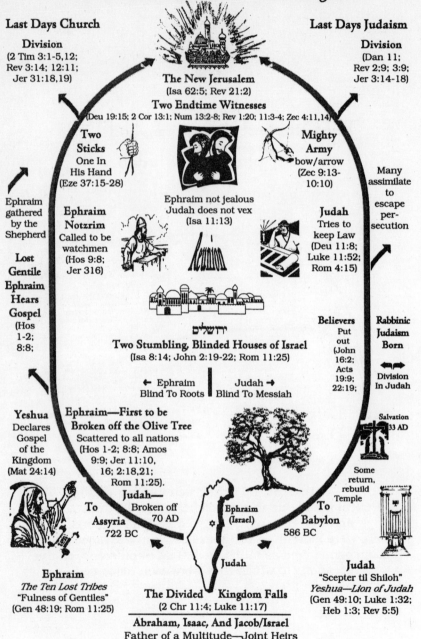

Last Days Church

Division
(2 Tim 3:1-5,12;
Rev 3:14; 12:11;
Jer 31:18,19)

Last Days Judaism

Division
(Dan 11;
Rev 2:9; 3:9;
Jer 3:14-18)

The New Jerusalem
(Isa 62:5; Rev 21:2)

Two Endtime Witnesses
(Deu 19:15; 2 Cor 13:1; Num 13:2-8; Rev 1:20; 11:3-4; Zec 4:11,14)

Two Sticks
One In His Hand
(Eze 37:15-28)

Mighty Army
bow/arrow
(Zec 9:13-10:10)

Ephraim gathered by the Shepherd

Ephraim Notzrim
Called to be watchmen
(Hos 9:8; Jer 316)

Ephraim not jealous
Judah does not vex
(Isa 11:13)

Judah
Tries to keep Law
(Deu 11:8; Luke 11:52; Rom 4:15)

Many assimilate to escape persecution

Lost Gentile Ephraim Hears Gospel
(Hos 1-2; 8:8;

ירושלים

Two Stumbling, Blinded Houses of Israel
(Isa 8:14; John 2:19-22; Rom 11:25)

Believers
Put out
(John 16:2;
Acts 19:9;
22:19;

Rabbinic Judaism Born

Division In Judah

← Ephraim
Blind To Roots | Judah →
Blind To Messiah

Yeshua
Declares Gospel of the Kingdom
(Mat 24:14)

Ephraim—First to be Broken off the Olive Tree
Scattered to all nations
(Hos 1-2; 8:8; Amos 9:9; Jer 11:10, 16; 2:18,21; Rom 11:25).

Judah—
Broken off 70 AD

Salvation
33 AD

Some return, rebuild Temple

To Assyria
722 BC

Ephraim (Israel)

To Babylon
586 BC

Judah

Ephraim
The Ten Lost Tribes
"Fulness of Gentiles"
(Gen 48:19; Rom 11:25)

The Divided   Kingdom Falls
(2 Chr 11:4; Luke 11:17)

Judah
"Scepter til Shiloh"
Yeshua—Lion of Judah
(Gen 49:10; Luke 1:32; Heb 1:3; Rev 5:5)

Abraham, Isaac, And Jacob/Israel
Father of a Multitude—Joint Heirs
(Gen 26:3; 28:4; 1 Chr 16:16-17; Heb 11:9,39,40; Gal 3:29)

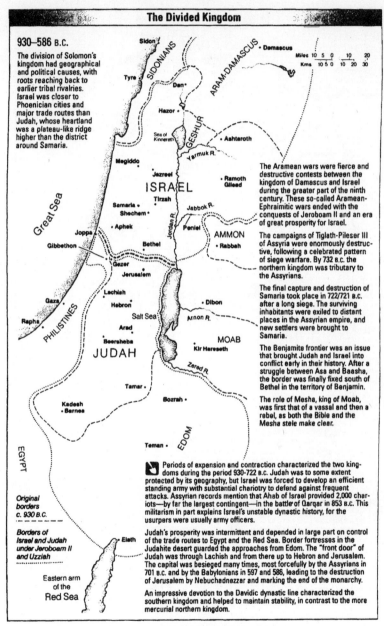

The Divided Kingdom

930–586 B.C.

The division of Solomon's kingdom had geographical and political causes, with roots reaching back to earlier tribal rivalries. Israel was closer to Phoenician cities and major trade routes than Judah, whose heartland was a plateau-like ridge higher than the district around Samaria.

Miles 10 5 0   10   20
Kms 10 5 0   10 20 30

The Aramean wars were fierce and destructive contests between the kingdom of Damascus and Israel during the greater part of the ninth century. These so-called Aramean-Ephraimitic wars ended with the conquests of Jeroboam II and an era of great prosperity for Israel.

The campaigns of Tiglath-Pileser III of Assyria were enormously destructive, following a celebrated pattern of siege warfare. By 732 B.C. the northern kingdom was tributary to the Assyrians.

The final capture and destruction of Samaria took place in 722/721 B.C. after a long siege. The surviving inhabitants were exiled to distant places in the Assyrian empire, and new settlers were brought to Samaria.

The Benjamite frontier was an issue that brought Judah and Israel into conflict early in their history. After a struggle between Asa and Baasha, the border was finally fixed south of Bethel in the territory of Benjamin.

The role of Mesha, king of Moab, was first that of a vassal and then a rebel, as both the Bible and the Mesha stele make clear.

Periods of expansion and contraction characterized the two kingdoms during the period 930-722 B.C. Judah was to some extent protected by its geography, but Israel was forced to develop an efficient standing army with substantial chariotry to defend against frequent attacks. Assyrian records mention that Ahab of Israel provided 2,000 chariots—by far the largest contingent—in the battle of Qarqar in 853 B.C. This militarism in part explains Israel's unstable dynastic history, for the usurpers were usually army officers.

Judah's prosperity was intermittent and depended in large part on control of the trade routes to Egypt and the Red Sea. Border fortresses in the Judahite desert guarded the approaches from Edom. The "front door" of Judah was through Lachish and from there up to Hebron and Jerusalem. The capital was besieged many times, most forcefully by the Assyrians in 701 B.C. and by the Babylonians in 597 and 586, leading to the destruction of Jerusalem by Nebuchadnezzar and marking the end of the monarchy.

An impressive devotion to the Davidic dynastic line characterized the southern kingdom and helped to maintain stability, in contrast to the more mercurial northern kingdom.

Original borders c. 930 B.C.

Borders of Israel and Judah under Jeroboam II and Uzziah

Eastern arm of the Red Sea

From the *New International Version Study Bible*, Grand Rapids: Zondervan Corporation. 1995. Used by permission.

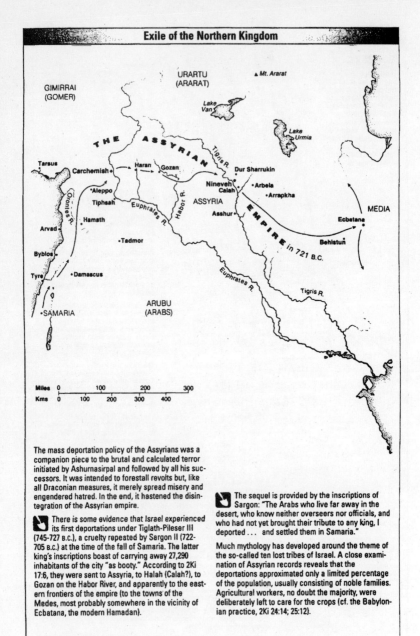

Exile of the Northern Kingdom

The mass deportation policy of the Assyrians was a companion piece to the brutal and calculated terror initiated by Ashurnasirpal and followed by all his successors. It was intended to forestall revolts but, like all Draconian measures, it merely spread misery and engendered hatred. In the end, it hastened the disintegration of the Assyrian empire.

There is some evidence that Israel experienced its first deportations under Tiglath-Pileser III (745-727 B.C.), a cruelty repeated by Sargon II (722-705 B.C.) at the time of the fall of Samaria. The latter king's inscriptions boast of carrying away 27,290 inhabitants of the city "as booty." According to 2Ki 17:6, they were sent to Assyria, to Halah (Calah?), to Gozan on the Habor River, and apparently to the eastern frontiers of the empire (to the towns of the Medes, most probably somewhere in the vicinity of Ecbatana, the modern Hamadan).

The sequel is provided by the inscriptions of Sargon: "The Arabs who live far away in the desert, who know neither overseers nor officials, and who had not yet brought their tribute to any king, I deported ... and settled them in Samaria."

Much mythology has developed around the theme of the so-called ten lost tribes of Israel. A close examination of Assyrian records reveals that the deportations approximated only a limited percentage of the population, usually consisting of noble families. Agricultural workers, no doubt the majority, were deliberately left to care for the crops (cf. the Babylonian practice, 2Ki 24:14; 25:12).

From the *New International Version Study Bible*, Grand Rapids: Zondervan Corporation. 1995. Used by permission.

Addendum:

Genetic Confirmation

by Michele Libin

*A**s for Me, behold, My covenant is with you, and you will be the father of a multitude of nations (Genesis 17:4).*

The evidence from Scripture clearly shows that Abraham had myriads of actual physical descendants. These descendants are alive today.

This article presents an overview of some of the recent scientific research that affirms what the Scriptures teach. The bulk of the evidence from genetic research shows that we all have common ancestors, and that everyone alive today has a high probability of having some of the genetic material of Abraham, Isaac, and Jacob, although the amount may be very small in some people.

"Behold, I am commanding, and I will shake the house of Israel among all nations as grain is shaken in a sieve, but not a kernel will fall to the ground" (Amos 9:9).

Where are the descendants of the Israelites who were deported to Assyria? Can we identify the descendants of these ancient Israelite peoples? Numerous writers have attempted to trace the migrations of the Ten Lost Tribes and the descendants of Joseph.

However, the science of molecular biology and genetics is beginning to provide some answers.

The Language of DNA

The God of Israel is the creator of the universe. Just as He has given us His words in Scripture, He has also provided "words" in the DNA that makes up our genetic code. These words consist of "letters," or chemical units, that are put together in a particular sequence. These units are called nucleotides, and it is their exact order on a chain of DNA that determines the unique characteristics of an individual.

The research that has been done in genetics is revealing some startling patterns about how groups of people pass their genetic material onto their offspring. This research is relevant to our study of "Who is Israel."

This article is a brief outline of the methods and procedures that are used in genetics research, plus some of the relevant highlights of the results. It is meant to be an introduction, not a comprehensive review of the literature.

How the Genetic Code is Transmitted

We all have 23 chromosome pairs in the nucleus of each of our cells. One member of each pair is contributed by the mother in her egg cell, the other is contributed by the father through his sperm. When they combine to form a fertilized egg, the DNA recombines to form a new individual with 23 distinct chromosome pairs of its own. This is basically how traits are passed from one generation to another.

One pair of chromosomes is different from the other 22 pairs. These are the ones that determine the sex of the child, and are known as the "X" and the "Y" chromosomes. Females have two X's, males have one X and one Y.

There Are Two Different Areas of Research:

1) Tracing populations through the Y Chromosome, which is only passed through the father.

2) Tracing populations through the "Mitochondrial DNA," which is only passed through the mother.

The Y Chromosome

Because the Y chromosome cannot exchange genetic material with the X, the Y of each male directly resembles his father, his grandfather before him, and so on.

The Y chromosome is a powerful tool in the study of the lineage of the male and the relationships between and among contemporary males. The comparative study of the genetic material on the Y chromosome is one of two main areas of genetic research having to do with populations.

Mitochondrial DNA

The second method for studying populations employs the Mitochondrial DNA.

It is contributed by the mother only, and is used because it lends itself to genetic sequencing techniques. It does not combine and recombine with other chromosomes.

The Mitochondrial DNA is a very small circular strand of DNA found in an organelle called the Mitochondria, which performs most of the energy producing tasks in our cells.

Because of its distinctive characteristics, geneticists have developed techniques for using it in their studies on how populations have interacted throughout history.

One early researcher, an evolutionist, postulated that all people on earth are descended from seven hypothetical women living in the distant past.[300]

Geneticists Study Patterns

The information that geneticists collect from their DNA studies of various individuals and groups is correlated to reveal patterns in populations throughout time. As the data about their biological relationships are studied, lineages begin to blend into common ancestors.

---

300 *The Seven Daughters of Eve*, Bryan Sykes, W.W. Norton & Co, N.Y., 2001.

An Overview of the Research

The following overview is excerpted from the book *Mapping Human History* by Steve Olson. [301] It provides a concise, current, and well-documented explanation of the work that has been done in this important area of research.

Tracing the Kohanim

"Since men pass their Y chromosome on to their sons, all of Aaron's sons would have had his Y chromosome, which they in turn would have passed on to their sons, and so on down the generations to the kohanim of today. Along the way, mutations would occur in the separate lineages derived from Aaron's Y chromosome, making the nucleotide sequences of Aaron's male descendants somewhat different from one another today. But the original haplotype [genetic blueprint] should still be visible, like a figure behind a translucent screen.

"A few years ago a team of geneticists...set out to find Aaron's Y chromosome. Using cells from the cheeks of about two hundred Jewish males from Israel, North America, and England, they looked for specific genetic markers along each man's Y. They found that Jews who did not identify themselves as kohanim had a broad assortment of Y-chromosome markers, no one of which was especially frequent. But of the kohanim, about 50% had a particular set of markers, indicating that all of their Y chromosomes descended from a common ancestor. The researchers called this genetic pattern the Cohen Modal Haplotype (modal in this case meaning most common). [302]

[They calculated that] "the man who carried the original chromosome lived about 106 generations ago. Within the margin of error inherent in the calculations, this easily falls withing the time frame when Aaron might have lived...." [303]

---

301 *Mapping Human History* by Steve Olson, Houghton Mifflin Co, Boston, 2002.
302 *Nature* 385 (1997):32, by Karl Skorecki and seven other researchers.
303 *Mapping Human History*, Hereafter *MHH*, "God's People," pp. 108-109.

The Jews and Other Middle Eastern Populations

[The Bible commands that the sons of Jacob were not to intermarry with non-Israelites]. "If this edict had been scrupulously observed since the time of Jacob—and if there had been no converts to Judaism—then all Jewish males would have Jacob's Y chromosome.

"Jewish history has obviously been much more complicated than that. In a recent study, a team of twelve researchers from the United States, Israel, England, and South Africa found that Jewish males have a wide variety of Y-chromosome haplotypes [genetic blueprints]—far too many to have come from a single man living anytime in the past few thousand years.   Rather, most of the Y chromosomes found in Jewish ales are the same as those found among many other men from the Middle East—Palestinians, Syrians, Lebanese, Saudi Arabians, and so on. The Jews and their neighbors all emerged from the same diverse pool of Middle Eastern people." [304]

"Studies of mitochondrial DNA sequences of Jewish females are even more diverse than the Y chromosomes of males, suggesting that non-Jewish women converted or married into the faith even more often than did men." [305]

The Story of the Lemba

"As Jews have scattered around the world, they have introduced their genes into populations not normally considered Jewish. The best-known example involves the Lemba, an ethnic group of black Africans...[who] say that their ancestors were Jewish, and [who] practice a number of Jewish-sounding rites, such as particular food taboos and circumcision.

"In 1997 a team of geneticists decided to take the

---

304 *Proc. of the Nat'l. Acad. of Sci.,* 97 (2000): 676769-74, by Michael Hammer and eleven other researchers,
305 *Human Biology* 65 (1993: 359-85, by Batsheva Bonne-Tamir and six others.
   MHH, "God's People" (pp. 109-110).

Lemba's claims seriously....[They found that] the majority of the Y-chromosome haplotypes among the oldest and most influential of the Lemba's clans were not just generic Middle Eastern chromosomes. They were the Cohen Modal Haplotype—the marker chromosome for the Jewish priesthood."[306]

Everyone Has Israelite Ancestors

"This connection between a group of black Africans and the Jews may seem surprising at first. Yet more and more of these kinds of genetic links will be found as more is learned about our genetic heritage. The forces of genetic mixing are so powerful that everyone in the world has Jewish ancestors, though the amount of DNA from those ancestors in a given individual may be small.

"In fact, everyone on earth is by now a descendant of Abraham...." [307]

Everyone is Related to Everyone Else

"Today tests are available only for mitochondrial DNA and the Y chromosome, but these tests detect only single lineages extending back into the past. Soon tests of genetic markers will reveal the full diversity of our ancestry. Geneticists will be able to show, for example, that a person received a piece of chromosome 21 from Jewish ancestors, a piece of chromosome 3 from African ancestors, and so on. At that point genetic tests may become distinctly less compelling, because they will simply demonstrate the obvious: *that everyone is related to everyone else....* "[308]

There are Limitations to Genetic Testing

"It may seem that such tests could unequivocally identify individuals as members of particular groups, functioning as a sort of genetic yellow star. But genetic

---

306 *American Journal of Human Genetics* 66 (2000): 674-86.
   MHH, "God's People," pp. 113-114.
307 *MHH,* "God's People," p. 114.
308 Ibid, p. 118.

research may turn out to have exactly the opposite effect. For example, no single genetic marker can indisputably prove that a person is Jewish. Even the Cohen Modal Haplotype, Aaron's Y chromosome, is found in all other Middle Eastern populations, both because of intermarriage and because *that haplotype existed before the Jews took shape as a people*....If a particular genetic marker were enough to make a person Jewish, the recounted Jewish population would grow manyfold....

[Remember, Abraham descended from those who lived in Ur of the Chaldees, or Babylon.]

"These observations about individuals and groups need to be treated carefully. Statistical associations can be made between collections of genetic markers and particular groups....But the associations will always be statistical because very few people will have exactly the same set of markers—and because the boundaries of the group will always be poorly defined. Our histories are too inter-connected to draw distinct lines between collections of people...." [309]

A Single Human Family

[Research into the genetic diversity of European and other western populations shows the same diversity and interconnectedness. For instance, investigators have found that] "The genes brought to Europe by modern humans were no different from those of the people who remained in the Middle East and Africa. [310]"

In his chapter on the settlement of the Americas, Olson writes, "Our DNA connects everyone to everyone after a couple of thousand years, so determining who is an ancestor of whom is far from straightforward." [311]

Finally, Olson concludes his book by summarizing the findings of geneticists:

---

309 Ibid, pp. 118-119.
310 *MHH*, "Who Are the Europeans?" p. 160.
311 *MHH*, "Settlement of the Americas," p. 195.

"Throughout human history, groups have wondered how they are related to one another. The study of genetics has now revealed that we are all linked: the Bushmen hunting antelope, the mixed-race people of South Africa, the African Americans descended from slaves, the Samaritans on their mountain stronghold, the Jewish populations scattered around the world, the Han Chinese a billion strong, the descendants of European settlers who colonized the New World, the Native Hawaiians who look to a cherished past. We are members of a single human family." [312]

Conclusions

In summation, if you feel you are descended from Israel, the evidence from genetic research demonstrates that it is statistically probable that you are related to some degree. Remember the conclusion we quoted earlier:

"Everyone on earth is by now a descendant of Abraham...."

Michele Libin has a B.S. degree in Biology and worked in Genetics research at the Univ. of Oregon Health Sciences Ctr. after graduation. She is now an Editor with Key of David Publishing and an Associate with Messianic Israel Ministries.

Resources:
Mapping Human History by Steve Olson, Houghton Mifflin Co, Boston & NY, 2002.
The Seven Daughters of Eve, Bryan Sykes, W.W. Norton & Co, N.Y., 2001.
Biblical Archeology Online, www.bibarch.com/Perspectives/1.2.
The Center for Genetic Anthropology Online, www.ucl.ac.uk/tcga.
Jewish Genetic Disorders, E.Abel, McFarland & Co., N.C., 2001.
Theory and Problems of Biochem., 2nd ed., McGraw-Hill, N.Y., 1998.

312 *MHH*, "The End of Race," p. 238.

Abbreviations & Bibliography

Abbreviations:
ArtScroll: ArtScroll Tanach Series
BDBL: New Brown-Driver-Briggs-Gesenius Hebrew-Aramaic Lexicon
NIV: New International Version Bible
NIV Study Bible: New International Version Study Bible
Strong's: Strong's Exhaustive Concordance
TAB: The Amplified Bible
TWOT: Theological Wordbook of the Old Testament
TNKH: Tanakh The Holy Scriptures

The following is a listing of writings used in making this book.

Adler, Mortimer J. *Ten Philosophical Mistakes.* NY: Macmillian, 1997.

Aharoni, Yohanan; Michael Avi-Yonah. *The Macmillan Bible Atlas.* NY: Macmillan, 1977.

Bacchiocchi, Samuele. *From Sabbath To Sunday.* Maplewood NJ: Hammond, 1979, 2000.

Barraclough, Geoffrey. *The Times Atlas of World History.* The Pontifical Gregorian University Press: Rome, 1997.

Beitzel. Barry J. *Moody Atlas of Bible Lands.* Chicago: Moody, 1985.

Berkowitz. Ariel & D'vorah. *Take Hold.* Chicago: First Fruits of Zion, 1999.

Brown, Frances. *The New Brown-Driver-Briggs-Gesenius Hebrew-Aramaic Lexicon.* Peabody, MA: Hendrickson, 1998.

Carta's Historical Atlas of Israel. Jerusalem: Carta, 1983.

Cohen, A. *Isaiah.* London: Soncino, 1987.

_____. *The Twelve Prophets.* London: Soncino, 1999.

DeHaan, M. R.. *The Chemistry of the Blood.* Grand Rapids: Zondervan, 1971, 1989.

Dowley, Tim. *The Kregal Pictorial Guide To The Bible.* Grand Rapids: Kregal Publications, 2000.

Eckstein, Yechiel, Rabbi. *What Christiand Should Know About Jews and Judaism.* Waco, TX: Word Books, 1984.

Edersheim, Alfred. *The Life and Times of Jesus the Messiah.* Grand Rapids: Eerdman's, 1979, 1997.

_____. *The Temple.* Grand Rapids: Kregal, 1997.

Edidin, Ben M. *Jewish Customs And Ceremonies*. NY: Hebrew Publishing, 1987.

_____. *Encyclopaedia Judaica, 16 Vols*. Jerusalem: Keter, 1972.

Even-Shushan, Avraham. *New Concordance of the Tanach*. Jerusalem: Sivan, 1983, 1999.

Fay, Frededrick L. *A Map Book For Bible Students*. Old Tappan, NJ: Revell, 1966.

Fellner, Judith. *In the Jewish Tradition, A Year of Food and Festivities*. Middle Village, NY: Jonathan David Publishers. 1995.

Frankel, Ellen, and Betsy Platkin Teutsch. *The Encyclopedia of Jewish Symbols*. Northvale, NJ: Jason Aronson Inc., 1992.

Gesenius' Hebrew-Chaldee Lexicon To The Old Testament. Grand Rapids. Baker, 1979, 2000.

Gilbert, Martin. *Atlas of Jewish History*. NY: William Morrow, 1993.

_____. *Israel: A History*. NY: William Morrow, 1998.

Green, Jay P. *The Interlinear Bible*, Hebrew, Greek, English. Grand Rapids: Baker, 1979.

Harris, R. Laird, Gleason L. Archer Jr., and Bruce K. Waltke, eds. *Theological Wordbook of the Old Testament, 2 Vols*. Chicago: Moody, 1998.

Hatch, Edwin, and Henry A. Redpath. *Hatch and Redpath Concordance to the Septuagint, 2 Vols*. Grand Rapids: Baker, 1983.

Holladay, William L. Editor. *A Concise Hebrew and Aramaic Lexicon of The Old Testament*. Grand Rapids: Eerdman's, 1991.

House of David Herald. White Stone, VA - Saint Cloud, FL: 1982-2000.

Interpreter's Dictionary of the Bible, 5 Vols. Nashville: Abingdon, 1983.

Jahn, Herb. *The Aramic New Covenant*. Orange, CA: Exegeses, 1996.

Jenkins, Simon. *Bible Mapbook*. Herts, England: Lion, 1985.

Knapp, Christopher. *The Kings of Judah & Israel*. Neptune NJ: Loizeaux, 1983.

Kolatch, Alfred J. *The Jewish book of Why*. Middle Village NY: Jonathan David Publishers, 1981, 1995.

_____. *The Second Jewish Book of Why*. Middle Village NY: Jonathan David Publishers, 1996.

Isaacson, Ben, Dr. David Gross, ed. *Dictionary of the Jewish Religion* Englewood, NJ: Bantam Books, 1979.

Lamsa, George M. *The Holy Bible From Ancient Eastern Manuscripts*. Nashville: Holman, 1968, 1984.

Leil, C.F.; F. Delitzsch. *Commentary on the Old Testament In Ten Volumes*. Grand Rapids: Eerdman's, 1981.

Lindsey, Robert. *Jesus, Rabbi, and Lord*. Oak Creek: Cornerstone, 1990.

_____. *Messianic Israel Herald*. Saint Cloud, 1999-2002.

Mordecai, Victor. *Christian Revival for Israel's Survival*. Jerusalem: 1999.

_____. *Is Fanatic Islam A Global Threat?* Jerusalem, 2002. Fifth Edition.

The New Encyclopaedia Britannica, 29 Vols. Chicago: Encyclopedia Britannica, 1985, 2003.

The New English Bible With the Apocrypha. Oxford, England: Oxford University Press, 1994.

New International Version Study Bible. Grand Rapids: Zondervan, 1985, 1995.

Newsome, James D. Jr., ed. *A Synoptic Harmony of Samuel, Kings and Chronicles.* Grand Rapids: Baker, 1986.

Pearl, Chaim, ed. *The Encyclopedia of Jewish Life and Thought.* Jerusalem: Carta, 1987.

Pfeiffer, Charles F., Howard F. Vos, and John Rea, eds. *Wycliffe Bible Encyclopaedia.* Chicago: Moody, 1983.

Richards, Lawerence O. *Expository Dictionary of Bible Words.* Grand Rapids: Zondervan, 1985..

Scherman, Nosson, and Meir Zlotowitz, eds. *Genesis. ArtScroll Tanach Series.* Brooklyn: Mesorah, 1987.

_____, Rabbis. *The Wisdom In The Hebrew Alphabet.* Brooklyn: Mesorah Publications, 1993.

Smith, William, L.L.D. *Smith's Bible Dictionary.* Peabody, MA: Hendrickson, 1997.

Strong, James. *The New Strong's Exhaustive Concordance.* Nashville: Thomas Nelson, 1984, 2002.

Stern, David H. *Jewish New Testament Commentary.* Clarksville, MD: Jewish New Testament Publications, 1995.

TenBoom, Corrie. The Hiding Place. Chosen Books

Tenny, Merrill, ed. *Zondervan Pictorial Encyclopedia of the Bible, 5 Vols.* Grand Rapids: Zondervan, 1976.

Thayer, Joseph Henry. *Thayer's Greek-English Lexicon of the New Testament.* Grand Rapids: Baker, 1983.

Thomas, Winton, ed. *Documents from Old Testament Times.* New York: Harper & Row, 1961.

Turner, Nigel *Christian Words.* Nashville: Thomas Nelson, 1981.

Unger, Merrill F. *Unger's Bible Dictionary.* Chicago: Moody, 1974, 1996.

Vaughn, Curtis, ed. *26 Translations of the Holy Bible.* Atlanta: Mathis, 1985.

Vincent, Marvin R. *Vincent's Word Studies of the New Testament.* McLean, VA: MacDonald.

Vine, W.E. *The Expanded Vine's Expository Dictionary of New Testament Words.* Minneapolis: Bethany, 1984.

Walton, John H. *Chronological Charts of the Old Testament.* Grand Rapids: Zondervan, 1978.

Webster's Third New International Dictionary, 3 Vols. Chicago: Encyclopedia Britannica, 1981.

Whiston, William, trs. *The Works of Flavius Josephus, 4 Vols.* Grand Rapids: Baker, 1974, 1992.

Wilson, William. *Wilson's Old Testament Word Studies, Unabridged Edition*. McLean, VA: MacDonald.

Wootten, Angus. The Restoration of the Kingdom to Israel. Saint Cloud, FL: Key of David, 2003.

_____. *Take Two Tablets*. Saint Cloud: Key of David, 2002.

Wootten, Batya Ruth. *In Search of Israel*. Lakewood, NY: Destiny Image/House of David, 1988.

_____. *Ephraim and Judah: Israel Revealed*. Saint Cloud: Key of David, 2002.

_____. *Israel's Feasts and their Fullness*. Saint Cloud: Key of David, 2002.

_____. *Who Is Israel?* Saint Cloud: Key of David, 2000.

Wuest, Kenneth S. *Weust's Word Studies From the Greek New Testament*. Grand Rapids: Eerdman's, 1981.

Yaniv, David. *Birth of the Messiah*. Lynnwood, WA: New West Press, Ltd. 1997.

Index

Batya Ruth Wootten

Batya and her husband, Angus, were early pioneers in the Messianic movement. Decades ago they began publishing the first Messianic Materials Catalogue, created to serve a fledgling new interest in Israel, the Jewish people, and relationships between Christians and Jews.

Batya read countless books about these subjects so she could write informed descriptions of them for the catalogue, and so discovered the great diversity of opinions about Israel's role in the world and about Israel's identity.

Hungering to truly understand "Israel," she began to cry out in desperation to her Heavenly Father, asking Him to show her *His* truth. As promised, He answered: "Call to Me and I will answer you, and I will tell you great and mighty things, which you do not know" (Jeremiah 33:3).

He began to open up the Scriptures to her, and His answers to her led to the book you now hold in your hands.

Batya's challenging books represent decades of study, discussion, and prayer on the crucial issues of identifying Israel, celebrating her feasts, and honoring Torah.

Many readers have given testimony about being transformed by her writings. Lives continue to be changed as they see the truth about both the houses of Israel— Judah and Ephraim. It is a truth that is helping to restore a brotherhood broken apart long ago.

Batya's emphasis on the need to show mercy and grace to both houses is helping to heal the wounds that began when Israel's Kingdom was divided into the Northern Kingdom of Israel and the Southern Kingdom of Judah.

Her book, *Israel's Feasts and Their Fullness,* also represents many years of meticulous research, study, and prayerful writing. Several people have said of it: "This is the best book about the feasts that I have ever read."

This important book is helping Believers to be liberated into glorious celebrations of the feasts.

Batya is married to her best friend, Col. Angus Wootten (Ret.), author of the visionary book, *Restoring Israel's Kingdom*, plus a guide to the Torah commandments, *Take Two Tablets Daily*. Together they have ten children who have blessed them with many offspring.

Working as a team, Angus and Batya moved forward from the early days of the *House of David Catalogue* and began publishing a Newsletter, the *House of David Herald*, plus a periodical magazine, *The Messianic Israel Herald*.

They also developed the informative Messianic Israel web sites: *www.mim.net* and *messianicisrael.com*, which in turn led to the founding of the *Messianic Israel Alliance*—a rapidly growing alliance of congregations and home fellowships that agree with "The Hope of Messianic Israel," the statement of faith of the Messianic Israel Alliance.

Together Angus and Batya continue to publish books that serve the growing army of Believers who are discovering the truth about their heritage. They work together to help raise up new leaders and to draw out their giftings.

For this assignment they have been uniquely prepared by the God of Abraham, Isaac, and Jacob.

We know you will be blessed as you read their writings.

"Let the one who is taught share all good things with him who teaches" (Galatians 6:6).
If through this book a good thing has been accomplished in your life, please write and share your good news with me.

Batya Wootten
PO Box 700217, Saint Cloud, FL 34770
e-mail: batya@mim.net

Who Is Israel?
Past, Present, and Future
by Batya Ruth Wootten

Who is Israel?

The Scriptural answer to that question is causing a renewal in the Body of Messiah. It is sparking a reformation in the Body of Messiah and inspiring Believers everywhere!

Believers are seeing that the way you define Israel sets the course for your interpretation of Scripture. And this book, which is now in its Third Edition, well explains the truth about "both the houses of Israel" (Isaiah 8:14)— Ephraim and Judah.

Reading this book will inspire and encourage you, even change your life. It will help you discover your own Hebraic Heritage. It will put your feet on the road to Zion. It will enable you to: Understand Israel, the Church, the Bible — The mystery of the "fullness of the Gentiles" — The "blindness of Israel" — The Father's master plan for Israel. It will answer: Why you feel something is missing in your life — Why you have a love for Israel and Jewish people — And why you feel an urge to celebrate the feasts of Israel.

This handbook will move you from religion to relationship. The Biblical truths unveiled in this volume will help: Put an end to "Christian" anti-Semitism and heal divisions in the Body of Messiah, as well as lead us back to our first love: Messiah Yeshua.

Includes Maps and Charts and an Addendum about current genetic research.

ISBN 1-886987-17-3   Paper, 288 pages $14.95

Available in Spanish!
¿Quién es Israel?

Based on our earlier Expanded Edition of *Who is Israel?*, this classic is also available in Spanish.
ISBN 1-886987-08-4   320 pages $14.95

Ephraim and Judah
Israel Revealed

by Batya Wootten

Ephraim and Judah: Israel Revealed. Inexpensive. Succinct. Easy-to-read.

This condensed overview of the material presented in the classic, *Who Is Israel?* includes maps, charts, and lists.

Like its parent, this book too is causing a stir among Believers. It is even encouraging a reformation in the Body of Messiah. It quickly clarifies misconceptions about Israel's Twelve Tribes.

This excellent tool helps non-Jewish Believers see that they too are part of Israel. It helps both the houses of Israel see how and where they fit into the Father's divine plan (Jer 31:18-19; Eph 2:11-22; Isa 8:14).

Especially created to be an inexpensive yet invaluable handout, this book readily outlines the essence of the phenomenal truth of the two houses of Israel. Quantity discounts available.

ISBN 1-886987-11-4   Paper, 80 pages, $ 3.95 plus shipping
3 copies for #10.00 — 10 for $25.00 — 25 for $50.00

Unlocking *your* future...

Books Distributed by—

Key of David Publishing

Write or Call for a Free Catalog
PO Box 700217, Saint Cloud, FL 34770
1 800 829-8777
All Book Prices Are Plus Shipping—Tripled for Overseas
Please add appropriate Shipping to all Orders

Restoring Israel's Kingdom
by Angus Wootten

What was the last question Messiah Yeshua's disciples asked their teacher as they stood on the Mount of Olives, knowing that He was about to depart? What mattered most to them?

As followers of Israel's Messiah, we must ask the question that mattered so much to His chosen twelve:

"Lord, is it at this time You are restoring the kingdom to Israel?" (Acts 1:6).

Yeshua's disciples had been trained by Him for more than three years. They asked this question because He taught them to pray to our Father in Heaven, "Your kingdom come. Your will be done, On earth as it is in heaven" (Matthew 6:10).

Since we are a people dedicated to bringing Yeshua's Kingdom to this earth, we must not lose sight of the vision that burned in the hearts of His first disciples. But we have done just that...

We lost sight of our heritage as part Israel and we lost sight of this important goal. However, the veil is now being lifted from our partially blinded Israelite eyes (Genesis 48:19; Romans 11).

Restoring Israel's Kingdom offers many challenging chapters: Are You Prepared? — Can We Make A Difference? — Learning the Lessons of History — A Brief History of Israel — Who Told You? — Who is a Jew? A Look at Israel's Bloodline — Our Hope of Glory and The Mystery of The Gentiles — The Way of the Gentiles — Ephraim, Once Again a Mighty Man — From Roman Roads to the World Wide Web — The Jubilee Generation — Restoring The Kingdom To Israel — The Messianic Vision — When Will Yeshua Return? — Preparing For The Final Battle.

This exciting book will help you keep your eye on the goal: The restoration of the Kingdom to the restored house of Israel.

ISBN 1-886987-04-1   Paper, 304 pages, $14.95 plus shipping

Take Two Tablets Daily
The 10 Commandments and 613 Laws

by Angus Wootten

"You're trying to put me under the Law!" This cry is often heard from Christians when they are presented with the laws and commandments of the God of Abraham, Isaac and Jacob.

Is their cry justified? This valuable book will help you thoughtfully examine the laws the Holy One gave to His people through Moses. Read it and see that the Father's instructions were given for the physical and spiritual guidance of His people. His judgments and precepts were not given to punish Israel, but to guide them as individuals and as a nation. They were given to enable the people of Israel to become strong, courageous, healthy, and blessed.

This handy guide conveniently lists the 613 laws, divided into Mandatory Commandments and Prohibitions (according to Jewish custom), plus the Scripture verse(s) from which each law is derived. Chapter titles include: Under the Law? — Yeshua's Attitude Toward the Law — Our Need For Law And Order — YHVH's Law or Man's Law? — Paul and the Law — Principles of the Protestant Reformation — What Should Be Our Attitude Toward the Law? — The Decalogue: The Ten Commandments.

YHVH's Word is like medicinal ointment, and nothing is more symbolic of His Word than the two tablets on which He wrote His desires for us. Taken daily, these "Two Tablets" will give us life more abundantly. This reference book should be in every Believers library. It is a must read!

ISBN1-886987-06-8   96 Informative pages, $4.95

Visit Our Cutting Edge Website

Messianic Israel Ministries
www.mim.net